ST. MARY'S COLLEGE OF MARYLAND LIBRARY

W9-ADF-601

KOREA AND THE OLD ORDERS
IN EASTERN ASIA

KOREA

AND THE OLD ORDERS IN

Eastern Asia

by

M. Frederick Nelson

NEW YORK / RUSSELL & RUSSELL

COPYRIGHT 1945 BY THE
LOUISIANA STATE UNIVERSITY PRESS

REISSUED, 1967, BY RUSSELL & RUSSELL
A DIVISION OF ATHENEUM HOUSE, INC.
BY ARRANGEMENT WITH LOUISIANA STATE UNIVERSITY PRESS
L. C. CATALOG CARD NO: 66–27132

MANUFACTURED IN THE UNITED STATES OF AMERICA

22477

PREFACE

The purpose of this study is to trace the international status of Korea, with particular accent on the years wherein that country functioned as an "international personality," having contacts with the Western nations. Since Korea simultaneously retained during this period a peculiar position as a member of a separate Asiatic family of nations, the problem also concerns the conflict resulting from the attempt of two systems to set the standard for Korea's international conduct.

Heretofore, Korea's diplomatic relations have been described and judged solely according to Western criteria. Little attempt has been made to interpret or to reconstruct the system of international relations which existed in the Far East before the West substituted its European legal order. Western writers have not undertaken to show the effect which membership in that Far Eastern order had upon the conduct of an area such as Korea. This study attempts, by the use of Far Eastern as well as Western standards, to explain some of the many seeming contradictions which punctuated Korea's short life as a member of the Western state system.

In analyzing Korea's diplomatic relations with the Western states, reliance has been placed mainly on the documents of the United States Department of State. This has been done because of the early diplomatic contacts between the United States and Korea, and the earnest attempts made by American diplomats to investigate and understand the relationship of Korea to China. It was the sympathetic attitude of these officials, and the efforts of other individual Americans to encourage aid and support for Korea, which led Koreans to regard the United States as an "elder brother" and as their protector in the Western world.

Chinese names have been Romanized according to the Wade-Giles system and Korean words according to J. S. Gale's *The Unabridged Korean-English Dictionary*. A Korean scholar was consulted where optional spellings were permissible. In certain cases, words which have acquired an accepted Western spelling were not altered.

The author wishes to express his appreciation to Dr. Paul M. A. Linebarger, under whose tutelage he developed an interest in the subject and under whose direction this study was originally made and submitted as a thesis in partial fulfillment of requirements for the degree of Doctor of Philosophy at Duke University. The author is also grateful to Professor Arthur N. Holcombe of Harvard University, and to Professors Robert R. Wilson and Paul H. Clyde of Duke University, who have read the manuscript and offered valuable criticisms. Professor Homer H. Dubs also read the entire manuscript and contributed translations of several important documents. More than this, he gave freely of his wide knowledge of the philosophy and early history of China.

Grateful acknowledgment is made to the publishers for permission to quote passages from the following works: Tyler Dennett, *Roosevelt and the Russo-Japanese War* (New York, Doubleday, Page Co., 1925); Tyler Dennett, *Americans in Eastern Asia* (New York, The Macmillan Co., 1922); W. E. Griffis, *Corea, The Hermit Nation* (London, Harper & Bros., 1905); Shuhsi Hsü, *China and Her Political Entity* (New York, Oxford University Press, 1926); Yoshi S. Kuno, *Japanese Expansion on the Asiatic Continent* (Berkeley, The University of California Press, 1937–40); G. T. Ladd, *In Korea with Marquis Ito* (New York, Charles Scribner's Sons, 1908); Owen Lattimore, *Manchuria, Cradle of Conflict* (New York, The Macmillan Co., 1932); P.M.A. Linebarger, *Government in Republican China* (New York, McGraw-Hill

Book Co., 1938); H. F. MacNair, *The Real Conflict Between China and Japan* (Chicago, University of Chicago Press, 1938); F. A. McKenzie, *The Tragedy of Korea* (New York, E. P. Dutton & Co., Inc., n.d.); F. A. McKenzie, *Korea's Fight for Freedom* (New York, Fleming H. Revell Co., 1928); H. B. Morse, *The International Relations of the Chinese Empire* (London, Longmans, Green & Co., Ltd., 1918); C. O. Paullin, *Diplomatic Negotiations of American Naval Officers, 1778–1883* (Baltimore, Johns Hopkins Press, 1912); F. M. Russell, *Theories of International Relations* (New York, D. Appleton-Century Co., Inc., 1936); F. L. Schuman, *Europe on the Eve* (New York, Alfred A. Knopf, Inc., 1939); Payson J. Treat, *Diplomatic Relations Between the United States and Japan, 1853–1895* (Stanford, Stanford University Press, 1932).

M. Frederick Nelson

CONTENTS

INTRODUCTION

KOREA, a country rich in age, culture, and national tradition, stands upon the strategic crossroads of East Asia, where military and naval power has focused since the dawn of history. Flanking the route of the northern people whose invasions have punctuated China's past, the peninsula also was for centuries the meeting place and battleground of the Chinese and Japanese empires. In later years America, Russia, and Britain joined the powers to whose strategy Korea is a fulcrum, and any present system directed to the maintenance of peace in the Pacific area involves the consideration of Korea's status and future role. While Korea's future in the world order, although planned, may not be definitely predicted, her past throws light on a broader and perhaps fundamental problem—the nature of state systems themselves.

The importance of the character of the system through which nations conduct relations with one another need not be emphasized to anyone who observes current affairs. The Western state system, now planetary in extent, no longer approves of many of the basic principles upon which international relationships previously depended. It has been said that "Among the artifacts of Western man which seem destined to disappear . . . is the whole system of international relationships which has hitherto prevailed in the Western world." [1] Whether or not this is to be fully borne out, the past decades have seen a definite contraction in the degree of community [2] existing among nations and in the effectiveness of the traditional order of international relations.

[1] F. L. Schuman, *Europe on the Eve* (New York, 1939), 513.
[2] The term "community" implies a social group with a certain solidarity and with common conceptions of value, as contrasted with a society of isolated

Korea offers a complete picture of the transition by an Asiatic area through several international orders or systems of international relations. In her relationship to China, Korea stood for centuries as the most perfect example of the peculiar Confucian order of Far Eastern international relations which preceded the Western state system. With the coming of the West, Korea attempted to maintain a double status, being simultaneously in the disintegrating East Asiatic system and in the ascendant system of the West. Forced into a role for which she was unprepared, that of an independent and sovereign state under Western international law, Korea, with traditions engendered by centuries of subservience as a junior nation in the East Asiatic order, suffered a painful and perplexing transition from legal independence back to subservience as a protectorate of Japan and ultimately to her extinction as a state. After 1910 the peninsula became an experimental ground for the first major step in the Japanese policy of creating a new order in the Far East.

In any reordering of Eastern Asia the tradition of the orders that have gone before should condition that which is to come. Especially is this true should world order be based upon regional communities of states with each region developing a unity greater than that possible on a world-wide scale. Furthermore, to view the Far East as explicable in purely modern terms is an error, since virtually every system finds some exponents in Eastern Asia today. With Japanese theocratic, feudalistic, and racialist ideas,[3] Pan-Sovietism, the democratic nationalism of Sun Yat-sen, Chinese race-nationalism (*min-tsu*), modern Philippine-American democracy, and nineteenth-century imperialism (not to mention Tibetan theocracy, Inner Mongol aristocratic feudalism, and outer

---

contending members. See Georg Schwarzenberger, "The Rule of Law and the Disintegration of the International Society," in *American Journal of International Law*, XXXIII (1939), 56–77.

[3] For some aspects of this question see M. Frederick Nelson, "Feudalistic Propaganda in Modern Japan," in *Amerasia*, II (1938), 444–51.

Mongolian pastoral democracy), we see that Asiatic affairs are confused by the simultaneous play of forces on several different levels of understanding. It is this complex of conflicts, of forces derived from the past and the present, as well as from the varied Eastern and Western heritages, which condition any system of East Asiatic security.

It is hazardous to deal with a problem that spans two spheres of thought as diverse as the Far East and the West, spheres which are separated by such formidable barriers as widely divergent language systems. Those studying the situation who are not familiar with the languages of the Far East must rely on translations for part of the materials used, and those translations, even though carefully made, inevitably convey the connotations of another language. Particularly is this true in a translation from the tongue of any civilization to that of a completely different one, as from Chinese into a Western language. For example, the relationship of Korea to China in the East Asiatic system was generally translated as "vassal" in the Western tongues, and endless misunderstanding arose as to the international status of Korea when she was found to lack those qualities which were held by the West to be the characteristics of a "vassal."

Therefore, in this work the attempt has been made to avoid peculiarly Western words (e.g., "state," "sovereignty," and "vassal"), the use of which would tend to project back onto a Far Eastern concept Western attributes which it did not possess, and to substitute simple translations of Chinese terms (e.g., "dependent nation"). In important passages an especial effort is made to attain a more literal rendition of the language used even at the risk of what seems to be repetition. Thus, it is believed that a truer picture of the subject will be secured, one which would be recognizable in both Western and Far Eastern spheres of understanding.

Korea's status throughout its long history is not explicable in purely legal terms; international law cannot adequately explain the status of an area which knew such law only for a brief period prior to its extinction as an international person. Therefore, though the international-law point of view remains, since it was in this light that the West viewed Korea and the whole Far East, the legal aspect has shared in the interpretation with the purely political. However, in place of a complete reconstruction of Western international law as it existed in the period of contact with Korea, such law is given in terms of what the diplomats in control of the foreign policies of nations at the time stated and presumably believed it to be.

This study does not pretend to include in its treatment all phases of Korean culture. It is primarily the political international status of Korea which is considered. Yet, to understand anything of the Far East, one must have some knowledge of the nature of its society and philosophy as well.

The preliminary approach to the subject requires, therefore, consideration of the Far Eastern world view, the nature of its government and its position in society, and the relations of those governments to each other. Consequently, this study first traces the growth of Korea from barbarism to brotherhood in the Confucian system and attempts a reconstruction of that system as it existed and confronted the eastward expansion of the Western powers in the latter part of the nineteenth century. In its second phase the study is concerned with the conflict of the two systems in Korea and with Korea's attainment of full membership in the Western state system. Finally, it considers the loss of statehood as Korea went under the protectorship of Japan and later became an integral part of that empire.

Part I

THE INTERNATIONAL SOCIETY OF CONFUCIAN MONARCHIES

CHAPTER I

CONFUCIAN FAMILISM AND THE IN-EQUALITY OF NATIONS

1. FUNDAMENTALS OF THE CONFUCIAN SYSTEM

UNFORTUNATELY, the Far East had little knowl-edge of the Western civilization which confronted it in the first half of the nineteenth century. Equally regrettable, however, was the lack of comprehension on the part of the Western peoples of the nature of society and government in the Far East. The application of Western terms to Asiatic in-stitutions led only to misunderstanding and confusion when these institutions failed to act in the manner of their West-ern counterparts. Since the East Asiatic peoples possessed a world outlook altogether different from Western thought of the time, this confusion was particularly apparent in the field of international relations. Furthermore, the nature of gov-ernment, the function of officialdom, and numerous other as-pects of the social organization differed greatly from those of the West.

The Chinese, and the Koreans as well, had for centuries fol-lowed a philosophy and code of ethics which had been so gen-eral in their diffusion as to constitute the mores of the people. Based primarily upon the writings of the great sage Confucius (Kung Fu-tzŭ, 551–479 B.C.), there had been constructed a complete philosophy of civilization which may be termed Con-fucianism,[1] though it was somewhat modified by the glosses

---

[1] "Confucianism" is used to express the thought structure of the Chinese, not just the writings of Confucius. Confucianism first became a state cult in

of the followers of Confucius and by rival schools of thought. The Confucian dogma was incorporated in a series called *The Classics,* knowledge of which became the highest standard of intellectual attainment and of proficiency in government. Apt quotation of them would win an argument or determine a course of action. In fact, their principles governed all human relationships and conduct in the Sino-Korean area.

For any complete understanding of political action in the Far East it is necessary, therefore, to devote some attention to the background of Confucian thought. It is only against this background that the social conduct, the actions of government, relationships among the countries of the Far East, and the conflicts of the Far East with the Western states can be properly understood.

According to the Confucian theory, the world is a single unit, natural in organization, with a set of hierarchical relationships ascending from the lowest man up to Heaven itself. Heaven is viewed as the source and the ancestor of all things. But the Chinese do not view Heaven as a paradise even though they believe it to be the abode of the spirits of selected emperors and sages. To them it is rather a presiding spirit or principle which is fundamentally moral in its nature and, therefore, analogous to Western concepts of fate or providence. It punishes and rewards, and its commands repose in the hearts of the people. For at least the later Confucians, who were less influenced by superstition, Heaven corresponds very nearly to the English word "nature." [2]

the Former Han dynasty (202 B.C.–A.D. 25). Its influence, however, diminished in the disunion which followed the downfall of that dynasty. After the rise of the T'ang dynasty (A.D. 620) the Confucian theory again came into prominence and in the Sung period, especially after the eleventh century, it attained a permanent position as the arbiter of the mores of the people. For the rise of Confucianism to dominance in China, see J. K. Shryock, *The Origin and Development of the State Cult of Confucius* (New York, 1932).

[2] Alfred Forke, *The World Conception of the Chinese* (London, 1925), 144, 147–48, 156; Fung Yu-lan, *A History of Chinese Philosophy* (Derk Bodde, trans.) (Peiping, 1937), 31; H. H. Dubs, *Hsüntze, The Moulder of Ancient Confucianism* (London, 1927), 62–63.

Confucianism makes all men subject to the will of Heaven and even an emperor must conform to the natural ordering of this will or lose his right to rule under Heaven's mandate. Man, therefore, occupies the position of having as his main duty the obligation to conform with Heaven's will, to fit himself into its natural order and thus attain peace and happiness. It was emphasized by Hsüntze,[3] however, that reasonable activities in conjunction with Heaven are productive of additional happiness, and in the *Book of Changes* (*I Ching*) it is said that man "may precede Heaven, and Heaven will not act in opposition to him." [4] However, the fact that unreasonable actions often produce unfortunate results reminds us that one can never be certain that he is actually anticipating Heaven. This illustrates the tenet in Confucian theory that there can be no bending of nature to man's will, but rather, only the limited field of "appropriate" actions within an established natural order.

This concept of a preordained natural order suggested that a definite relationship existed between all material things and that, in every situation, proper conduct depended upon the status of the actors. In the structure of society five fundamental relationships were postulated, and man's entire existence was embraced within them. The first relation, male and female or husband and wife, evolved from the original existence of Heaven and earth. The second relation, derived from the first, is that of father and son; the third that of elder brother and younger brother. The fourth and fifth are those of friend and friend, and of sovereign and minister (or subject). These relationships are held to be as permanent as the universe. Peace and order exist automatically when the husband is truly a husband, the wife truly a wife, the sovereign

---

[3] Hsüntze is followed as a Confucian authority because of his position as "The Moulder of Confucianism." See *The Works of Hsüntze* (H. H. Dubs, trans.) (London, 1928), viii, and Dubs, *Hsüntze, The Moulder*, xiii.
[4] *The Sacred Books of the East* (F. Max Müller, ed.) (Oxford, 1879–1910), XVI, App. IV, 417.

truly a sovereign, and so on.[5] By appropriately conforming to relationships which man finds in his social existence, one would follow Heaven's will and would receive Heaven's blessings.

But not all men are wise, or able to discern within their hearts the behavior true to each of the five relations. Furthermore, men are born with desires and are constantly seeking the satisfaction of them. Means for the satisfaction of desires are naturally scarce, while the craving for satisfaction is without measure or limits, hence contention between men. Contention leads to disorder and confusion, and disorder and confusion to poverty. Therefore, from their wisdom and knowledge of the true order of things, the ancient Sage-Kings interpreted and set down the rules of proper conduct or propriety known as *li*.[6] *Li* is held to be more than a set of arbitrary rules conjured from men's minds; rather it is the natural rules which govern even the relation of Heaven and earth, and of the stars and the seasons as well. The rules of *li* were discovered, not made, by the ancient sages. *Li* is termed the greatest of all principles, for "He who follows it will be preserved; he who does not follow it will be destroyed." [7]

The fundamental element in the rules of proper conduct (*li*) and, in fact, in the whole system of Confucian thought, is that of inequality.[8] Because of the relation of the natural desires of each man "to be as honourable as the Emperor and so wealthy as to own the country," [9] and the disorder

---

[5] *The Works of Hsüntze,* 135–36. Here is the basis of *Cheng ming,* the doctrine of "rectification of names," wherein actions or the natural order of things was achieved if the ideas attached to a name conformed to its natural and original meaning. See L. S. Hsü, *The Political Philosophy of Confucianism* (London, 1932), Chap. III.

[6] *Li* has usually been translated as "rites" or "ceremony," neither of which expresses its true meaning. For the Far East *li* means the entire code of ethics. See L. S. Hsü, *The Political Philosophy,* 93–99, and *The Sacred Books of the East,* XXVII, 9–11.

[7] *The Works of Hsüntze,* 224.

[8] See Dubs, *Hsüntze, The Moulder,* Chap. XIV.

[9] *The Works of Hsüntze,* 65.

which would result from man's attempt to achieve these rare satisfactions, nature has decreed inequalities or the distinctions of superior and inferior in all relations.

As soon as there was heaven and earth, there was the distinction of above and below (superior and inferior); when the first wise king arose, the country he occupied had the division of classes. . . . The ancient kings established the rules of proper conduct . . . to divide the people, to cause them to have classes of poor and rich, of noble and inferior, so that everyone would be under someone's control. . . .[10]

This theory, that everyone and everything should be under someone's direction, illustrates the hierarchical nature of the Confucian system. Within the extremes of the lowest and the highest, everyone has inferiors below him and superiors above. Responsibility and benevolence descend from above, and obedience and respect ascend from below—all emanating from or culminating in the emperor, or Son of Heaven, who, in turn, looks to Heaven as his superior and as the bestower of his mandate to rule. Banishment of inequality, according to Confucian theory, would mean a return to a state of barbarism and chaos wherein men's desires have no limits.[11] Therefore, desire is subordinated to the distinctions of superior and inferior; and this subordination attains advantageous social relations under conditions imposed by innate nature. This does not mean that men are unequal in their original capacities. In fact, the Confucians democratically maintain the theory of equal capacities for all men. The aristocracy in which they believe is a moral one, based on equality in capacity but inequality in development.[12]

With a natural order of society in which man's whole social duty is embraced in five great relationships, with a hier-

[10] *Ibid.*, 124.

[11] *Works of Mencius* in *ʌ ne Chinese Classics* (James Legge, trans.) (London, 1861–72), II, 318.

[12] Dubs, *Hsüntze, The Moulder*, 250–52.

archical scale of inferiors and superiors ascending to the emperor, with each inferior controlled by a superior, and with *li*, the rules of proper conduct, embracing all of these relations, the position of the emperor and the nature of government (in the Confucian sense) become apparent. Government is formally the indoctrination of inferiors by superiors with the rules of proper conduct. The downward flow from Heaven of these doctrines is conceived to be the force which will preserve natural order in society. Government is thus not an artificial creation based on the fiat of law, but is the entire ethics of society. Just as the seasons are natural to Heaven, and wealth is natural to the earth, so government is natural to man.[13] Its sole object is to keep men within the natural rules of conduct, to prevent the disorder that will result when men stray from the "way." [14] Or, as Confucius expressed it, "To govern is to rectify." [15] To Hsüntze, "The rules of proper conduct (*li*) are the greatest thing in government . . . ; they are the foundation of strength and security. . . . They are the utmost of human morality." [16]

The emperor is the apex of the Confucian system. As the supreme man, he is Heaven's substitute on earth, and his relation to his subjects is similar to that of Heaven to earth.[17] All men are his children, and to protect them and prevent them from straying from the natural way is the purpose of his existence.[18] Since the emperor views the people as a great family, the rules of proper conduct between parent and child are applied in the relation of sovereign and subject. But though Heaven creates the emperor, and though the emperor rules under Heaven's authority, the mandate of Heaven,

---

[13] *The Works of Hsüntze*, 174.
[14] *Tao*. For discussion of *tao*, see Fung, *A History of Chinese Philosophy*, 177–80.
[15] *Analects* in *The Chinese Classics*, I, 122.
[16] *The Works of Hsüntze*, 216, 225.
[17] Forke, *The World Conception*, 75.
[18] "The Great Declaration" in *The Chinese Classics*, III, 2, 281–97.

through which a dynasty keeps the throne, is not unshakable. For "Imperial Heaven," states the *Book of History,* "has no predilections. It always allies itself to the virtuous." [19] When disorder and calamities attest the disfavor of Heaven, the right of rebellion is recognized and asserted by those seeking to overthrow a dynasty.[20]

The method whereby men are to be brought to observe the rules of *li* is in sharp contrast with Western methods of carrying out governmental policy. As the emperor deserves to be emperor only as long as he remains virtuous and in accord with Heaven's rules of propriety, so all officials of the empire are likewise to be models of proper conduct. Logically, then, no rigid, lifeless laws are needed to set the standard for the conduct of the people. Instead, the example of virtue in the official hierarchy which ascends to the all-virtuous Son of Heaven is to be so overwhelming as to compel acquiescence.

Here is a "government of men"—virtuous men—who are not respected and followed for the power they may possess as much as for the model they present. Each inferior views his superior as a model, and from the emperor down, government is not force but instruction. By proper example and instruction in the principles of *li,* all men are to cultivate a sense of shame [21] which will cause them to comply with the proper rules. Only when they lack this sense of shame and cannot be swayed by reason and instruction, is punitive power to be exercised. In theory, the emperor is a teacher and model primarily and a ruler only in extreme cases.

Silence concerning the concept of law in Confucian theory is not the result of ignorance. Other Chinese advocated a regime wherein one impersonal standard is set by law, and

[19] *The Shu King* (W. G. Old, trans.) (London, 1904), 239. Cf. *ibid.,* 98.

[20] See statement of T'ang when overthrowing the Hsia dynasty and that of King Yu of Chou upon the overthrow of the Shang, in "The Announcement of T'ang" and "The Great Declaration" in *The Chinese Classics,* III, 1, 184–90, 2, 281–97.

[21] More understandable, perhaps, as a consciousness of "face."

obedience secured by force. Such a school existed in the third and fourth centuries B.C., and their theories became the basis for the government of the Ch'in dynasty (221–206 B.C.). The tyranny possible under a rule of law designed for the benefit of the rulers rather than for the welfare of the people was well illustrated during this era. With the overthrow of the Ch'in dynasty by revolution, government by law and force was definitely replaced by theories of self-control through teaching and example.[22]

The doctrine of control through example, of conquering through virtue, throws the problem of the control of society back upon the individual. If the empire is in disorder, the emperor is at fault; he has presumably failed to cultivate virtue within himself. If a family is disrupted, the parent is lacking in sufficient virtue and knowledge of the rules of proper conduct. Therefore, the man who would govern (*i.e.*, enforce the rules of proper conduct) must first rectify himself with Heaven's way. An often quoted passage of Confucius illustrates this expanding nature of individual virtue.

Their hearts being rectified, their persons were cultivated. Their persons being cultivated, their families were regulated. Their families being regulated, their states were rightly governed. Their states being rightly governed, the whole empire was made tranquil and happy. [23]

War is therefore incompatible with Confucian theory, which requires that an unsubmissive people should be conquered by a display of civil culture and virtue, not coerced by force.[24] When a ruler invited Confucius to teach military tactics, the Sage refused and left the state of so unrighteous

---

[22] For rise and fall of the Legalist school, see Derk Bodde, *China's First Unifier* (Leyden, 1938), 191–99, and Fung, *A History of Chinese Philosophy*, Chap. XIII.

[23] "The Great Learning" in *The Chinese Classics*, I, 223.

[24] *Analects, ibid.*, 173.

a monarch.[25] Mencius also denounced offensive war, except for the punishing of unrighteousness. The fighting which occurred in the Spring and Autumn Epoch (770–473 B.C.) was all unrighteous; those who boasted of their military skill were termed "great criminals," and the ministers who advised the use of force were "robbers of the people." [26]

In this renunciation of war the Confucian theory was supported by the theories of all the other major schools of thought in China, with the exception of the short-lived Legalists.[27] "Laotze's quietism led him to pacificism; Micius (Motzǔ) adopted Confucius' dislike of war and made pacificism one of the cardinal tenets in his creed. China presents the unique picture of a country in which practically all important philosophical opinion was against war. . . ." [28] However, Confucian theory in one respect encouraged civil as opposed to international warfare by its doctrine of the Mandate of Heaven. Whenever a ruler's government decayed, some person felt justified in raising the standard of revolution. Though civil war was common in China, foreign conquest was viewed as being in a different category and was not justified by Confucian doctrine. Genuinely Confucian dynasties avoided foreign aggrandizement.

2. EAST ASIATIC INTERNATIONAL THEORIES

The Confucian theory viewed the whole world as a single unit. As Confucius expressed it, "Within four seas" all men are brothers.[29] Since the control exercised by the emperor was that of a teacher and a model of proper conduct, it inevitably

---

[25] *Ibid.*, 158.
[26] *Works of Mencius, ibid.*, II, 316, 354–55.
[27] See pp. 9–10.
[28] Dubs, *Hsüntze, The Moulder*, 266–67.
[29] *Analects* in *The Chinese Classics*, I, 117. The phrase "all under Heaven" was also used to suggest the world which the Son of Heaven controlled.

diminished as the outlying areas were reached where the non-Chinese inhabitants, being semi-civilized, paid less heed to emperors who sought to conquer by virtue.

The area of China proper, where all men abided by the rules of propriety, was termed *Chung Kuo*, the "Middle Kingdom." Most who lived outside the area were termed barbarians. The latter term did not necessarily denote savagery; it meant rather those who had not acquired Chinese customs and dress, who did not observe the proprieties, and who were not amenable to reason. Such people actually possessed a lower degree of civilization, according to Confucian standards, and were therefore classed as rude. There were four main groups of barbarians, the *i*, those of the east, the *man* of the south, and the *jung* and *ti* of the west and north, though the terms *man-i* or *jung-ti* or even *i* alone were used to denote barbarian tribes in general.[30]

The surrounding tribes, not being civilized enough to enable their members to feel a voluntary sense of shame and to submit to the reason and teaching of the Middle Kingdom, presented a perplexing problem. No actual intergovernmental relations in the Confucian sense could exist between China and these people to whom government by benevolence and reason was not understandable. Consequently, these barbarians were looked upon as something less than men at their full stature, who had occasionally to be dealt with, to be sure, but who were to be treated in the kindly and benevolent spirit one would exercise toward lesser animals or young and unruly children.[31] This attitude is expressed by an old saying

[30] *The Chinese Classics*, Vol. III, Pt. I, pp. 142–48, nn. 18–22. See H. A. Giles, *A Chinese-English Dictionary* (Shanghai, 1912), 674, 720, 952, 1357.

[31] This particular idea even constituted a problem set by the palace examiners to test the literary ability and orthodoxy of opinions of the scholars competing in the year 1061, the subject being "Those Who Rule-by-Benevolence Do Not Govern-by-Reason the Barbarians." Su Tung-p'o, an eminent poet-essayist, stated the theory when he wrote: "Barbarians may not be governed by the Government-by-Reason of the Central State. They must be regarded as resembling birds and beasts. To apply to them great

that "When a *hsiu t'sai* (scholar of the first degree) meets a soldier eye to eye, although the former has reason, his arguments will not be clear." [32]

As time passed, however, through immigration, social intercourse, and conquest, the once rude barbarians within the Far Eastern areas surrounding the Middle Kingdom were brought gradually within the Confucian realm of thought. Eventually they developed scholars who brought them the Classics, they adopted *li* as their rule of conduct, and they came to respect the civilization and might of China, thus exemplifying the fact that China's most enduring conquests have been cultural, not military. Confucius himself had said that it was desirable to treat those barbarians who had become Chinese in a Chinese manner,[33] that is, with Government-by-Reason. No new theory needed to be evolved, therefore, for the intergovernmental relations of Confucian states. "All within the four seas" and the "Middle Kingdom" were rather vague terms, and with the whole world being in theory subject to the emperor, there was no definite point at which

---

Government-by-Reason must result in vast confusion. The early Rulers . . . comprehended this; hence, by non-use of Government-by-Reason, governed the Barbarians."

This attitude toward those less civilized than themselves was equally well illustrated at a date two centuries earlier than that at which Su Tung-p'o wrote, when Han Yŭ, upon hearing that the emperor was making preparations to receive with great ceremony a bone of Buddha, submitted a memorial which indicates that it was not only the lack of understanding on the part of the barbarians which governed their treatment, but also a fear of diluting the heaven-directed natural order with barbarian customs.

Nor was this theory found only in the early ages. As a matter of fact, it did not apply when the peripheral barbarians became Confucianized, as will be pointed out, but it was again revived when Westerners who came to take the place of the once untutored surrounding tribes were accordingly treated with condescending benevolence and with non-use of Government-by-Reason. See H. F. MacNair, *The Real Conflict Between China and Japan* (Chicago, 1938), 15–16, 19–20.

[32] *Ibid.*, 17–18.

[33] *Spring and Autumn Annals,* cited by H. F. MacNair in "Some Observations on China's International Relations," in *Journal of the North China Branch of the Royal Asiatic Society,* LVI (1925), 8.

one passed from the confines of China into the periphery, from Confucianism into barbarism.

When civilized and Confucianized groups rose from the barbarians, the Confucian system was merely extended to them. The emperor would then attain the attitude described in the Classics, which was to view all in the Middle Kingdom as one man, as a *person* in that *family of persons* which comprised "all under Heaven." [34] Here is the basic theory of Confucian international relations. The rules which were to govern this Far Eastern family were the same natural rules, the same code of *li*, that governed the individual family. Here, much more than ever existed in the West, was an international family in the true meaning of the word—natural, governed merely by a further extension of the principles which made up East Asiatic social existence. Since inequality was an essential element in the natural family, these principles were likewise projected into the international sphere. Consequently, China— the superior, the Middle Kingdom—was surrounded by inferior or lesser members who looked to her and were viewed by her as younger brothers or children in the international family.

The rules which governed the relation between the Confucian nations were not definite and uniform. Each situation as it arose was judged according to the principles of *li*. The control by China, the superior, was that of teaching and admonition, of presenting herself as the model for the lesser countries to follow. Chinese influence, and the relationship of the lesser states, varied from rather close supervision, such as China exercised over Korea, to occasional ceremonial contacts such as those with Siam and Burma. This distinction was recognized in Chinese theory by the classic conception of the various domains extending outward from the Central domain of the emperor, each varying in degree of civilization and in obligations to the imperial power according to the dis-

[34] *Lichi* in *The Sacred Books*, XXVII, 379.

tance of the domain from China. The "Tribute of Yu" in the *Book of History* lists these domains (*fu*) as: first, the imperial domain (*tien-fu*), surrounded successively by the feudal domain of the nobles, princes, and bureaucrats (*hou-fu*); the peace-seeking domain (*sui-fu*), into which the cultivation of learning and the proprieties extended only halfway; the domain of restraint (*yao-fu*); and the wild domain (*huang-fu*).[35] Whether this arrangement actually ever existed is doubtful,[36] and by Han times it certainly ceased to be anything more than a point of reference in literary use.[37] Varying treatment among the lesser nations, or at different times toward the same nation, was supported by the Confucian principle which held that the superior, under ordinary circumstances, should not exercise his utmost authority, but should reserve it for emergencies.[38]

However, certain general rules were followed, which had for their purpose the preservation of the natural familial relation. One of the most important was the old theory of the extension of control and the maintenance of supervision by virtue and by the voluntary submission of the lesser nation. While it is true that this theory was often violated and that force was frequently used to compel submission or to restore order within a lesser nation, it is nevertheless important to notice that this force was used mainly either to secure recognition of some new Chinese dynasty as truly holding the mandate of Heaven, or to chastise an area which had strayed from the proper rules of conduct and had allowed disorder to rise among its people. The Classics are replete with examples of how ancient emperors had failed in bringing certain areas under their control by force, only to succeed when they

[35] See "The Tribute of Yu" in *The Chinese Classics*, Vol. III, Pt. I, pp. 142–51.

[36] *Ibid.*, 148.

[37] Pan Ku, *The History of the Former Han Dynasty* (H. H. Dubs, trans.) (Baltimore, 1938), II, Introduction to Chap. VIII.

[38] See pp. 91, 148 n.

rectified themselves, put their own area in order, and allowed the tales of their virtuous government to bring recalcitrant groups to voluntary submission.[39]

The ruler of the lesser nation accepted investiture from the Chinese emperor in the form of a seal to be used as a badge of office. After the death of the lesser ruler of the inferior country, the Chinese emperor would bestow on him a post-humous title.[40] In rare cases the succession to the throne might be interfered with and a more virtuous heir set up to rule.[41] For use in dating all official documents, the lesser state would each year receive a calendar arranged in terms of the reigning dynasty of China, and the Chinese emperor would also send letters for the instruction and admonition of the lesser king.

Relations were maintained by periodic visits of a Chinese envoy and by return visits by a mission of the lesser nation. The unequal status in this interchange of envoys is particularly well brought out in the commentary of Tso-ch'iu Ming, a disciple of Confucius, who stated:

When a great state goes to a small one it (the smaller) rears a high structure (for the large state's reception). When a small state goes to a great one it (the great one) should construct a booth. . . . When a great state visits a small one it should do five good things: be indulgent to its offenses, pardon its errors and failures, relieve its calamities, reward it for its virtues and laws, and teach it where it is deficient. There is thus no pressure on the small state. It cherishes (the great) state's virtue, and submits to it, fondly as one goes home. On this account a high structure is reared, to display the merit (of the great state), and to make it known to posterity, that they may not be idle in the cultivation of virtue. When

[39] See, for example, "The Counsels of the Great Yu" in *The Chinese Classics,* Vol. III, Pt. I, pp. 52–67.

[40] W. H. Wilkinson, *The Corean Government Constitutional Changes, July 1894 to October 1895, With an Appendix on Subsequent Enactments to 30th June 1896* (Shanghai, 1897), App. V, p. 153.

[41] Pan, *The Former Han Dynasty,* II, Introduction to Chap. VIII.

a small state goes to a great one, it has five bad things to do. It must explain its trespasses, beg forgiveness for its deficiencies, perform governmental services, and contribute its proper dues and attend to its seasonal commands . . . it has to double its various offerings, to felicitate (the great state) on its happiness, and show condolence with it in its misfortunes.[42]

The envoys from China were no mere messengers. Their credentials were half of a set (the other half having been previously given to the lesser nation) which, when presented and matched, carried a restricted power of command over the lesser ruler. When the superior nation had decided on a military expedition for the purpose of "correction," the inferior nation could be required to furnish both men and supplies.[43] Other practices were the custom of having for education at the Chinese court a son of each of the lesser nations' kings and, in rare cases and as a special favor, the granting to rulers of lesser countries women of the Imperial Household to be their wives.[44]

The most obvious indication of the relationship between China and the lesser nations appeared in the so-called tribute missions periodically sent by the lesser states to China. The principle was an old one derived from the idea that all areas should contribute services and pay homage to the Son of Heaven in accordance with a gradation based on the concentric, ideal, classic arrangement.[45] According to Confucian mythology, in the most ancient times the domains near-by offered slaughtered victims daily; the next distant domains offered monthly sacrifices; and the outposts of civilization offered thanks seasonally. Among the more civilized barbarians of the east and south tribute was offered yearly. Among the less cultured, and, consequently, the less dominated, tribes

[42] Quoted in F. M. Russell, *Theories of International Relations* (New York, 1936), 23.
[43] Pan, *The Former Han Dynasty*, II, Introduction to Chap. VIII.
[44] *Ibid.*
[45] See p. 15.

of the north and west, acknowledgment of the emperor's over-lordship occurred only upon the ascension of a new ruler.[46] All homage and gifts of areas outside of China proper, how-ever, continued to be termed tribute, even after these one-time barbarians had taken over Chinese customs.

Aside from any religious base which the paying of this graded homage to the emperor may have contained, there was another element which leads to the conclusion that the tribute missions were also designed as an early form of inter-change of goods between the vast reaches of the empire, and as an encouragement to the production of varied products throughout its breadth. It is recorded in the *Shu-ching* that when a large hound, a curiosity because of its size and train-ing, was sent as tribute, the disapproval of the great guardian of the emperor was expressed in a memorial setting forth the correct subjects of tribute. Here the great guardian stated that tribute should be "the produce of their parts . . . cloth-ing, food and implements of use." He admonished the em-peror "not to deal in unprofitable things and not to neglect those that are worthy." Moreover, the emperor should "not set value on strange productions, nor belittle those that are useful. . . . Dogs and horses, except in their natural coun-tries, should not be reared. If rare birds and creatures are not bred in the country, and you do not set a false value on for-eign products," the guardian warned, "then strangers will be admonished." [47]

While it is true that this tribute came to consist of mate-rials other than the usual products of the country, its con-tribution did not cease to resemble an economic transaction. China, the superior, generally gave in return presents of more worth than the offerings of the inferiors. Thus the system served as a subsidy to the lesser states and encouraged un-controlled areas to come into the Chinese orbit.

[46] *The Works of Hsüntze*, 196–97.
[47] *The Shu King*, 174–75.

Finally, the tributary mission was an act acknowledging the seniority of China in the Confucian family of nations, though China apparently had no desire to use this acknowledgment for the direct control of internal affairs. If a lesser ruler kept the peace, endeavored to live as the model for his people, and fulfilled the few duties which his subordinate position required, he was autonomous. Theoretically, Far Eastern government, both imperial and international, involved the enforcement of the rules for proper conduct (the doctrine of *li*) through passive example. Power politics, on the other hand, which employs force as a legitimate agent of diplomacy, was definitely rejected by Confucian thought. This attitude is explained by the fact that extinction of a country by conquest was considered akin to the murder of one individual by another. Thus Confucian theory was basically pacifistic.

It should be mentioned, however, that those who controlled the affairs of China under Confucian principles were not merely theorists, but often practical politicians as well. For Confucianism was a very flexible doctrine, and within its many volumes of Classics could be found precedent for a wide variety of conduct. Even though those in control of government acknowledged Confucian theory as their guiding principle, they were able to use it to accomplish their own ends instead of merely conforming passively to fixed tenets.

A second qualification which should be noted is the fact that the theory itself was rejected or ignored at times as a guide for the administration of government. At other times when the entire theory was not put aside, certain portions of it were not made effective. For instance, the Ch'in rulers (221–206 B.C.) based their government upon legalist theories, and the period of disorganization after the downfall of the Han dynasty also saw a decline in the authority of Confucianism. The first T'ang Emperor was not a Confucian, but a Taoist. Later in the T'ang dynasty, however, Confucian doctrines again came into prominence, and from the eleventh century on, this philosophy became altogether dominant in China as the ethics of its people and as the guide for governmental policy.

Followed as a guide for the preservation of the order decreed by Heaven in all affairs—personal, familial, national, and international—these principles of Confucianism constituted the source book for scholars and officials. Since governmental employment depended on scholarship, which in turn was determined by a knowledge of Confucian principles, it was inescapable that Confucianism practically guided governmental administration.

With its natural world order, its idea of government by indoctrination and example rather than by law and compulsion, and with its definite formula prescribing relations with peoples beyond the Middle Kingdom, Confucian theory should be viewed as the ideological background for the early history of the Korean peninsula.

CHAPTER II

EARLIEST SINO-KOREAN RELATIONS
(TO 108 B.C.)

1. Chao-hsien before the Han Dynasty

THE origin of the kingdom of Chao-hsien, the earliest name by which the Korean area is known, is shrouded in myth. Although tradition dates the founding of the kingdom as early as 1122 B.C.,[1] the earliest authentic reference to the area is found in Han dynastic histories. There Chao-hsien is recorded as being definitely in contact with Chinese civilization in the period of disorganization in China known

---

[1] The Shang books in the *Book of History*, and the Korean histories which were later written from the Chinese texts, attribute the founding of Chao-hsien to the Viscount of Chi (Chi-tzŭ), whose name is said to have been Tzu-hsü-yu. This mythical person was the uncle and counselor to the last of the Shang emperors, Chou Hsin. Chi-tzŭ is described as refusing, despite ill-treatment by his sovereign, to serve under the succeeding dynasty, the Chou, whom he viewed as usurpers. After giving the first Chou ruler, Wu, advice on the conduct of government (see "The Great Plan" in *The Chinese Classics*, Vol. III, Pt. II, pp. 320–44), Chi-tzŭ is said to have migrated with 5000 of his followers to the Korean peninsula and established the kingdom of Chao-hsien. Chi-tzŭ brought with him men skilled in poetry, music, medicine, and trades, and established order through the promulgation of the "Eight Laws" defining the proper relationships among a people until then completely barbaric.

Although the Koreans claim Chi-tzŭ as the founder of their state, the only authority for his existence and migration to Korea is in the Shang books in the *Book of History*. These books, however, are fabrications written in Chou times as propaganda to justify the overthrow of the Shang by the Chou. The migration of Chi-tzŭ and his relations with the Shang and Chou are of no historical value. See H. G. Creel, *Studies in Early Chinese Culture* (Baltimore, 1937), 89. For accounts of the mythical Chi-tzŭ, see the "Viscount of Wei," "The Great Plan," in *The Chinese Classics*, Vol. III, Pt. I, pp. 273–79, Pt. II, pp. 320–44; and H. G. Appenzeller, "Ki Tza, The Founder of Korean Civilization," in *Korean Repository*, II (1895), 81–87.

as the *Chan Kuo* or "Fighting States" (473–221 B.C.).[2] The infiltration of Chinese culture into Korea came mainly by the land route. However, since Liao-tung and the north Korean areas were blocked off by the Jehol hills from direct contact with the Yellow River basin, the seat of Chinese civilization, much of the early penetration of Chinese culture reached the peninsula secondhand through the barbarian tribes of Manchuria. The first direct contact was through the kingdom of Yen, a north-Chinese area and one of the many kingdoms into which China was divided in the Spring and Autumn and Fighting States Epochs (770–221 B.C.).[3] In its expansion to the north and east around the Gulf of Po-hai, this kingdom of Yen overran the Liao-tung region including Chao-hsien, erected fortifications at the boundaries of the latter area, and established officials to administer it.[4] When the Ch'in dynasty was able to weld the contending kingdoms into a unified empire, Yen succumbing in 241 or 239 B.C., the Chao-hsien area became part of the Liao-tung command-ery.[5] Later, upon the rise of the Han dynasty (202 B.C.), the Chao-hsien territory was considered too distant to be pro-tected without great effort; so at least part of it was then abandoned, and the P'ei River [6] was again set as the boundary of Chinese authority.[7]

Through the kingdom of Yen, Chao-hsien received its in-itial contacts with the superior culture of the Chinese. After

[2] Pan Ku, *Han-shu Pu-shu* (History of the Former Han Dynasty) (Wang Hsien-ch'ien, ed.) (Changsha, 1900), Chap. XCV, p. 18b.

[3] Albert Herrman, *Historical and Commercial Atlas of China* (Cambridge, 1935), 14–16.

[4] Pan, *Han-shu Pu-shu*, Chap. XCV, p. 18b.

[5] *Ibid.* A commandery was a district corresponding administratively to the Ch'ing dynasty's province under an administrator appointed by and respon-sible to the emperor.

[6] Chavannes, in his introduction to Se-Ma Ts'ien's history, states that the P'ei River is what is the present Ta-tung River in Korea. Se-Ma Ts'ien, *Les mémoires historiques* (Edouard Chavannes, trans.) (Paris, 1895), I, lxxxvi. Herrman, *Atlas of China*, 22–23, shows it as the Yalu.

[7] Pan, *Han-shu Pu-shu*, Chap. XCV, p. 18b.

the fall of this kingdom and during later political upheavals in China, fugitives sought immunity in Chao-hsien. Though these Chinese immigrants were absorbed by the native stock, they undoubtedly contributed to the culture of the region.

2. THE WEI DYNASTY

The King of Yen, having become a subordinate ruler of the Han empire, rebelled in 195 B.C. against the Emperor Kao-tsu and fled northward into the territory of the Huns.[8] One of his followers, Wei Man, with a band of over a thousand men and some barbarians whom he compelled to join him, fled eastward across the frontier, the River P'ei, into the vacant border lands. With the aid of Chinese adventurers and fugitives from the former kingdoms of Yen and from neighboring Ch'i, Wei Man brought the territory of Chao-hsien partly under his control and set himself up as king with Wang-hsien (Pyeng-yang) as his capital town.[9] The account of this usurpation in the *Han-shu* is enlarged by the traditional Korean version which tells how Wei Man, fleeing from defeat in Yen, was given refuge in Chao-hsien by Ki Chyun, the king, and made "Guardian of the Western Frontier." This kindness he repaid by marching on Ki Chyun's capital and, under the pretense of protecting the king, deposing Ki Chyun and in 193 B.C. setting himself up as ruler.[10]

Wei Man then proceeded to strengthen and enlarge his newly won kingdom. In the time of the Han Emperor Hsio-hui and of the Empress of Emperor Kao (194–180 B.C.), the Grand Administrator of the Liao-tung Commandery recommended an arrangement whereby Wei Man should be recognized as a semi-dependent, semi-independent ruler outside the Chinese realm. By this arrangement Wei undertook to keep

[8] *Ibid.;* Pan, *The Former Han Dynasty,* I, 143.
[9] Pan, *Han-shu Pu-shu,* Chap. XCV, p. 18b.
[10] J. H. Longford, *The Story of Korea* (London, 1911), 52–53; W. E. Griffis, *Corea, The Hermit Nation* (London, 1905), 16.

the barbarians beyond the border from raiding Chinese territory, and he was in turn to be recognized as the only agency
through which the barbarians could approach the throne of
the Middle Kingdom.[11] The emperor approved this disposition of the Chao-hsien area and, through the support of both
troops and subsidies from China, Wei Man was able to reduce
to his control all the surrounding petty principalities.[12]

By the time Wei Man's grandson Wei Yu-ch'ü came to the
throne, Chao-hsien had grown to an area of several thousand
li square, and a constantly increasing stream of Chinese adventurers and immigrants had added to its culture. Wei Yu-
ch'ü had never gone, however, to pay homage to the Chinese
emperor, and he had blocked the border to envoys from Ch'en-
han, a southern Korean area, desirous of submitting an address and of "seeing the Emperor's face." This latter action
was doubtless justified under the previous agreement by
which representations to the emperor from such areas could
be made only through Chao-hsien.

In 109 B.C. the Chinese Emperor Wu dispatched to Chao-
hsien an envoy named Shê Ho to reprove Wei Yu-ch'ü for
his neglect and to secure from him an admission of China's superiority. The King of Chao-hsien, however, refused to go to
the Chinese court. Returning disgruntled and empty-handed,
Shê Ho, when nearing the frontier, caused his charioteer to
assassinate the Chao-hsien prince, Chang, who was escorting

[11] Pan, *Han-shu Pu-shu,* Chap. XCV, p. 19a.
[12] E. H. Parker, "On Race Struggles in Corea" [translated from Chao-hsien
chapters in *Early Han-shu* (200 B.C.–A.D. 1) and *After Han-shu* (A.D. 1–
A.D. 200)], in *Transactions of the Asiatic Society of Japan,* XVIII (1890),
160. *Transactions of the Asiatic Society of Japan* hereafter cited as *TASJ.*
Imperial troops aided in an expedition in 128 B.C. when a Prince of Wei,
Nun-Lu, rebelled against Chao-hsien. A Chinese expedition under P'eng Wu
conquered the area and set up Chinese administration, but withdrew, returning the area to Chao-hsien in 126 B.C. *Ibid.,* 160 n. Cf. Pan, *The History of the
Former Han Dynasty,* Vol. II, Chap. VI, pp. 10a, 10b. For practice of payment of subsidies to barbarians as inducement to keep the peace, see *ibid.,*
Introduction to Chap. VIII.

him to the border.[13] Having saved his reputation by falsely reporting that he had killed a general of Chao-hsien, Shê Ho received from the trusting emperor the appointment of "Chief Commandant of the Eastern Section of Liao-tung," the territory adjacent to Chao-hsien. But Wei Yu-Ch'ü avenged the prince's murder by invading this area and killing Shê Ho. He then retired to his kingdom to prepare for the inevitable wrath of the Han Emperor.[14]

3. THE END OF ANCIENT CHAO-HSIEN

The Han Military Emperor (Wu Ti) was not slow to retaliate for the killing of Shê Ho. Recruiting from his empire the criminals under death sentence,[15] he dispatched two large armies under Yang P'u and Hsün Chih. Hsün Chih was to march overland through Liao-tung, and Yang-P'u by sea across the Gulf of Liao-tung.

The ensuing campaign is an example of poor strategy and incompetence due to jealousy between the commanders and local sentiments of the two armies. Yang P'u's troops arrived first, vainly attempted to invade Wei Yu-ch'ü's capital, and presently fled in confusion to the mountains. Meanwhile, the troops of Hsün Chih met those of Wei Yu-ch'ü in the mountain passes and were likewise forced to retreat. Emperor Wu then sent a second envoy with reinforcements to secure the submission of Wei Yu-ch'ü, who now realized the overwhelming power of the Chinese. Wei Yu-ch'ü promptly received the envoy with respectful apologies, indicated his willingness to acknowledge the superiority of the emperor, and agreed to send his heir to China as a token of submission. But as the Chinese envoy and the king each suspected the other of

---

[13] Parker, "On Race Struggles in Corea," *loc. cit.*, 160.

[14] Pan, *The Former Han Dynasty*, Vol. II, Chap. VI, p. 26b.

[15] *Ibid.;* Lucien Gibert, *Dictionnaire historique et géographique de la Mandchourie* (Hong Kong, 1934), 867.

treachery, and further, since it appeared that the Chao-hsien heir-apparent had more than 10,000 well-armed troops in the entourage to accompany him, the heir of Wei Yu-ch'ü was not allowed to enter Chinese territory and both parties again resorted to force. Blundering tactics and non-cooperation between the two Han commanders, however, delayed the downfall of the Chao-hsien capital. Hsün Chih, suspecting that Yang P'u was about to make a private agreement with Wei Yu-ch'ü, arrested his colleague and seized his army. Finally in 108 B.C. the subjects of Wei Yu-ch'ü assassinated their ruler and surrendered to the Chinese. The two generals were punished for their mismanagement, Hsün Chih by public execution and Yang P'u by being deprived of all honors and titles.[16]

The subdued kingdom of Chao-hsien, which ceased to exist in 108 B.C., was divided by the Han Emperor into the four commanderies of Lo-lang, Lin-t'un, Hsüan-t'u, and Chên-p'an, each administered directly by the imperial government. Within a quarter of a century, however, the two commanderies of Lin-t'un and Chên-p'an were abolished, their areas either being incorporated with the other commanderies, or possibly left without Chinese control.[17]

This account of ancient Chao-hsien indicates that at an early date at least the northern part of the Korean peninsula had come into contact with Chinese civilization. Despite

---

[16] For this expedition against Chao-hsien, see Pan, *The Former Han Dynasty,* Glossary sub "Wei Yu-ch'ü," "Yang P'u" and "Hsün Chih"; and Parker, "On Race Struggles in Corea," *loc. cit.,* 159–66.

[17] See Pan, *Han-shu Pu-shu,* Chap. XCV, pp. 20a–21b; Pan, *The Former Han Dynasty,* Glossary sub "Lo-lang," "Lin-t'un," "Hsüan-t'u" and "Chên-p'an"; and Herrman, *Atlas of China,* 22–23, for discussion and description of these areas. Emperor Wu's successor abolished these commanderies in the general retrenchment which followed his ambitious reign. Lo-lang and Hsüan-t'u, however, continued to be centers of Chinese influence in the Korean peninsula throughout the Later Han period. For the extent of Chinese culture which existed in Korea in Han times, see G. B. Sansom, "An Outline of Recent Japanese Archaeological Research in Korea in Its Bearing Upon Early Japanese History," in *TASJ,* VI, 2d series (1929), 5–19.

myths of earlier Chinese migration and control, the region cannot be said at such times to have attained a degree of Chinese culture high enough to warrant Chao-hsien's inclusion in the Confucian world order in a role other than that of *barbarian*, for its people were not considered amenable to reason. Chinese policy, as illustrated by the agreement with Wei Man, was to secure the pacification of the borders by obtaining the personal allegiance of the chieftains of the uncivilized tribes. Border chieftains were also partially brought within the Chinese system by investiture from the emperor. Since the emperor, as protector and pacifier of each border area and of the more distant lands, theoretically ruled over the whole world, these border chieftains, through the titles granted them by the emperor, became superior to more distant barbarian areas. Each could approach the Middle Kingdom only through his superior. Thus in theory, a hierarchy descended from the Middle Kingdom out to the most remote corners of the earth, the farthest being the most inferior, and each being responsible for those below.

The invasion was little more than aggression, though it was based on Wei Yu-ch'ü's refusal to acknowledge the overlordship of the Middle Kingdom. The earlier agreement with Wei Man had designated Chao-hsien as the overlord of the barbarians beyond the border, and their allegiance to China was through Chao-hsien, not directly to the emperor. The demand that Wei Yu-ch'ü allow the more distant barbarians direct access to the emperor was, therefore, in violation of the earlier agreement with Wei Man putting them under the control of Chao-hsien. Yet, as Chao-hsien was, presumably, part of the wild domain, its ruler should have come once in his lifetime to the Chinese court in a formal manner. His refusal to do this broke the personal arrangement between himself and the Han Emperor. Nevertheless, Han aggrandizement was hardly justified under Confucian theory, despite the fact that barbarian Chao-hsien could not be dealt with through reason.

CHAPTER III

CHINA, JAPAN, AND THE KOREAN BALANCE OF POWER (TO A.D. 1280)

1. KAOKULI AND THE THREE HAN

AFTER the ancient kingdom of Chao-hsien had been destroyed and divided into four commanderies by the Han Emperor Wu in 108 B.C., an area known as Kaokuli (Ko-ko-rai) [1] was included in the northeast commandery of Hsüan-t'u. Kaokuli had been settled at a remote time by people from the Fuyü area [2] just south of the Sungari River in Manchuria,[3] but it had been occupied for at least two centuries before the Christian Era by peoples known as Weimai.[4] Since this region is described in Chinese works as being well developed in comparison with the nomadic barbarian lands around it, the presence of some Chinese culture there is indicated. For instance, the people lived in stockaded cities with palaces and granaries, were orderly and honest, wor-

---

[1] Parker, "On Race Struggles in Corea," *loc. cit.*, 186; Herrman, *Atlas of China*, 22–23. "Kokorai" is the Korean pronunciation of the Chinese characters.

[2] Gibert, *Dictionnaire*, 177. Kaokuli also appears to have been called Nan (south) or Tsu-pen Fuyü. For history of this area, see Hiroshi Ikeuchi, "A Study on the Fuyü," in *Memoirs of the Research Department of the Toyo Bunko*, VI (1932), 23–60.

[3] Longford, *Korea*, 57; Herrman, *Atlas of China*, 18–19.

[4] Gibert, *Dictionnaire*, 175. The legends point to a tribe even farther north called T'o-li or So-li, where a miraculously-born infant named Tung-ming so aroused the rulers' envy with his supernatural nature as he grew up that Tung-ming left in fear and went southward. He entered the Fuyü country and, resembling a predicted monarch, became their king. See Parker, "On Race Struggles in Corea," *loc. cit.*, 167; J. S. Gale, "Korean History (Translations from the Tong-gook T'ong-gam)," in *Korean Repository*, II (1895), 324; Griffis, *Corea*, 19–20.

shiped Heaven, and observed the etiquette of the table.[5] Fuyü is important because it was from there that Chu-mêng, a supposedly miraculously-born son of the Fuyü King Ch'uṇwa, came south into the area of Kaokuli and in 37 B.C. set up a kingdom.[6] Chu-mêng established his capital at Kuonei-ch'êng on the headwaters of the Hun-kiang, a tributary of the Yalu River,[7] and took for his family name "Kao," which was the first character of the name of the region.[8] His successors, slowly expanding southward into the Korean peninsula, ruled until A.D. 668.

At the time that the kingdom of Kaokuli was being established in the northern part of the Korean peninsula, new alignments were also appearing in the southern part. This much more backward region was traditionally divided into three *han* or tribal districts known as the *Ma-han*, the *Ch'ên-han*, and the *Pien-han*. No boundaries may be fixed for these areas other than general locations which placed Ma-han on the west, Ch'ên-han on the east, and Pien-han on the south.[9]

[5] Parker, "On Race Struggles in Corea," *loc. cit.*, 168–69.

[6] Gibert, *Dictionnaire*, 402. The fact that identical legends are told of the birth and migration of Tung-ming to Fuyü and Chu-mêng to Kaokuli, tends to show that the latter legend was a subsequent invention, presumably from Chinese sources, to add majesty to the line of Korean monarchs.

[7] *Ibid.*, 24, 403.

[8] Gale, "Korean History (Translations . . .)," *loc. cit.*, 321–27. Certain traditional accounts state that the name of Kaokuli was applied only after 37 B.C., when a Fuyü leader named Kao coupled his name with that of a legendary tribe north of Fuyü called Kuli or Korai, and applied the combination to the newly formed kingdom. These accounts, however, ignore the fact that the name was applied to a part of the Hsüan-t'u commandery of Emperor Yu of the Han dynasty before this migration. Therefore, the most reasonable story appears to be that wherein the migrating Fuyüs assumed the name of the area to which they came, their kings taking "Kao" as their family name. Gibert, *Dictionnaire*, 24. Gibert says that the name originally came from that of a mountain in the area, and Griffis quotes a Japanese writer who derives the name from a passage in *The Chinese Classics* referring to high mountains. Both Longford and Griffis, however, have the name originating with the state's founder in 37 B.C., despite a record of its existence in 108 B.C. *Ibid.*, 403; Longford, *Korea*, 59; Griffis, *Corea*, 23.

[9] Parker, "On Race Struggles in Corea," *loc. cit.*, 207; Griffis, *Corea*, 30. See also R. K. Reischauer, *Early Japanese History* (Princeton, 1937), II, 37.

Of the three the Ma-han was the largest, comprising fifty-four clans or tribes. Its territory appeared to extend up the whole western half of the Korean projection to the Ta-tung River on the north, and tradition held that this *han* had once ruled the entire southern part of the peninsula. Though the Ma-han people understood tillage, sericulture, and the making of cloth, they were much less advanced than the north Korean tribes who were in closer contact with China. The Ma-han had no cities; they built their houses of mud in the shape of a grave mound, with an opening or door in the top. They were not acquainted with the polite formalities such as obeisance, did not separate the sexes, and knew nothing of how to ride oxen or horses. They placed no value on gold, jewels, rugs, or embroidery, esteeming only pebbles and pearls as dress and ear ornaments, and their worship was of a primitive nature.[10] Among the clans of the Ma-han, history records one made up of Chinese refugees who had crossed to the peninsula at some remote time and who bore the name of Pai-chi, meaning the "many crossers." [11]

Ch'ên-han, though comprising only twelve tribes, was further advanced than either of its neighbors. This condition was attributed to a legendary Chinese ancestry, for the elders of Ch'ên-han claimed that they were Ch'in refugees who had fled to the *han* areas to avoid forced labor in China and that their land had once extended from sea to sea until the Ma-han, in occupying the western coast, had relegated them to the east. Living in a land described as "fat and fair and suited to the five cereals" and having a background of Chinese civilization, the Ch'ên-han were prosperous. They alone were skilled in the production of iron; and since the surrounding states all purchased it, iron is said to have become the sole medium of exchange. The Ch'ên-han people, with graded

[10] Parker, "On Race Struggles in Corea," *loc. cit.*, 207–208.
[11] Gale, "Korean History (Translations . . .)," *loc. cit.*, 323; Longford, *Korea*, 63.

ranks of chieftains, lived in city-like enclosures. They used domestic animals, observed the proper forms in marriage, and appear to have more closely approached a civilized existence than either the western or southern *han*.[12]

Little is known, however, of the territory to the south called Pien-han. Its people are recorded as being similar to the Ch'ên-han in dress and in the practice of living in cities, but their language and some of their customs were different. For instance, some of the Pien-han are said to have borrowed the practice of tattooing [13] from the bordering people of Wo (Japan).

About the time that Kaokuli was founded in the northern part of the peninsula, the three traditional regions in the south were in process of merging into two kingdoms called Pai-chi and Hsin-lo.[14] Later, the small tribe of Pai-chi, the "many crossers" in the Ma-han clan, was able to extend its sway and eventually to give its name to the whole area. The actual founding of the kingdom of Pai-chi is credited, however, to Wên Tsu, a son of the founder of Kaokuli, Chu-mêng, by his second wife; [15] but when Chu-mêng's firstborn came from Fuyü in search of his father and was received and proclaimed as heir, Wên Tsu and another brother, sons of a later marriage, went south and founded a second kingdom in Pai-chi in 19 B.C. By A.D. 9, according to Korean records, Wên Tsu had completed his conquest of the Ma-han.[16]

Little is known of the founding of Hsin-lo by the union of Ch'ên-han and Pien-han. Korean history fixes the date, however, as 57 B.C. and attributes a supernatural birth to its first king.[17]

[12] Parker, "On Race Struggles in Corea," *loc. cit.*, 209–10.

[13] *Ibid.*, 210–11.

[14] In Korean, Pakche and Silla; in Japanese, Haiksai or Kudara and Shinra or Shiragi.

[15] Gibert, *Dictionnaire*, 431; Parker, "On Race Struggles in Corea," loc. cit., 214.

[16] Gale, "Korean History (Translations . . .)," II, *loc. cit.*, 327.

[17] *Ibid.*, 323–24.

At the beginning of the Christian Era the Korean peninsula was divided into three kingdoms—Kaokuli in the north,
Pai-chi on the west, and Hsin-lo on the east. Wedged in between Pai-chi and Hsin-lo on the southern tip of the peninsula
was the area of Kaya, known to the Japanese as Mimana,
which was gradually absorbed by Hsin-lo.[18]

Although the influence of China on Kaokuli was continu-
ous from about 100 B.C. to at least A.D. 200,[19] it should be
noted that no official influence of the Chinese empire—Chinese administration, Chinese armies, nor the officially sponsored Chinese culture, which was considered the hallmark of
human advancement—had been extended to the two southern kingdoms. These southern kingdoms, to be sure, had a
tradition of past Chinese immigration, particularly notice-
able in Hsin-lo, but they lacked any consciousness of definite
status within the Far Eastern world order. Consequently,
despite any Chinese influence which may have survived from
ancient Chao-hsien, despite proximity to the Middle Kingdom, and despite the southern legends of early migrations,
the Korean peoples could, at the time of Christ, be classed
by Chinese standards only as semi-barbarians. Some writers
have held that the supposed effect of early connections must
long since have been overwhelmed by the native civilization.[20]

For the first few centuries after their founding the three
kingdoms were to learn little from China except the art of
war. They submitted before overwhelming Chinese force
when it was presented, but they acknowledged the superiority of China only temporarily and when no other course was

[18] Yoshi S. Kuno, *Japanese Expansion on the Asiatic Continent* (Berkeley,
1937–40), I, 12, 193–95; W. G. Aston, "Early Japanese History," in *TASJ*,
XVI (1889), 43; H. B. Hulbert, "The Ancient Kingdom of Karak," in *Korea
Review*, II (1902), 541–46.

[19] Sansom, "An Outline of Recent Japanese Archaeological Research . . . ,"
loc. cit., .7.

[20] H. B. Hulbert, "Korean Survivals," in *Transactions of the Korean Branch
of the Royal Asiatic Society*, I (1900), 27–30. *Transactions of the Korean
Branch of the Royal Asiatic Society* are hereafter cited as *TKBRAS*.

open. Following the classic principle which recognized that barbarians could be dealt with only by "non-use of Great Government-by-Reason," [21] China relied mainly on force to extend her authority far enough to preserve order and protect the Middle Kingdom. The Chinese did not seek direct administration of these territories, but rather the "protection of the hedges" of China. Accepting and requiring tribute from areas which were conquered or which voluntarily submitted, to maintain order they used the method of securing the submission of the barbarian chiefs and then conferring upon them titles denoting a responsibility to China as protector of the outlying regions. By thus bringing the barbarian chieftains partially within the Chinese system, it was possible to keep the borders quiet, even though the people themselves were not "amenable to reason."

2. KAOKULI, PAI-CHI, AND HSIN-LO

Kaokuli displayed its warlike nature almost immediately after its foundation. Wang Mang, who had usurped the Chinese throne, called on the second of the Kaokuli kings, Lyu-ri [22] (19 B.C.–A.D. 17), for troops to support an expedition against the Huns. Lyu-ri not only refused to comply but also, to emphasize his recalcitrance, occupied part of Hsüan-t'u commandery, nominally under Chinese control.[23] While records show that a punitive expedition was sent against Kaokuli, Wang Mang's vengeance was the official removal of the title of King from Lyu-ri and the changing of the name of Kaokuli to Hsiakuli, "Kao" signifying "high" and "Hsia" meaning "low." [24] The successors of Lyu-ri, nevertheless,

[21] See pp. 12–13.
[22] The titles of the Korean rulers are Romanized according to J. S. Gale, *The Unabridged Korean-English Dictionary* (Seoul, 1931).
[23] Hiroshi, "A Study on the Fuyü," *loc. cit.*, 25; Gibert, *Dictionnaire*, 404.
[24] Parker, "On Race Struggles in Corea," *loc. cit.*, 187 n., states, however, that the name "Kao" was merely a family name and had no connection with its antithesis "Hsia." Cf. Gibert, *Dictionnaire*, 401.

34   KOREA AND THE OLD ORDERS

pursued similar tactics against China and also against their Manchurian neighbors.[25] Though other reports recount a submission to the Han dynasty and a regranting of the title of King, removed by Wang Mang,[26] and even though mention is made of aid to China against revolts in the northwest,[27] the exploits of the third Kaokuli king, Kung (A.D. 53–145), show no evidence of submissiveness. Raids are said to have been made by him in Liao-tung in 105 and in Hsüan-t'u with Ma-han allies in A.D. 118.[28] After his defeat by armies led in person by the administrators of the Liao-tung and Hsüan-t'u commanderies, Kung, while making a pretense of submission, ambushed his pursuers and also sent troops to attack the unguarded cities his opponents had left behind.[29] In the last year of his life Kung was beaten in an attempted invasion of Hsüan-t'u, and his successor, Syu-Syüng, surrendered to the Chinese.[30]

When the Later Han dynasty fell (A.D. 220) and the Wei dynasty came to power in North China, Kaokuli took advantage of the confusion attending the dynastic change and

[25] Gibert, *Dictionnaire*, 425.
[26] Parker, "On Race Struggles in Corea," *loc. cit.*, 188.
[27] Griffis, *Corea*, 24.
[28] Parker, "On Race Struggles in Corea," *loc. cit.*, 189.
[29] *Ibid.*
[30] *Ibid.*, 190–91; Hiroshi, "A Study on the Fuyü," *loc. cit.*, 31. Hsüan-t'u commandery, to the north and east of Kaokuli, seems to have been the area against which Kaokuli directed most of its attacks. It was the farthermost area to the northeast over which China exercised direct control. Aside from its remoteness, it lacked the protection of the wall which ran along the north border of Liao-hsi and then south to meet the sea at the Yalu River. Herrman, *Atlas of China*, 23. Situated in the angle formed by Hsüan-t'u to the north and Liao-tung to the west, Kaokuli could raid northward into Hsüan-t'u at will, and westward across the barrier into Liao-tung if desiring a bolder venture. Should pressure from the two areas be exerted simultaneously, as it later was, it was simple to retire southward into the peninsula. When the defenses of Hsüan-t'u were strengthened in the second century by the organization of six tribes of agricultural garrisons, the tenth Kaokuli king, Yün Wu (197–226), moved his capital from the headquarters of the Hun southward to Wan-tu, near the present town of Tsi-an-hien on the right bank of the Yalu River. Parker, "On Race Struggles in Corea," *loc. cit.*, 191; Gibert, *Dictionnaire*, 404.

extended its control westward into Liao-tung. The king, Wu-Wui-Kü (A.D. 227–247), also established friendly relations with the Chinese kingdom of Wu in the Yangtze valley as a diplomatic move against the Wei dynasty. Later, after remonstrance by the Wei kingdom, Wu-Wui-Kü abandoned this alliance and in A.D. 238 even aided the Wei armies in their campaigns in Liao-tung.[31] In the latter part of his reign he again resorted to forays into Liao-tung. Retaliating swiftly, the Wei governor of Yu province invaded Kaokuli and in A.D. 242 destroyed its capital. The chastened king then moved his capital farther south into the peninsula to Pyeng-yang on the banks of the Ta-tung River.[32]

Though the Wei kingdom of China was short-lived (221–265), the Kaokuli kings had little opportunity again to push toward the north and west. After the death (290) of the Chin monarch Wu, successor to the Wei rulers, barbarians swept down from the north into Liao-tung and westward into the Yellow River basin. For more than a century thereafter, in the period known as the "Barbarian Rebellion" (317–439), the north of China was a battleground.[33]

In 342 Kaokuli blocked easy access of the Hsien-pi barbarians to the Yu-wên, their enemies in southern Manchuria. Mujung Kuang, the Yen ruler whose dynasty these bar-

[31] Gibert, *Dictionnaire*, 404.
[32] Hulbert, "Korean Survivals," *loc. cit.*, 179.
[33] Shuhsi Hsü, *China and Her Political Entity* (New York, 1926), 10. Hsü states that after the Mujungs went from the Liao-tung area into the Yellow River basin and after the Tobas conquered all the area in 439, a Manchurian tribe named Kaokuli came down into the commanderies of Lo-lang, Hsüan-t'u, and Tai-fang and founded the kingdom of Kaokuli, thus dating the founding of the kingdom about A.D. 439 instead of 37 B.C. The Kaokuli had not merely "cast a covetous eye" upon the area before A.D. 439, as Hsü states, but, as shown above (page 29, n. 8), they had been living in it since 37 B.C. The Kaokuli were not one of those later groups who came south after the death of the Chin Emperor Wu; instead they had arrived at least two centuries earlier. The driving of the Kaokuli back across the border several times, as Hsü states, could mean only the southern border beyond which the Kaokuli retired when the Mujungs came down from the north. See E. B. Price, *Russo-Japanese Treaties of 1907–1916* (Baltimore, 1933), 7.

barians had set up in China, invaded Kaokuli from the east and north and forced the Kaokuli king to recognize the Mujung superiority, for which recognition the submissive ruler received the official title of Governor over several areas.[34]

Defeated in the north, Kaokuli was more successful in its southward expansion and, during the confusion of the Barbarian Rebellion in China, had spread southward into Lolang commandery as far as the Tai-fang area.[35] The outlying areas of China had ceased to be attractive raiding ground; moreover, the overwhelming power of the Middle Kingdom was such that a country like Kaokuli could never be safe if it either stayed too close to China's ever-expanding influence or tried to push it back. The result was that from the end of the fourth century the relations of China and Kaokuli, aside from the nominal acknowledgment of superiority required from semi-barbaric peripheral areas, revolved around the intercourse of the three peninsula kingdoms of Kaokuli, Pai-chi, and Hsin-lo. In their intercourse each would bid for the support of the powerful Middle Kingdom.

Japan, or the Kingdom of Wo, also was active in the affairs of the peninsula, not as a second powerful nation playing against China on the Korean checkerboard, but as a fourth minor kingdom. Recognizing China as her superior,[36] Japan sought Chinese approval of her desire to expand in the southern part of the Korean peninsula in order to forestall the advance of Kaokuli. In its memorial to the Chinese emperor,

---

[34] Gibert, *Dictionnaire,* 405.

[35] This area had been lately created as a separate district from the southern part of Lo-lang by the Chin rulers (265–316), but the southwestern Korean kingdom of Pai-chi had pre-empted it, barring Kaokuli's southward moves. The occupation of these areas officially designated as Chinese commanderies may be explained by the fact that the barbarian dynasties in China, hard pressed by later arrivals on their borders, constructed defensive walls rather than the earlier offensive ones, thus contracting and attempting to solidify rather than expand their holdings. Under these tactics the northeast commanderies were abandoned. Gibert, *Dictionnaire,* 405; Shuhsi Hsü, *China,* 8–9, 11.

[36] Kuno, *Japanese Expansion,* 225.

the Japanese government described Kaokuli as the "powerful enemy nation" which interfered with their reaching the imperial throne in order to pay due respect.[37] Through the dominated coastal area of Kaya (Mimana), and through alliances with the Korean kingdoms, Japan constituted a factor in the affairs of the peninsula for a century or more, though she was never able to destroy Kaokuli.

When Kaokuli turned southward in her expansion after the disastrous defeat at the hands of the Hsien-pi Mujungs, she encountered the strong western kingdom of Pai-chi, which had entered into friendly relations with Japan as early as 365.[38] The first Kaokuli excursion into Pai-chi (369) was made when Pai-chi and Japan were engaged in joint effort against the third Korean kingdom, Hsin-lo (Silla), an area which had been experiencing Japanese raids since 14 B.C.[39] and which had in 344 refused Japan's offer of peace through a matrimonial alliance.[40] This reconnoitering raid of Kaokuli brought repercussions the following year when a Pai-chi army invaded Kaokuli, placed the capital at Pyeng-yang under temporary siege, and killed the king.[41] Though the two succeeding Kaokuli kings were able merely to continue an armed truce with Pai-chi, a still later ruler, King Tam Tük (392–412), bore and merited the title of Kuang-k'ai-t'u-wang, "King who expanded the territory of his realm." [42] In 395 Tam Tük moved northward and westward into areas abandoned by the barbarian north Chinese dynasties and subdued various tribes in his path.[43] In the following year he constructed a large fleet and attacked Pai-chi by sea.[44] Hoping

[37] *Ibid.*
[38] Aston, "Early Japanese History," *loc. cit.*, 61–62.
[39] Kuno, *Japanese Expansion*, 214–15.
[40] *Ibid.*, 216.
[41] Gibert, *Dictionnaire*, 408.
[42] *Ibid.*, 428.
[43] *Ibid.*, 409; Shuhsi Hsü, *China*, 11.
[44] Gibert, *Dictionnaire*, 409. This attack was made by sea evidently because Pai-chi is recorded as having constructed a defensive wall along its

to exercise dominance over Kaokuli, Mujung Pao (396–398), a ruler of the Later Yen dynasty, a line which had assumed the title of Emperor of China in A.D. 386,[45] approved the exploit of Tam Tük and conferred on him the title of "Governor of P'ing-chou (a province in south Jehol) and King of Liao-tung and Tai-fang." Japanese influence on Pai-chi, evidenced by the fact that the Pai-chi king had sent his son to Japan as hostage in 397,[46] led to an alliance between Japan and Pai-chi, its objective being opposition to Hsin-lo and Kaokuli. To succor Hsin-lo, who asked aid to recover territory lost to the Japanese, and to punish Pai-chi for violation of her previous submission, Kaokuli again moved southward, defeating the Japanese who were in Kaya and the Tai-fang region, and forcing the Pai-chi king to renounce his Japanese alliance.[47]

The success of Kaokuli was due not only to her own warlike propensities but also to her diplomatic finesse which prevented Chinese aid to her opponents. To this end she established relations with the several kingdoms contending for the dominance of China, offered tribute to the court of the southern Ch'in kingdom in 413, for which titles were conferred on her ruler Kü Ryün,[48] opened relations with the northern Wei kingdom under the Tobas and with the southern Sung,[49] and sent an envoy in 465 to congratulate the new Toba emperor, Hsien-wen of the northern Wei dynasty.[50] These precautions of being friendly with several of the Chinese kingdoms proved of benefit to Kaokuli in her later conflicts in the Korean peninsula. For instance, the refusal of the Wei rulers to give aid

---

northern border a decade earlier, thereby forestalling land attacks. J. S. Gale, "Korean History (Selections from Native Writers)," in *Korean Repository*, III (1896), 186.

[45] Herrman, *Atlas of China*, 29; Gibert, *Dictionnaire*, 232.

[46] Aston, "Early Japanese History," *loc. cit.*, 63.

[47] Gibert, *Dictionnaire*, 410.

[48] Parker, "On Race Struggles in Corea," *loc. cit.*, 194.

[49] Gibert, *Dictionnaire*, 410.

[50] Parker, "On Race Struggles in Corea," *loc. cit.*, 193.

to Pai-chi against Kaokuli in 474 enabled the king of Kaokuli to overrun Pai-chi, take its capital, put to death its king and his sons, and set up his own brother to rule at a new capital farther south.[51]

During the sixth century Kaokuli attained her largest extent. In the north her territory reached up the east coast above the forty-second parallel to the Tu-man River, and in the west it included the entire Liao-tung peninsula. Southward the borders ran to the Im-chin River just north of the capital city of Pai-chi on the west coast, and on the east about as far down into the Hsin-lo area as the thirty-seventh parallel. Hsin-lo, Pai-chi, and the Japanese-controlled Kaya (Mimana), each constituted a triangular wedge on the east, west, and south, respectively, and all were surmounted on the north by the expanding Kaokuli.[52]

The disunity which had existed in China since the downfall of the Han dynasty, and which had caused inattention toward affairs within the Korean peninsula, was coming to an end during the latter part of the sixth century. The Duke of Sui, late adviser to the throne of Northern Chou, and subsequently its usurper, was able in 589 to reunite into a compact empire the long-contending kingdoms.[53] Even before the unification Kaokuli, diplomatically astute, had established cordial relations with the Sui, and her king, Wün (590–617), was confirmed in his titles by the first Sui Emperor Wên.[54]

It is difficult, in the light of these early cordial relations, to understand the action of the Kaokuli king in leading a foray beyond the Liao-tung River into the Liao-hsi area and sacking a town in Jehol province in 598.[55] Perhaps he sus-

[51] Cf. Kuno, *Japanese Expansion,* I, 10, for the Japanese version of this invasion. See also, Aston, "Early Japanese History," *loc. cit.,* 68; Parker, "On Race Struggles in Corea," *loc. cit.,* 216–17.

[52] See Herrman, *Atlas of China,* 31–32.

[53] G. N. Steiger, *A History of the Far East* (Boston, 1936), 94–95.

[54] H. B. Hulbert, "Korean History," in *Korea Review,* I (1901), 233.

[55] Gibert, *Dictionnaire,* 26, 411.

pected the rapid flow of Chinese customs and influence into the other two Korean kingdoms, particularly into Hsin-lo,[56] and feared that a united China would not long tolerate a disunited and disordered peninsula.[57] It was this raid, however, which was the initial cause of the downfall of Wün's kingdom.

The position of the Sui dynasty (589–619 A.D.) with reference to its northeastern neighbors was more difficult than that of the Former Han dynasty (202 B.C.–A.D. 25) had been. For hundreds of years no regular policy governed the relations between China and this region. In the first place, the northeastern kingdoms had developed a local sentiment from centuries of warfare. Furthermore, the Sui dynasty was not, as the Han rulers had been, in possession of the zone of semi-civilization that lay between the two sections.[58] If the northeastern regions had remained peaceful, the Sui dynasty would probably have been content with only the nominal control which came from the acknowledgment of its superiority by the petty kingdoms. Such an attitude is indicated by the fact that, as a result of the Kaokuli raid, the first Sui emperor sent only a letter of remonstrance to the king of Kaokuli which stated in part:

Although the people and the territory of the out-of-the-way kingdom of your highness are insignificant, they are just the same my people and my territory. If we were to depose your highness, we could not leave the post vacant and would have to select some one to fill it. Should your highness be able to cleanse your heart, modify your conduct, and hereafter act in conformity with the fundamental laws of the empire, we would already have had a good minister, and why should we trouble ourselves to send other talents! In administering laws, the rulers of old were guided above all by the principle of justice; reward is for the good, and punishment for the evil. The people within the four seas will know what we do.

[56] See pp. 43 ff.
[57] Cf. Longford, *Korea*, 68 ff.
[58] Shuhsi Hsü, *China*, 15.

If we impose armed forces upon your highness without a just cause, what would they think of us? We hope your highness will consider what we have said and desist from further designs. . . .[59]

Since the letter apparently had no effect, Emperor Wang dispatched an army of 300,000 overland through Shanhai-kwan and a strong fleet to attack the capital on the Ta-tung River, thus following the strategy used by Emperor Wu of the Han dynasty six hundred years earlier.[60] However, storms at sea disrupted the naval force before it reached the Korean coast, and the overland army was besieged by torrential rains which made roads impassable for both men and supply wagons. Meanwhile the king of Kaokuli, greatly frightened by the approaching army, sent excuses for his act, and the Chinese expeditionary force was recalled.[61]

In 607 Emperor Yang of the Sui dynasty, to test the sub-missiveness of Kaokuli, ordered its king to appear at his court. Upon the king's refusal, a massive force was again fitted to attack Kaokuli by both land and sea. Setting forth southward across the Yalu River in 612, the troops were said to extend in an unbroken line for 320 miles, requiring forty days to pass one point.[62] Nevertheless, the resistance of the besieged Koreans, their feigned submission, a lack of provisions, and a waning enthusiasm among the Chinese troops, despite their initial successes, caused the return journey of this expedition to become a rout.

The Kaokuli troops so harried the retreating Chinese at every strategic point that, of the 305,000 men who crossed the Yalu River, only 2,700 recrossed to the safety of the main body.[63] With winter approaching, the army returned to China and the following year attempted only the conquest of the

[59] Ibid., 16.
[60] See pp. 25 ff. It is possible that the size of this and of the later Sui armies, as well as the number of casualties, is exaggerated.
[61] Gibert, Dictionnaire, 26, 411; Longford, Korea, 69–70.
[62] Hulbert, "Korean History," loc. cit., I, 235.
[63] Ibid., 239.

Liao-tung area. Even before this conquest was completed, however, the emperor was called back to deal with a rebellion fomented in his own capital by Yang Hsüan-kan.[64] In 614 a new army and new tactics were employed, and Kaokuli, its resources depleted in the previous campaigns, was forced to send an envoy with the submission of its king.

The Emperor Yang then recalled his troops, ordered the king of Kaokuli to appear at court the following winter, and kept the Kaokuli envoy as a hostage for the king's appearance.[65] When the recalcitrant ruler did not appear, the emperor had the envoy killed. Presently, before another expedition against Kaokuli could be prepared, a new revolt arose, the Emperor Yang was assassinated (in 618), and his dynasty was replaced by that of the T'ang.[66] Kaokuli was now in possession of even the land route to the peninsula, a route paralleling the Gulf of Liao, as far south as Shanhaikwan.[67]

This long period, extending from the beginning of the Christian Era to the end of the sixth century, may be described as one wherein the relations between China and the Korean area reached no approximation of that ideal and harmonious status envisaged in the Confucian conception of the world order. With disorganization in China eclipsing Confucian influence, and with the recurrent pressure and invasions of barbarians from the north constantly cutting off the Korean kingdoms from China proper, no definite political relationship was long maintained.

The general attitude taken by China, regardless of the dynasty in power, was that the Korean area was one inhabited by barbarians who had, however, the beginnings of civilization. But as barbarians, the Koreans could not enjoy Government-by-Reason, and the policiy pursued was merely an

[64] *Ibid.*, 240.
[65] Gibert, *Dictionnaire*, 412.
[66] *Ibid.*, 27.
[67] Herrman, *Atlas of China*, 35.

attempted preservation of peace and order. This was accomplished through bringing these people partly within the Chinese system by conferring titles and honors on their leaders, trusting mainly to the sobering effect of such titles and of imperial admonitions to prevent border raids. When this form of control failed, force was used to bring about a change of heart in the barbarian leaders or, failing that, force deposed the leader.

The Korean kingdoms themselves had as yet no conception that their "natural position" in the world order was one of voluntary submission to China's superiority. However, they knew, though they did not understand, the Chinese theories; and Kaokuli was particularly adept at submission in the face of superior force, only to violate its promise as soon as the threat was withdrawn. As a matter of fact, the many dynastic changes in China in this period and the existence of more than one ruler claiming to be the rightful Son of Heaven left a field wherein power diplomacy rather than Confucian theories dominated the situation. Nevertheless, the infiltration of the Chinese literature and culture into these barbarian areas was slowly winning for China the position of ascendancy which force could not compel.

3. HSIN-LO AND THE GROWTH OF CHINESE CULTURE

Coincident with the rise of a unified China under the Sui and the subsequent T'ang dynasty, there occurred on the Korean peninsula the rise to power and culture of the heretofore unimportant kingdom of Hsin-lo (Silla). This area, with the traditions of settlement by Chinese immigrants and of a period of sovereignty over all of South Korea,[68] is known in the early centuries mainly for the numerous onslaughts she suffered at the hands of the Japanese.[69] The Japanese writers

[68] See pp. 30–31.
[69] Facing, as it did, the coasts of Japan, many of the early raids were prob-

state that Hsin-lo, known to them as Shinra or Shiragi, was the first Korean area to be reduced by them to the status of a tributary.[70] Successive expeditions of the Japanese to the coast of Hsin-lo, with scarcely more than a decade between any two of them,[71] confirm the Japanese complaint that she "frequently ignored the authority of Japan" and cast doubt on the actual exercise of that authority despite the records of its existence.[72] Hsin-lo's traditional enemy, however, was Pai-chi, the western Korean kingdom whose relations with Japan were more cordial, and the kingdom through which Japan sought to extend her control on the peninsula. Hsin-lo and Kaokuli, therefore, generally aligned themselves together, Hsin-lo playing a passive role in the southward expansion of Kaokuli into Pai-chi and calling for the assistance of Kaokuli when attacked by Pai-chi or Japan.

Up to the sixth century of the Christian Era, Hsin-lo had been less affected than the other Korean kingdoms by Chinese influence, notwithstanding the legend of early Chinese migrations to her territory.[73] Though the Confucian Classics and Buddhist writings had been introduced into Kaokuli as early as A.D. 372 and into Pai-chi in the same century, it was not until the beginning of the sixth century that they found their way into Hsin-lo.[74] At that time Hsin-lo underwent a phenomenal growth in both culture and power, which was to make her within two centuries the master of the entire peninsula.[75]

---

ably of a private piratical nature, but those such as that of A.D. 121, which required 1000 men to repel, show that even at that date they were a constant menace to the life of Hsin-lo. See Aston, "Early Japanese History," *loc. cit.,* 48.

[70] Kuno, *Japanese Expansion,* 5.
[71] See Aston, "Early Japanese History," *loc. cit.,* 69–70.
[72] Kuno, *Japanese Expansion,* 5, 8.
[73] Parker, "On Race Struggles in Corea," *loc. cit.,* 221.
[74] Maurice Courant, "Introduction to the 'Bibliographie Coreene'" (Mrs. W. Massy Royds, trans.), in *TKBRAS,* XXV (1936), 34.
[75] With the Japanese-administered area of Kaya (Mimana) to the south, Hsin-lo, at the opening of the sixth century, constituted only a small triangle

This sudden growth may have been caused partly by the waning of Japanese power in Korea under the pressure of a reunited China, and by the disorganization preliminary to and accompanying the Taikwa reforms in Japan.[76] Thus relieved from Japanese attacks on her coasts and from encroachment by Japan's ally, Pai-chi, Hsin-lo could devote herself to internal development. However, the main cause appears to have been the conscious reorientation of her international policy. From the very beginning of the sixth century Hsin-lo turned toward China for inspiration and aid rather than to the warlike Kaokuli,[77] whose recognitions of Chinese supremacy were only temporary and were occasioned by expediency rather than by any genuine admiration. But China may also have played more than a passive role in Hsin-lo's change of front and subsequent growth. Since any expansion of imperial prestige to the northeast was blocked by the strong Kaokuli kingdom, the emperors of reunited China, particularly those of the T'ang dynasty, courted Hsin-lo as a power to balance Kaokuli on the peninsula and to serve as a valuable ally for the pacification of the whole area.[78]

The way in which this orientation of Hsin-lo toward China began definitely marked the change of policy. In the year 503 the name of the country was fixed and transcribed in Chinese characters, and its king, Chi Teung, dropped his native title for the Chinese appellation of *Wang*.[79] About the same time,

---

on the eastern coast with its base extending from parallel 35 to parallel 37½. Herrman, *Atlas of China*, 32.

[76] For the Taikwa reforms, see James Murdoch, *A History of Japan* (London, 1925–26), I, Chap. V.

[77] While it is true that the aid of Kaokuli had earlier saved Hsin-lo from extinction at the hands of Pai-chi, Kaokuli, in her subsequent southward expansion, did not limit her ambitions to Pai-chi alone.

[78] Longford, *Korea*, 75; Kuno, *Japanese Expansion*, I, 16.

[79] Courant, "Introduction to the 'Bibliographie Coreene,'" *loc. cit.*, 32–33. The official titles of earlier kings had been, progressively, Chü-hsi-kan, Tz'u-tz'u, Ni-shih, and Ma-li-kan, native words which were transcribed into Chinese. "Wang" is translated as "king." Parker, "On Race Struggles in Corea," *loc. cit.*, 220.

the *Sam Kuk Sa Kui* [80] also begins to record some of the titles of officials in conformance with Chinese organization.[81]

4. UNIFICATION OF THE KOREAN PENINSULA

With the rise of the T'ang dynasty, Hsin-lo entered into even closer collaboration with China. The prevading nature of the flow of Chinese culture into Hsin-lo during this period is illustrated by the fact that even in the twentieth century the prefix "T'ang," when applied to works of art, literature, and coins in Korea, meant "Chinese," and the term "T'ang-yang" was the equivalent of "prosperity." [82] The Chinese court headdress and ceremony were adopted, and Buddhism and the Classics, already known, were diligently studied.[83] A present from T'ai-Tsung, the second T'ang Emperor, consisting of a picture of a peony, led to the adoption of that flower as the king of flowers in Korea. In 651 the king of Hsin-lo sent his sons to China to wait on the T'ang Emperor, and one of the sons, a noted scholar, was there made Minister of the Left.[84] So diligent was the cultivation of the Chinese culture in Hsin-lo that it became referred to by the T'ang rulers as "The Superior Man's Nation." [85]

The early T'ang emperors, evidently recalling the recent defeats of the Sui rulers in the Korean peninsula—defeats which contributed no small part to the downfall of that dy-

[80] The earliest of Korean dynastic histories, written in the eleventh century. See Courant, "Introduction to the 'Bibliographie Coreene,'" *loc. cit.*, 83; M. N. Trollope, "Corean Books and Their Authors," *TKBRAS*, XXI (1932), 24.

[81] Courant, "Introduction to the 'Bibliographie Coreene,'" *loc. cit.*, 33; Parker, "On Race Struggles in Corea," *loc. cit.*, 221; Hulbert, "Korean Survivals," *loc. cit.*, 29–30.

[82] Griffis, *Corea*, 47; J. S. Gale, "The Influence of China Upon Korea," *TKBRAS*, I (1900), 12.

[83] Courant, "Introduction to the 'Bibliographie Coreene,'" *loc. cit.*, 34; Longford, *Korea*, 75.

[84] Gale, "The Influence of China Upon Korea," *loc. cit.*, 5.

[85] Hulbert, "Korean Survivals," *loc. cit.*, I, 45.

nasty [86]—showed no desire to enter the Korean arena. Moreover, since the rulers of all three of the Korean kingdoms had made formal acknowledgment to the T'ang dynasty and had been confirmed in their titles,[87] the emperor appeared to be satisfied with the status quo. But the Korean kingdoms themselves, particularly Kaokuli, confident after its defeat of the Sui armies, soon conspired to break the peace. In 641 the Kaokuli king, Kün-Mu, who had established friendly relations with the T'ang rulers, was assassinated by his minister Kai-So-Mun. The regicide then placed the deceased king's nephew Chang (642–668) on the throne but actually conducted affairs of state himself. In spite of the advice of ministers who desired to use this occasion for an invasion, T'ai-Tsung (627–649), the T'ang Emperor, made no move to intervene in this domestic matter.[88]

But in 643 representatives from Hsin-lo appeared at the T'ang court and informed the emperor that Kaokuli, in league now with its old enemy Pai-chi, was seeking to disrupt the communications between Hsin-lo and China, thus blocking Hsin-lo's access to the T'ang court. Since Hsin-lo was the most progressive Korean state, and the only one which had adopted Chinese forms and civilization, the emperor was anxious to preserve such a valuable ally. He therefore sent an ambassador to Kaokuli to remonstrate, but Kai-So-Mun, the *de facto* ruler, treated the envoy with insolence and even cast him into prison.[89] Accordingly, the emperor personally formed and commanded a great army, with barbarian auxiliaries, and invaded Liao-tung in 644. City after city fell after stubborn resistance, but the approach of winter caused the besieging forces to be recalled from the city of An-shih before any advance was made into the Korean peninsula

[86] Gibert, *Dictionnaire*, 412.
[87] Gale, "The Influence of China Upon Korea," *loc. cit.*, 5.
[88] Gibert, *Dictionnaire*, 27, 413.
[89] Hulbert, "Korean History," *loc. cit.*, I, 274, 278.

proper.[90] In 647 a second expedition was sent which destroyed several cities in Liao-tung and then returned. Two years later the Emperor T'ai-Tsung died.[91]

Though the minister who murdered his king continued to rule in Kaokuli, the peninsula enjoyed a decade of peace. The rising power of Hsin-lo and Japan's waning influence in the peninsula, however, caused Kaokuli and Pai-chi to draw together in another alliance to crush Hsin-lo. Again Hsin-lo appealed to China against this coalition, and the T'ang Emperor Kao Tsung (650–683) dispatched an army by sea to the coasts of Pai-chi. Aided by the Hsin-lo troops on the east and by the disorganization resulting from the incapacity of the Pai-chi rulers, the emperor's forces subdued the kingdom after a short battle in 660; [92] whereupon the king of Pai-chi fled to Kaokuli. His remaining son and other members of his family, together with many prisoners, were taken to China, and Pai-chi became temporarily a province under a Chinese governor.[93]

In 663 a revolt occurred in which another son of the last Pai-chi king, long a hostage in Japan, was returned by the Japanese with a strong army in an attempt to save their influence in the peninsula. The T'ang and Hsin-lo armies, then on the southern border of Kaokuli, quickly executed a forced march southward and, cooperating with the T'ang fleet off shore, overwhelmingly defeated the Japanese on land and sea. As a result, Japan withdrew from Korea, not to return for almost a thousand years.[94] China relinquished her direct control as soon as order was re-established, and in 665 the deposed king's son, captured five years before, was sent back to rule as "Prince of Tai-fang." [95]

---

[90] Gibert, *Dictionnaire*, 28, 413. Longford, *Korea*, 76, locates the town of An-shih in the peninsula only forty miles north of the capital.
[91] Gibert, *Dictionnaire*, 414.
[92] *Ibid.*, 29, 414; Longford, *Korea*, 78.
[93] Kuno, *Japanese Expansion*, 18, 20; Gibert, *Dictionnaire*, 29.
[94] Kuno, *Japanese Expansion*, 19–20, 234.
[95] Shuhsi Hsü, *China*, 17.

Kaokuli was not long in following Pai-chi into extinction. The minister Kao-So-Mun, who had controlled the kingdom since 642, had died. The son who succeeded him to power, Nam-Saing, was opposed by the two younger sons Nam-Kun and Nam-San. To save himself, Nam-Saing sent in his submission to China and was reinstated in 666 as Governor of Liao-tung and Pacifier of Pyeng-yang. His authority existed, however, only in the north, since the powerless king of Kaokuli, under the control of the other brothers, occupied the capital at Pyeng-yang.[96] The T'ang ruler seized the opportunity caused by this dissension to invade the last unsubmissive parts of the peninsula. Hsin-lo threw her forces against the southern border of Kaokuli, while China attacked from the north; and the kingdom of Kaokuli ceased to exist in 668. In 676 the defeated king was set up as a petty ruler in Liaotung, though he was later deposed for plotting with the northern barbarians. Eventually he was taken to China, where he died in 682.[97] In 687 the grandson of the twice-deposed king was created "Prince of Chao-hsien," and in 698 he was dispatched to rule in Pyeng-yang.[98]

Though conquered and reorganized by China, the Korean area did not long remain under any actual Chinese administration. It has been mentioned that the administration of the territory of Pai-chi was ended in 665.[99] The protectorate in Kaokuli also ceased to exist as its headquarters moved gradually westward toward the confines of China, finally being transferred in 676 from Pyeng-yang to the Liao-tung area, out of the Korean peninsula.[100] The T'ang-shu describes the short period of Chinese administration of this region as a very benevolent one. "Great care was taken of the old and the orphanage (sic); capable men were appointed to office. Loy-

[96] Gibert, Dictionnaire, 414.
[97] Ibid., 415.
[98] Shuhsi Hsü, China, 17–18.
[99] See p. 48.
[100] Li Chi, Manchuria in History: A Summary (Peiping, 1932), Map 2.

alty, filial piety, chastity and faithfulness, were especially encouraged. Thus all the educated learned to appreciate the culture of the Empire. . . ." [101]

That the T'ang rulers sought merely peace and order in the peninsula and not a definite unification of the area is indicated by their action in reinstating the conquered rulers in the various separate commanderies. The remaining kingdom of Hsin-lo, however, took advantage of the Chinese withdrawal, and also of China's domestic troubles, to extend its sway into the territory of its former enemies. During a disturbance in China attending the death of the Emperor Kao Tsung (650–683), Hsin-lo annexed most of the former Pai-chi area,[102] and when a great rebellion occurred at the end of the reign of Hsuan-Tsung (713–755), she moved northward into former Kaokuli as far as the Yalu River.[103] But since the Chinese control was withdrawn from the area northeast of the Yalu, this region had been pre-empted by P'o-hai, a new kingdom which had expanded southward from Manchuria. It consisted of a tribe known as the Mo-ho, together with North Kaokuli refugees and persons left by the earlier Chinese invasions.[104] This nation, also taking advantage of the disturbances in China, had moved into northern Kaokuli down to about the fortieth parallel, thus blocking further northward expansion of Hsin-lo.[105] Yet in the peninsula proper Hsin-lo was paramount.[106]

For the next two hundred years the history of the Korean peninsula is the story of the progress of Hsin-lo in the refinements of the Chinese civilization. That the Koreans were apt pupils is shown by a comment of no less a person than Em-

[101] Quoted in *ibid.*, 26.

[102] Shuhsi Hsü, *China*, 18.

[103] *Ibid.*

[104] Gibert, *Dictionnaire*, 756–57; Parker, "On Race Struggles in Corea," *loc. cit.*, 182 ff.; Herrman, *Atlas of China*, 39.

[105] Herrman, *Atlas of China*, 39; Shuhsi Hsü, *China*, 18.

[106] Kuno, *Japanese Expansion*, I, 20; Griffis, *Corea*, 49. Griffis records an unsuccessful attempt of Hsin-lo to invade P'o-hai in 733.

peror Tai-Tsung of the T'ang dynasty, who considered Korea "a country of educated gentlemen." [107] Unhampered by competition for survival, all its energies could be devoted to non-militaristic progress. Relieved of Japanese raids or pretense of dominance, Hsin-lo showed Japan neither fear nor respect; [108] to China, the source of her culture, she dutifully sent acknowledgments of inferiority. As early as 684 the noted Korean scholar Sul-chong had edited and prepared the Confucian Classics for his people. It was he who invented the *Ni-tu*, a system of arbitrary signs introduced through the margins of a Chinese text to aid the Korean reader in applying the proper endings and connectives.[109] The prevalence of Chinese culture, even at this date, is illustrated by the advice of Sul-chong to the Hsin-lo monarch wherein Chinese examples alone were used in admonishing him. The viewing of natural phenomena as omens of social disorder, a practice advocated in the Confucian Spring and Autumn Classic, was also prevalent.[110]

The Hsin-lo capital, Kyüng Chyu, was

a brilliant center of art and science, of architecture and of literary and religious light. Imposing temples, grand monasteries, lofty pagodas, halls of scholars, magnificent gateways and towers adorned the city. In campaniles, equipt with water-clocks and with ponderous bells and gongs, which, when struck, flooded the valley and hilltops with a rich resonance, the sciences of astronomy and horoscopy were cultivated. As from a fountain, rich streams of knowledge flowed from the capital of Shinra [Hsin-lo]. . . .[111]

The charm of the entire country is applauded by the account of an Arab merchantman written in 851. Here the Arab asserts that men never leave once they had arrived in "al-Sila"

[107] E. H. Parker, "A Chinese View of Corea," in *Chinese Recorder*, XVIII (1887), 72.
[108] Kuno, *Japanese Expansion*, I, 242.
[109] H. B. Hulbert, "The Itu," in *Korean Repository*, V (1898), 47–54.
[110] Gale, "The Influence of China Upon Korea," *loc. cit.*, 7.
[111] Griffis, *Corea*, 48.

(Hsin-lo), a country which, he stated, "sends gifts to the lord of China and says that if they did not do so the heavens would not send them rain." [112]

But the long period of peace and security sapped the vitality of the line of Hsin-lo rulers and the prosperity of the country declined. The brilliance of the capital city continued, but the provinces were neglected and the peace of the kingdom was broken by uprisings.[113] At the end of the reign of Queen Chin Syüng (888–898),[114] who parceled out her kingdom to favorites, uprisings occurred both in the north and in the southwest. Kung Yüi, a monk of royal blood, overran at first a region north of the Ta-tung River within the P'o-hai kingdom and then extended his sway into Hsin-lo proper.[115] In 906 another rebel, Li Chin Syün, proclaimed in the southwest the kingdom of Later Pai-chi.[116] A lieutenant of Kung Yüi, Wang Kün, who claimed descent from the rulers of old Kaokuli, replaced the rebel monk and in 918 proclaimed himself king of Kao-li (Ko-rai), the name of this kingdom being a contraction of *Kaokuli*.[117] During all of this confusion the king of Hsin-lo continued to rule in a shrunken area on the east coast, the peninsula again being divided roughly on the lines of the earlier three kingdoms.

In 935, however, after Wang Kün had defeated the ruler of Later Pai-chi, the king of Hsin-lo, the fifty-seventh of his line, resigned his throne and handed his authority over to Wang Kün, who founded a dynasty which ruled Korea until 1392. The new king set up his capital at Sung-to on the west-

[112] Quoted in Kei Won Chung and G. F. Hourani, "Arab Geographers on Korea," in *Journal of the American Oriental Society,* LVIII (1938), 658.

[113] Longford, *Korea,* 84.

[114] For an account of Hsin-lo's three female sovereigns, see F. Ohlinger, "The Three Female Sovereigns of Korea," in *Korean Repository,* I (1892), 223–27.

[115] Hulbert, "Korean History," *loc. cit.,* I, 370; Longford, *Korea,* 85.

[116] Gibert, *Dictionnaire,* 420.

[117] *Ibid.* This term had, however, been used in reference to Kaokuli as early as the seventh century. See Parker, "On Race Struggles in Corea," *loc. cit.,* 176 n.

ern coast, just north of the outlets of the Han and Im-chin rivers, and became the ruler of the reunited peninsula extending northward but stopping at the Ta-tung River, the boundary which had existed since 668.[118]

5. SINO-KOREAN RELATIONS, 935–1280

Though the Chinese empire was disrupted after the downfall of the T'ang dynasty, Wang Kün continued relations with the various petty Chinese dynasties which came into power. In 923, several years before he conquered the peninsula, Wang Kün had acknowledged Hsin-lo's allegiance to China.[119] Later, upon unification of the peninsula, his title as King and the state's name as Kao-li were confirmed. At the same time the imperial calendar, which recorded time in terms of the Chinese imperial reigns, was adopted for Korean use.[120] In 958 the Chinese examination system for securing government officials was reinaugurated,[121] the subjects dealing with the Confucian Classics exclusively,[122] and a recently arrived Chinese scholar named Shuang-chi appears to have set up the recruitment system for the united Kao-li.[123] Wang Kün, an ardent Buddhist, encouraged the spread of that faith, making it the official religion.[124] When the Sung dynasty was founded in China in 960, succeeding the last of the weak "Five Dynasties," close relations allowed the brilliant culture of the Sung empire to flow into Kao-li. The degree to which the peninsula had progressed from barbarian ways to an emulation and admiration of the Chinese culture is aptly

[118] Gibert, *Dictionnaire,* 420.
[119] Shuhsi Hsü, *China,* 26.
[120] Gale, "The Influence of China Upon Korea," *loc. cit.,* 9.
[121] The kingdom of Hsin-lo, however, had employed such examinations as early as the end of the eighth century. H. B. Hulbert, "National Examination in Korea," in *TKBRAS,* XIV (1923), 11.
[122] Gale, "The Influence of China Upon Korea," *loc. cit.,* 9.
[123] Hulbert, "National Examination in Korea," *loc. cit.,* 13.
[124] Griffis, *Corea,* 66.

summarized in a statement made by the scholar Ch'o Seung-no in proposing a set of rules to the sovereign Syüng-chong, who came to the throne in 982. The eleventh of these rules reads: "In poetry, history, ceremony, music and the five cardinal relationships let us follow China but in riding and dressing let us be Koreans." [125]

But the relations between China and Kao-li stood little chance of further development and regularization, for the "barbarian" Kitans (*Ch'i-tan*) had created a vast empire in the north, and were pressing down on China, forcing the Sung dynasty southward and disrupting its communications with Kao-li. The Kitan chief, A-pao-ki, had assumed the title of Emperor in 916 and named his dynasty the Liao. In 926 the Kitans conquered the kingdom of P'o-hai north of Kao-li and then swept west and south into China proper.[126] Kao-li used the destruction of P'o-hai as an opportunity to move northward up the west coast toward the Yalu River. The attention of the Kitans was drawn to Kao-li in 985 when the Sung dynasty, seeking to oust the invaders from China, called on Kao-li to assist by an attack westward. Invaded by the Kitans, Kao-li was forced to renounce her allegiance to the Sung dynasty, and in 991 she acknowledged the superiority of the Kitans and agreed to follow their calendar-year periods (*nien hao*).

Another invasion of Kao-li by the Kitans occurred in 1010 when the Kao-li king Muk-chong was assassinated. Though his successor, Hyün-chong, sent an ambassador to the Sung ruler asking protection and affirming anew the recognition of the superiority of the Chinese empire, the Sung aid did not appear. Beaten again, Kao-li was forced in 1022 to reaffirm her allegiance to the Liao dynasty.[127]

As the Kitans shifted their center of power from South

[125] Gale, "The Influence of China Upon Korea," *loc. cit.*, 9.
[126] Gibert, *Dictionnaire*, 35–36.
[127] *Ibid.*, 421.

Manchuria to North China, Kao-li's relations with them became less vital. Any respite, however, that Kao-li may have enjoyed from ambitious northern neighbors was short-lived, for a new threat developed to the northeast in the expanding tribe known as the Nüchen. This tribe had occupied the northeast portion of the Korean peninsula for a long time, but since the Kitans had sought to control only the right bank of the Yalu River, the Nüchen had expanded southwest from the Tu-men River district. This blocked the efforts of Kao-li to annex the northeast area after the fall of P'o-hai.[128] Though the Nüchen had, when weak, even paid tribute to Kao-li,[129] their rise to power after the fall of the P'o-hai kingdom was so serious a threat that in 1033 the Kao-li king constructed a protective wall across his northern boundary. This wall, which shows conclusively that Kao-li did not at the time extend northward to both the Yalu and Tu-men rivers,[130] started on the left bank of the Yalu near the river mouth and ran southeast to the sea below Yüng-Heung.[131]

The Kitan (Liao) dynasty of North China remained at peace with Kao-li, and relations of the latter with the Sung dynasty were even re-established.[132] The need for Kao-li's defense against the rising Nüchen was, however, becoming increasingly apparent. Attempting to expand north of the wall, the king of Kao-li, Whui-chong, was defeated by the Nüchen in 1107 and forced to agree to a solemn compact accompanied by sacrifices to Heaven, wherein the wall was acknowledged as Kao-li's northern border. When the Nüchen later overthrew the Liao dynasty and set up their own Chin dynasty (1115), this area north of the wall was known as Ho-lan province.[133] The boundary agreement between the Chin

---

[128] *Ibid.*, 422.
[129] *Ibid.*, 376–77.
[130] Cf. Longford, *Korea*, 87–88; Griffis, *Corea*, 68.
[131] Gibert, *Dictionnaire*, 377, 422.
[132] *Ibid.*, 422.
[133] *Ibid.*, 381.

rulers and Kao-li held as the Chin dynasty spread into China. Before a century had passed, however, a new band of northern peoples, the Mongols, were to succeed in conquering the Middle Kingdom. They were also destined to affect the affairs of the Korean peninsula to a greater degree than any Chinese dynasty had done.

Though Korea had surrendered completely to the influence of Chinese culture within the three centuries between the T'ang and the Mongol dynasties and while under the leadership of Hsin-lo, it should be pointed out that close governmental relations between China and Korea were not even then consistently maintained. The control of parts of China by barbarian dynasties from the north did not encourage the people of the peninsula to acknowledge willingly the superiority of these rulers.

Yet the Koreans were to such a degree Sinified that they recognized their country's status as inferior to that of the Middle Kingdom. A pure Chinese dynasty, such as the Sung, received their voluntary acknowledgment, while the claims of the barbarians were resisted. Thus, after the Kao-li kings had sought investiture of their authority by the Sung rulers and had adopted the Sung reign titles voluntarily, the Liao dynasty found it necessary on two occasions to use force to break this relation and to bring about an acceptance of Liao superiority. Then as soon as the Liao rulers became more deeply involved in China and less in southern Manchuria, Kao-li seized the opportunity to acknowledge again the Sung dynasty as their true superior. It is clear too that this action of Kao-li cannot be taken as a mere bid for military aid, for the Sung emperors were in no position to give aid to those separated from them by their enemies; and further, such aid, though asked for, had not been previously given.[134]

The acknowledgment by Kao-li can be understood only as being based on the position of the Sung dynasty as the legiti-

134 See p. 54.

mate heirs of the superior culture. When a new group of barbarians, the Mongols, apparently less civilized than either the Kitans or the Nüchen, became masters of China, they too were rejected. An area which centuries before had been termed the "gentleman's country" could not admit voluntarily the superior position of a people so obviously uncouth. The Mongols, on the other hand, failed to comprehend the mutually acceptable relations which former dynasties had maintained with the Korean peninsula. Thus, with ill will on both sides, Kao-li was to suffer constant invasion, control, exploitation, and virtual annexation by the Mongol dynasty. The regularization of relations on principles of propriety was re-established again only with the accession of a pure Chinese dynasty, the Ming.

CHAPTER IV

KOREA AND THE MONGOL CONQUEST
(TO A.D. 1368)

1. EARLY CONTACTS WITH THE MONGOLS

CHINESE civilization, introduced into Korea during the
T'ang period, also brought to that country the refinements which had sapped the vigor of Chinese dynasties. By
the thirteenth century the Wang dynasty in Korea was already succumbing to these enervating effects. Buddhism,
which the founder of the dynasty had encouraged, had honey-
combed the kingdom, and the monks exercised a powerful
influence over the king and the government. Chyung Mong-
chu, a Kao-li Confucian scholar, was moved to remark that
"All the incense lights burn to Buddha. From house to house
they pipe to demons, but the little hut of the teacher (Confucius) has its yard o'ergrown with grass, for no one enters
there." [1] The political situation was further complicated by
the fact that the civil and the military officials constituted
opposing classes; and one of them would occasionally wrest
control of the kingdom from the monks. Since their sympathies were with the cult of Confucianism, the civil and
military factions finally united against the court-favored
Buddhism. At the time of the Mongol rise to power in China,
the government of Kao-li was in the hands of a military man,
General Choi Ch'ung-Hün, the king, Heui-chong, being a
figurehead. [2]

[1] Gale, "The Influence of China Upon Korea," *loc. cit.*, 13.
[2] Longford, *Korea*, 106–107; H. B. Hulbert, "The Mongols in Korea," in
Korean Repository, V (1898), 133–34; M. N. Trollope, "Kang-Wha," in
TKBRAS, II (1901), 26.

The first contact of Kao-li with the Mongols was in 1212, when the Kao-li envoy to the Chin court of China was slain by Mongols who had penetrated southward to a position commanding the road to Peking. Two years later they had so threatened China that the Chin Emperor sent envoys to Kao-li to demand supplies of rice and horses. Kao-li, not too friendly to the Chin rule and wary of a possible dynastic change, publicly refused the requested aid, though the envoys were allowed to purchase supplies privately.[3] The most immediate danger to Kao-li, however, was not from the Mongols but from hordes of Kitans who, fleeing from the Mongols, sought safety and plunder in the peninsula. The action of Kao-li against their Kitan enemies so greatly pleased the Mongols that, after pacification of the area, all of north Korea and south Manchuria were handed over to Kao-li to rule.[4]

But the Koreans made little effort to conceal their dislike for the uncouth Mongols. The arrogant actions of the Mongol envoys cooled any early desire of Kao-li to make friends with these semi-barbarian invaders. Relations became further strained by their exorbitant demands for tribute. When a Mongol envoy on his way back to China was killed in 1225, all relations ceased and Kao-li prepared for the inevitable invasion.[5] Genghis Khan, the Mongol chieftain, who was at the time engaged in subduing the Tangut kingdom, died before he could turn toward Kao-li,[6] but his successor Ogotai (Emperor T'ai-tsung) launched the expedition in 1231.[7] The Mongols pushed quickly to the Kao-li capital, and the king, Ko-chong, submitted without siege. Leaving seventy of their number to act as political residents, the invaders withdrew after plundering the territory south of the capital.[8] The next

[3] Hulbert, "The Mongols in Korea," loc. cit., 134.
[4] Ibid., 135–36.
[5] Ibid., 136.
[6] Steiger, The Far East, 363–64.
[7] Gibert, Dictionnaire, 423.
[8] Trollope, "Kang-Wha," loc. cit., 28; Hulbert, "The Mongols in Korea," loc. cit., 137.

year (1232) the Kao-li king and his court fled to Kang-wha, an island at the mouth of the Im-chin River,[9] abandoning his country and his completely disorganized subjects to the Mongols.[10] Since anarchy reigned and the Mongol residents could stay in power only with the constant aid of troops which were needed for other conquests, the Mongol ruler repeatedly ordered the Kao-li king to return from his island sanctuary to the capital and resume control over the country. The native monarch finally made some effort in 1233 to reduce the peninsula to order, but the Mongols found it necessary in 1235 to pacify the country by actual occupation and settlement. By the following year they had established seventeen permanent camps in the northwest and numerous additional garrisons southward throughout the peninsula.[11] Repeated efforts were made to force the Kao-li king off the island of Kang-wha, but strong fortifications and the unfamiliarity of the Mongol horsemen with sea fighting effectively prevented his removal.[12] The mainland, however, was time and again plundered by the Mongols, and the people of Kao-li who escaped slaughter fled to the mountains or to islands off the coast.

After thoroughly ravaging the country in 1238, the Mongols were content for a few years to issue frequent orders to the Kao-li king to come off his island retreat and bow before their ruler. Finally in 1252 Mangu, who at that time acceded to the throne of China, issued an ultimatum to the king in regard to his seclusion on Kang-wha. In 1253, hearing that the island was being more heavily fortified, the Chinese ruler sent General Ya-gol-da with a force which again overran the peninsula, and arrayed itself before the king's island. When the general offered to withdraw his forces if the king would

[9] See Trollope, "Kang-Wha," loc. cit., 1–36, and E. B. Landis, "Notable Dates of Kang-Wha," in Korean Repository, IV (1897), 245–48, for history of this island.

[10] Hulbert, "The Mongols in Korea," loc. cit., 138.

[11] Ibid., 138–39.

[12] Ibid., 142; Longford, Korea, 111–12.

come out of his hiding place for a parley, the king consented and signed an agreement whereby he would "gradually" withdraw from Kang-wha and destroy its fortifications and palaces. The terms also specified that a Mongol prefect would be established in each province and that 10,000 Mongol troops were to be quartered in and supported by Kao-li. When the king assented, the armies were withdrawn, but the murder of a native who had aided the Mongols, and the king's reluctance to leave Kang-wha, brought a new series of devastations under the most ruthless of the Mongol invaders, General Chala-ta. The Mongols continued to govern the north of the peninsula through Kao-li renegades with fortified camps set up throughout the country. So weak had Kao-li become that the Mongol General Cha-la-ta in 1258 felt free to ravage the country with only a thousand men.[13]

2. SUBMISSION OF KAO-LI

The aging Kao-li king, Ko-chong, seeing in the north of his kingdom the growth of permanent Mongol agricultural settlements, and also the construction, by the hitherto land-bound Mongols, of war boats for operations against his island, finally agreed to submit and sent his son and heir to China as a token of capitulation.[14] On his journey southward to where Mangu had been fighting the Sung armies, the prince received information that Mangu had died and that a Mongol general was contemplating revolt. Hurrying northward, he informed Kublai of these events and, upon the death of his father, the king of Kao-li, he was rewarded by being returned to his homeland in great honor, with an entourage of high Mongol officials.

Known now as King Wün-chong, the former prince gave all evidences of allegiance. He sent his son to China,[15] and

13 Hulbert, "The Mongols in Korea," *loc. cit.*, 138–42.
14 *Ibid.*, 171.
15 *Ibid.*, 172–73; Trollope, "Kang-Wha," *loc. cit.*, 30.

the Mongol forces and "political residents" were withdrawn. Soon, however, the presence at the Mongol court of Korean renegades who had the ear of the khan caused the wealth of Kao-li to be exaggerated and its king to be suspected by the Mongol court. Forced to come to Peking in 1263, the discredited ruler was there accused of bad faith.[16]

In 1265 it was a Kao-li renegade who first suggested that the Mongols extend their sway to Japan.[17] A beginning was made, but a storm at sea and the reluctance of the Kao-li king to take part in such an enterprise prevented the arrival of the first Mongol mission to that country. The Mongol emperor, suspecting Korean failure to cooperate, sent his envoy to Kao-li in 1266 with orders that the envoy himself and a Kao-li aide be dispatched immediately to Japan. The king complied, but the two emissaries were treated in Japan with marked disrespect.[18]

Meanwhile the Kao-li king was fast losing the favor of Kublai,[19] and affairs within the peninsula were also disturbing. The king had long been under the control of one Kim Chyun, his minister. To free himself, he secured the minister's death by contriving with a courtier, Im Yun, only to have the courtier attempt to seize the throne himself. Another complication arose when a portion of the king's troops plundered Kang-wha and also raised a rebellion in the south. Kublai, who desired order in the area which was to be his corridor for the projected invasion of Japan, forthwith adjudged the king unable to rule his country and sent a Mongol commissioner to Song-to to assume control of affairs until order was restored.[20]

In 1270, the year the Mongols proclaimed their dynasty as the Yüan, the Kao-li king presumably gave up all attempts to resist the Mongol influence. At that time he sought to in-

[16] Hulbert, "The Mongols in Korea," *loc. cit.*, 173.
[17] *Ibid.*
[18] *Ibid.*, 173–74. See text of Kublai's letter to Japan. Shuhsi Hsü, *China*, 32.
[19] Hulbert, "The Mongols in Korea," *loc. cit.*, 174.
[20] *Ibid.*, 176.

gratiate himself with the Mongol rulers of China, and thus to prop his own throne. Moving his capital back to Song-to and disbanding the regiments defending Kang-wha,[21] he went to the court of the Yüan emperor and asked that the "political residents," formerly established by the Mongols in each Korean province, be returned. He also asked that a daughter of Kublai be given as wife to his son.[22] These requests were granted, and when Wün-chong died in 1274, there began a period in which the Mongol wives, fathers-in-law, and grandfathers dominated the Kao-li kings and their policies. Eventually the court and the official class were swung over completely to the Mongol dress, coiffure, and customs, and when the entire Kao-li royal family visited Peking in 1279, the union between the two courts was significantly sealed with gay festivities.[23]

The Mongols, in preparing for the invasion of Japan, mercilessly exploited the resources of Kao-li. Though they were not sailors, the Koreans were, and the Kao-li king was ordered to construct 1,000 boats and to furnish 4,000 bags of rice and a contingent of 10,000 troops. His protests were overruled, and a Mongol commissioner was sent to oversee the work.[24] Later, in 1270, the king was ordered to establish rice fields to feed the armies and to furnish oxen, seed grain, and 6,000 plows. Again the protests of the king were ignored, though 10,000 pieces of silk were sent as payment.

The vanguard of the army of invasion soon arrived in Kao-li bringing 33,000 additional pieces of silk to pay for their sustenance. But silk was of little use in a poverty-ridden country which had yet to recover from the earlier Mongol raids; and in the famine which followed, Kublai was forced to send 20,000 bags of rice to the starving inhabitants.[25]

[21] Landis, "Notable Dates of Kang-Wha," loc. cit., 246.
[22] Trollope, "Kang-Wha," loc. cit., 30.
[23] Hulbert, "The Mongols in Korea," loc. cit., 179.
[24] Ibid., 175.
[25] Ibid., 176–77.

After the failure of the first expedition against Japan in 1274, the demands on Kao-li were repeated, and lives and materials were again squandered in a second attempt at conquest. Kublai even contemplated a third invasion and made further demands on Kao-li; but the reports of the defeats, the impossibility of squeezing further supplies from Kao-li, and the internal situation in China caused the plan to be dropped in 1288.[26]

This did not end the series of disasters, for incursions into Kao-li by the wild tribe of Ha-tan rebels from China, with the Mongol troops in pursuit, so ravaged the already prostrate country that famine was rife again. Rice sent from China for relief was divided among the officials and men of influence; the people were left to starve.[27]

The kings of Kao-li, now thoroughly Mongol in spirit, preferred to spend their time in Peking rather than in their own capital, and Kao-li experienced misgovernment far worse even than that of China during the Mongol decline. The Kao-li kings had so far departed from any recognition of their proper functions that commissioners had to be sent from China to administer the country.[28] A provincial government was set up to rule alongside the corrupt native one, and in 1323 even the abolition of the dynasty and the complete annexation of the area to China were discussed.[29] The disgraces of the Kao-li kings culminated in the career of Ch'ung-hye, who ascended the throne in 1340. Under Mongol authority, he was shamefully paraded through the length of the kingdom to a place of exile.[30]

---

[26] *Ibid.*, 203.
[27] *Ibid.*, 203–204; Trollope, "Kang-Wha," *loc. cit.*, 30.
[28] Hulbert, "The Mongols in Korea," *loc. cit.*, 204.
[29] Shuhsi Hsü, *China*, 27.
[30] *Ibid.;* Hulbert, "The Mongols in Korea," *loc. cit.*, 205.

3. DECLINE OF THE YÜAN

When Chu Yüan-chang, the founder of the Ming dynasty, crossed the Yangtze and set up his capital at Nanking in 1356,[31] the Mongol power had so declined that it was no longer feared in Kao-li, though a pretense was made of satisfying the Mongol demands for troops to stem the rebellions in the north.[32] This lack of fear may be illustrated by the action of the Kao-li governor of Chul-la province when a Mongol envoy came to Kao-li to burn incense on the mountain tops in an effort to secure divine aid to save the declining power of the Mongol line. The governor showed his courage by throwing the envoy into prison and killing his son. This act, which in previous years would have brought swift retaliation, went unpunished by the decaying Yüan dynasty.[33] There were numerous other signs of the Mongol decline. For instance, under King Kong-min (1352–1374) Kao-li reoccupied the lands from Pyeng-yang up to and even beyond the Yalu River, the Ha-tan province of the Mongols having been abandoned at an earlier date.[34] Moreover, as far as his Mongol blood and surroundings would allow, the king attempted to disentangle himself from the disintegrating Yüan dynasty; but his order forbidding the Mongol coiffure led to a revolt of the Mongol party which was quelled only by numerous assassinations. Then Lady Chi, a Kao-li beauty who was full consort of the Mongol emperor, and who controlled the court at Peking, also attempted to depose Kong-min, but the resistance was so strong that her order was countermanded.[35] One incident concerning both Kao-li and the Mongols further illustrates the relative impotence of the latter. As contending

[31] Steiger, *The Far East*, 291.
[32] G. H. Jones, "Sketches of a Hero," in *Korean Repository*, V (1898), 321–22; Hulbert, "The Mongols in Korea," *loc. cit.*, 205.
[33] Hulbert, "The Mongols in Korea," *loc. cit.*, 205.
[34] Gibert, *Dictionnaire*, 423.
[35] Jones, "Sketches of a Hero," *loc. cit.*, 324.

forces in China always spilled over into Kao-li, the peninsula as far south as the capital was ravaged by the "Red Heads," a force of rebels against the Yüan. After capturing Peking, the "Red Heads" attempted the conquest of Kao-li but were finally defeated by the Koreans unaided. This showed conclusively that the Yüan were no longer masters even of China, much less of Kao-li.[36]

The relationship between Kao-li and the Yüan dynasty did not follow the practice of earlier dynasties; in fact, "international" relations would hardly have been an apt designation for it. Up to the time of the Yüan dynasty, though Kao-li had suffered many invasions and often was made to submit through force alone, the traditional formalities between the rulers were observed when peace was established. The administration of the country was always left to the local monarch, and the proprieties were followed consistently in the relations of envoys and tributary missions. But the Mongols, from their first rise to power, paid little heed to Confucian practices concerning Korea, since they viewed the peninsula merely as a source of plunder and exploitation. From the beginning to the end of the Mongol occupation the relations between the two governments were of a purely military nature,[37] and Kao-li became an integral part of the Mongol empire in everything but name. The floggings imposed on the ministers of Kao-li, the control exercised through Mongol commissioners and provincial residents, the deposition of its kings, and the imminent abolition of the kingship itself, all indicate that the kingdom was actually assimilated by China during this period. By the Mongols, as Kublai wrote to Japan, the relation of Kao-li to the Yüan dynasty was actually described as "that of master and servant." [38] By the Koreans the Mongol

[36] *Ibid.*, 321–23.
[37] H. B. Hulbert, "The Korean Alphabet," in *Korean Repository*, I (1892), 6.
[38] Shuhsi Hsü, *China*, 32.

interlude was considered one of barbarian domination. A native writer recorded it thus:

The Barbarian Yüan destroyed the Sung dynasty, took possession of all the empire and ruled for a hundred years. Such power in the hands of vandals was never seen before. Heaven dislikes the virtue of the barbarians. Then it was that the great Ming empire, from mid-heaven, in communication with sages and spirits of the past set up its reign of endless ages. [39]

[39] Quoted in Gale, "The Influence of China Upon Korea," *loc. cit.*, 11.

CHAPTER V

RESTORATION OF THE CONFUCIAN NORMALITY (TO 1866)

1. FOUNDATION OF CHAO-HSIEN AND THE LI DYNASTY

SINCE the native kings, dominated by Buddhist monks, made little pretense of ruling Kao-li, the Mongolized Wang dynasty continued to exist there after the Ming dynasty was established in China in 1368. The Ming line, however, being Chinese rather than barbarian, reverted to Confucian practice and discontinued the "master and servant" relation of direct provincial control which the Mongols had imposed upon Kao-li. The first Ming emperor merely announced his ascension to the imperial throne as a means of soliciting Kao-li's acknowledgment of her inferior relation to his dynasty. Kong-min (1352–1374) of Kao-li accordingly sent his congratulations, returned the seal given him by the Mongol Yüan dynasty, and received from the Ming emperor confirmation of his status as king of Kao-li, together with "a Silver Seal, with the antient Privileges of offering up solemn Sacrifices to the Gods of the Rivers and Mountains of Corea." [1] Informed that the Kao-li king devoted himself to Buddhism to the neglect of government, the emperor also sent a present of books which included the Classics, the Four Books, and a political history, and he transmitted a personal letter of admonition which stated:

[1] J. B. Du Halde, *The General History of China* (R. Brookes, trans.) (London, 1736), IV, 409; Chang T'ing-yu and others, *Ming Shih* (History of the Ming Dynasty) (Wuchang, 1877), Chap. CCCXX, p. 1a.

The rulers of old paid special attention to the defence of the country, to the means of subsistence of the people, and to the maintenance of a proper place as the centre of government. We have learnt that, on the contrary, your highness has sheltered your people with no wall, abandoned the land of P'o-hai as waste, and housed even the person of your highness in mean huts. We can hardly consider this advisable. The important functions of government are the vicarial and the military. If one devotes himself to the offering of prayers to Buddha instead, let him acquaint himself with the fate of Wu-ti of the Liang dynasty. The kingdom of your highness is adjacent to the Nuchens on the north and to the Wo tribe on the south. May your highness neglect no vigilance.[2]

The new emperor also sent an envoy to Kao-li with suggestions for a better scheme of governmental examinations.[3]

The decadent line of Wang, however, paid little heed to the emperor's admonitions. Even ceremonial homage was refused to the emperor in 1379,[4] and in 1387 Kao-li ignored his ruling fixing her northern frontier at the Yalu River.[5] As a matter of fact, the king, against the wishes of his advisers, refused to give up that area on the right bank of the Yalu which Kao-li had pre-empted as the Yüan power declined, and he even ordered his general, Li Süng-kyüi, to march north and resist the Ming ruler. It was this act which brought an end to the dynasty, for the general rebelled, returned to the capital, and placed a puppet on the throne.[6] Later he himself became the first of the Li dynasty, rulers of the Korean peninsula until 1910.

Li Süng-kyüi, also known as Li Tan, appears to have been the most commanding Korean personality in the period of the Yüan dynasty's collapse. It was he who defeated the "Red Heads" and who turned back a Mongol army sent to depose

[2] Chang, *Ming Shih*, quoted in Shuhsi Hsü, *China*, 9.
[3] Hulbert, "National Examination in Korea," *loc. cit.*, 17–18.
[4] Du Halde, *History of China*, 409.
[5] Chang, *Ming Shih*, Chap. CCCXX, p. 2a.
[6] *Ibid.*

Kong-min,[7] but when ordered to invade territory claimed by the Ming emperor, he realized the futility of such a venture, and his address to his soldiers [8] so won them over that he and the army returned to the capital. He then exiled the king to Kang-wha and, during a counterrevolt, removed the tablets of the king's ancestors from their shrine and forbade further sacrifices to them, thus extinguishing the line. Li Tan then proclaimed himself king.[9]

Known in history as Tai-cho,[10] this founder of the Li dynasty ascended the throne in 1392. As his first act he sought from the Ming emperor authorization of his right to rule. To this end the Kao-li censors addressed a report to the emperor recounting the corruptness of the Wang dynasty, its lack of an able heir, and the refusal of Li Süng-kyüi to advance to the border against the Ming armies. The report concluded by stating: "The people both within and without the capital are devoted to Süng-kyüi, so the Ministers and the elders of the people have requested him to become their sovereign, and the Emperor's approval is asked." [11]

The reply of the emperor, in purely Confucian terms, was as follows:

Kao-li is a small region in the far east, and is not under the rule of the Middle Kingdom (*fei Chung-Kuo so chih*).[12] Let the Board

---

[7] Jones, "Sketches of a Hero," *loc. cit.*, 319–27.

[8] See Griffis, *Corea*, 78.

[9] *Ibid.;* Chang, *Ming Shih*, Chap. CCCXX, p. 2a.

[10] The dominating character in the titles of all the Li dynasty kings was always Cho or Chong. Cho means "founder" or "progenitor" and is given to those kings who have successfully surmounted difficulties or obstacles in their reigns. Chong has the meaning of "exemplar" and is given to those kings whose reigns were peaceful and undisturbed. These two terms are equivalent to the Chinese *tsu* and *tsung*, which have formed part of many emperors' posthumous names in China ever since the Han dynasty. G. H. Jones, "Historical Notes on the Reigning Dynasty," in *Korean Repository*, III (1896), 343. The character for the family name of the Li dynasty has also been Romanized as *Yi* or *Ye*.

[11] Chang, *Ming Shih*, Chap. CCCXX, translated in W. W. Rockhill, *China's Intercourse with Korea from the XVth Century to 1895* (London, 1905), 7.

[12] It is statements such as this, while understandable in the light of East Asiatic theory, which were viewed by the legalistic West as an admission of Chao-hsien's complete independence.

of Rites inform it that so long as its rule is in conformity with the will of Heaven and in harmony with the hearts of men, and so long as it creates no strife on our borders, so long will its people be allowed to go and come and the Kingdom will enjoy happiness; but we have no investigation to make in the matter (of the change of dynasty).[13]

Accordingly, when King Tai-cho returned the seal of King Kong-min and asked for one in his own right and also for a new name for his kingdom, the Ming emperor invested him and, as the official designation for Korea, revived the name "Chao-hsien" by which the legendary kingdom of Chi-tzŭ was known.[14]

Breaking completely with the previous dynasty, Tai-cho in 1394 created at the town of Han-Yang, fifty-three miles south of Song-to, a new capital, which became popularly known as "the capital" or Seoul.[15] He substituted Confucianism for Buddhism as the official creed, erected at the capital the Confucian College Hall as a government department of education in 1398,[16] and in 1413, blaming the presence of widespread famine on the non-Confucian teachings current in the kingdom, made a huge fire of the texts of Buddhist writings. Tai-cho also abolished the custom of building Buddhist monasteries at the graves of kings.[17]

Governmental reorganization also was undertaken on the Chinese model, and the Ming dynasty's code of punishments was adopted for Chao-hsien.[18] The peninsula was divided into eight provinces, the previous decentralization being replaced

[13] Chang, *Ming Shih*, Chap. CCCXX, translated in Rockhill, *China's Intercourse with Korea*, 7.
[14] Chang, *Ming Shih*, Chap. CCCXX, p. 2a; cf. Du Halde, *History of China*, IV, 410.
[15] Jones, "Historical Notes on the Reigning Dynasty," *loc. cit.*, 344; see J. S. Gale, "Han-yang (Seoul)," *TKBRAS*, II (1902), 1–43, for history of Han-Yang (Seoul).
[16] Jones, "Historical Notes on the Reigning Dynasty," *loc. cit.*, 344, 393.
[17] H. B. Hulbert, *The History of Korea* (Seoul, 1905), I, 302, 305.
[18] Jones, "Historical Notes on the Reigning Dynasty," *loc. cit.*, 347.

by direct control from the capital. Many new schools were established, and the examination system, now freed from Buddhist adulterations, was reinstituted for both civil and military officers. Thus strengthened, the army was able to resist more successfully the depredations of Japanese pirates, who had revived their ancient practice of raiding the Korean coast.[19]

The relations of Chao-hsien with China were regularized according to the principles of proper conduct between nations as prescribed in the Chinese Classics. That these ancient rules were still followed is attested by the refusal of the tribute sent to the emperor by King Tai-chong (1401–1418), the third king of Chao-hsien. Since this tribute consisted solely of sea-eagles, which were not among the prescribed "products of the country," it was refused by the Chinese emperor, who thus duplicated the attitude reported as follows in the Chapter "Hound of Li," of the *Book of Chou:* "Precious stones and rare creatures are not what I like; let him not any more present them." [20] It is also recorded that the first memorial of King Tai-cho was refused and its framer banished because the document was not written in terms proper for addressing the Son of Heaven, and that a later monarch was deprived of the return gifts which the emperor had previously presented because he addressed the emperor in terms not proper and lacking respect.[21] In this connection it is interesting to note also that repeated efforts were made by Chao-hsien to secure an alteration in the Chinese histories of the statement that the founder of the Li dynasty was a usurper rather than a king by popular acclaim.[22] These examples show clearly

---

[19] Hulbert, "National Examination in Korea," *loc. cit.,* 20; Longford, *Korea,* 127. Fusan and two other ports were opened for limited trade to the Japanese for government missions, but the entry of these foreigners through any other ports was forbidden. Hulbert, *History of Korea,* I, 306.

[20] Du Halde, *History of China,* IV, 410. See p. 18.

[21] *Ibid.,* 410, 423.

[22] Chang, *Ming Shih,* Chap. CCCXX, pp. 3b, 4a.

enough that the relations between Chao-hsien and China were conducted on the basis of the rules of proper conduct between the superior and inferior according to the classic theory of *li,* rather than on the principle of military domination which the Mongols practiced.

One of the envoys sent to Chao-hsien in 1487 to announce the death of the Emperor Hsiao-tsung and the ascension of his successor, wrote an account of his visit which further illuminates the relationship between the two nations. According to this account, the Chinese envoys were met at the south gate of the Chao-hsien capital where a hall, the *Tai-P'yüng-Kwan,* had been constructed for their reception and entertainment. The king himself, in ceremonial robes and with his ministers in full attendance, proceeded to the reception hall to welcome these representatives of the emperor with due ritual. As the Chinese envoy recorded it:

When the message arrives, the king puts on his ceremonial robes and crown and comes out to meet the ambassador. The ministers with pins in their headgear stand like ibises in attendance, while old and young gather on the hills to see, and towers and gates are filled with people in gaudy dress, houses are decorated and music is wafted on the morning breeze, drums beat, flags fly, incense goes up like mist in the morning air, peach and plum blossoms give color and a noise of moving horses and chairs is heard. The Stone Sea-lions bask in the sun that rises from the sea.[23]

The first of three feasts given in the *Tai-P'yüng-Kwan,* the *Ha-ma-yün* (alighting feast), was then held to conclude the welcoming reception.[24]

On the following day, after inquiries by the king through his ministers concerning the health of the honored visitors, the envoys, with secretaries constantly in attendance to record their words, were transported to the royal palace where the king and court received them. As they approached, the

[23] Quoted in Gale, "Han-yang (Seoul)," *loc. cit.,* 36.
[24] *Ibid.,* 40.

king bowed and the entire assemblage three times called out "Long live the Emperor." Other ceremonies were then performed, at the close of which all present were facing in the direction of the imperial palace at Peking. Next, after the ceremony of arranging gifts and seating envoys, the king of Chao-hsien said:

> Our little kingdom may well serve as fence and wall and still do disgrace to the wide and limitless favor of the Emperor. Even though all one's heart be in it it be favor impossible to repay, though we die we shall never be able to make recompense. We sing the songs of Chu, that tell of the grace of heaven; we pray that as the day comes round so may blessings fall upon the Emperor. We also intone the happy sayings of the Seupsang (Book of Poetry) and we proclaim the ceremonies of the Book of Spring and Autumn which says, "the various states must first see to the rectitude of the individual man." May glory ever be in the presence of his Imperial Majesty.[25]

The imperial message read, the king thanked the envoys, who replied: "Because our Imperial Master has confidence in the devotion and allegiance of the Eastern Kingdom we regard you as different from all other states."[26] The envoys then returned to their reception hall, where they were joined by the king. Each of the pleasantries exchanged during the feast which followed arose from a quotation in the Classics. The correctness of the procedure caused the envoys to observe that "We heard heretofore that his majesty was a scholar and a rarely-gifted gentleman. Now that we see him we know it to be so." After a sojourn of five days the king appeared to see the envoys on their way, "being very gracious and particular in his form of ceremony."[27]

[25] *Ibid.*, 38.
[26] *Ibid.*
[27] *Ibid.*, 37-41.

2. THE JAPANESE INVASION

The friendship and admiration which Chao-hsien felt for China was to serve it in good stead during the Japanese invasion toward the end of the sixteenth century. The Japanese had been allowed to trade at three Korean ports which were opened shortly after the founding of the Li dynasty, and an official Japanese mission had been received at each place. However, in the seventh year of the reign of Chung-chong (1506–1543) intercourse with Japan was practically stopped because of Japanese riots which had to be forcefully suppressed. In 1572, upon receipt of a friendly message from Japan, the southern port of Fusan was reopened to Japanese trade but not to official intercourse with the Japanese government.[28]

In a dream of the invasion of China through Chao-hsien, Hideyoshi, the famous Japanese warrior who had already unified Japan, saw both the answer to his own ambitions and a means of diverting from civil strife the Japanese soldiery, now restless and useless in the first peace Japan had known for centuries.[29] As his plan of conquest showed, Hideyoshi aspired to the rule of the entire Far East, not from the islands of Japan, but from Peking.[30] His procedure was altered, however, from that traditionally followed by invaders of China in that before he had ascended the throne of the Middle Kingdom he summoned to pay homage those nations who acknowledged the superiority of that area.

First among the areas called upon to submit to Japan was Chao-hsien,[31] whose land and whose soldiers Hideyoshi hoped to use in conquering China. Though negotiations were opened

[28] Hulbert, *History of Korea*, I, 338.

[29] G. H. Jones, "The Japanese Invasion," in *Korean Repository*, I (1892), 12–13.

[30] See Kuno, *Japanese Expansion*, App. 36, pp. 314–17.

[31] *Ibid.*, 300–14, for Hideyoshi's letters to Liu-ch'iu, Formosa, the Philippines, and India.

and envoys and presents exchanged, the attempt to secure the aid of Chao-hsien was sharply refused, the plan to conquer China being termed by the Chao-hsien ruler akin to "measuring the ocean in a cockle-shell" or "a bee trying to sting a tortoise through its armour." [32] In 1591 the king of Chao-hsien wrote to Hideyoshi in part as follows:

> You stated in your letter that you were planning to invade the supreme nation (China) and requested that our Kingdom (Korea) join in your military undertaking. . . . We cannot even understand how you have dared to plan such an undertaking and make such a request of us. . . . For thousands of years, from the time of yore when Chi-tzu, the founder of the Kingdom of Korea, received the investiture from the Chow dynasty, up to our own time, our kingdom has always been known as a nation of righteousness. . . . The relation of ruler and subject has been strictly observed between the supreme nation and our kingdom . . . generation after generation, we have reverently adhered and attended to all duties and obligations due from a tributary state of Chung-Chao (China). . . . Our two nations have acted as a single family, maintaining the relationship of father and son as well as that of ruler and subject. . . . We shall certainly not desert "our lord and father" nation. . . . Moreover, to invade another nation is an act of which men of culture and intellectual attainments should feel ashamed. . . . We would conclude this letter by saying that your proposed undertaking is the most reckless, imprudent, and daring of any of which we have ever heard.[33]

Nevertheless, invasion followed in 1592. The Japanese swept up the peninsula as far as Pyeng-yang before aid was sent by China, who was suspicious that Chao-hsien might actually have connived with the Japanese. After a time, their lines of communications severed by the Korean fleet, and their retreating columns harassed by guerilla bands, the Japanese negotiated a truce. Later, however, hostilities were re-

---

[32] W. G. Aston, "Hideyoshi's Invasion of Korea," in *TASJ*, VI (1878), 234.
[33] Quoted in Kuno, *Japanese Expansion*, 303–304.

sumed, but upon the death of Hideyoshi, the invaders quit the peninsula, concluding seven years of intermittent struggle. Chao-hsien was again at peace, but desolated.[34]

Friendly relations were established between Japan and Chao-hsien in 1609 through the mediation of the Daimyo of Tsushima. Forging a correspondence between the shogun and the Chao-hsien king and personally increasing the gifts sent from Chao-hsien to Japan, the Daimyo caused each country to believe it had won out in the peace negotiations.[35] The two countries agreed to a new exchange of courtesies by which each should send congratulatory missions to the other at the time of great national events, though the expense of the missions from Chao-hsien to Japan were to be borne by the Japanese. This custom, observed more often after the family of Hideyoshi had been succeeded by the Tokugawa clan, was the basis for eleven missions sent to Japan on the ascension of a new shogun, while similar missions were dispatched to Chao-hsien on the ascension of a king. The financial burden of the missions, however, proved too heavy for Japan, and in 1763, hoping to reduce the cost, she presumed to receive a Korean delegation on the island of Tsushima between Chao-hsien and Japan. Chao-hsien then discontinued the custom.[36]

It should be noted that this custom of exchanging courtesies involved no Japanese claims of superiority over Chao-hsien. Neither did it demand tribute, a prerogative Japan had not asserted since the seventh century. Chao-hsien was, in fact, on terms of equality with Japan, and Japan recognized Chao-hsien's relation to China. Despite this fact, some writers, confusing Hideyoshi's campaign with the early dominance by

---

[34] For detailed accounts of the Japanese invasion see Aston, "Hideyoshi's Invasion of Korea," *loc. cit.*, VI, 227–45; IX, 87–93, 213–22; XI, 117–25. See also Jones, "The Japanese Invasion," *loc. cit.*, 10–16, 46–50, 116–21, 147–52, 182–88, 217–22, 308–11.

[35] I. Yamagata, "Japanese-Korean Relations After the Japanese Invasion of Korea in the XV Century," in *TKBRAS*, IV (1913), 1–11.

[36] Kuno, *Japanese Expansion*, 8, 239.

Japan over the area of Kaya (Mimana), have wrongly inferred that Japan had suzerain power over Korea prior to 1894.[37]

3. KOREA AND THE MANCHUS

Though the restoration of peace in Chao-hsien gave time for rehabilitating the country, that peace was soon to be broken, this time by the recurrence of dynastic changes in China. Another tribe from the area north of Chao-hsien, the Manchus, was moving south, destined to replace eventually the ruling dynasty of China.[38] Within two years after friendly relations were re-established with Japan, Chao-hsien was advised by China to prepare her military forces against the expanding Manchus.[39] Accordingly, in 1619 Chao-hsien sent twenty thousand men to assist the Ming army opposing the invaders. When both the Ming and Chao-hsien forces were defeated, the Manchu chieftain, recognizing the relationship between China and Chao-hsien, freed the remaining five thousand soldiers with an admonition to the king of Chao-hsien which said: "The Mings sent troops to rescue you from the Japanese, and therefore, I do not feel aggrieved at your aiding the Mings against me. I return you the prisoners. King, beware!" [40] Despite the warning, Chao-hsien remained loyal to the declining Ming dynasty even though the land route to Peking was in Manchu hands and though tribute missions to China were forced to go by sea.[41]

But the Manchus, with eyes on Peking, could brook no

[37] *Ibid.*, 21, 234.

[38] For the rise of the Manchus, see J. R., "The Rise and Progress of the Manjows," in *Chinese Recorder*, VII (1876), 155–68, 235–48, 315–29; VIII (1877), 1–24, 196–208 (conquest of Korea), 361–80. See also the recent study by Franz Michael, *Origin of Manchu Rule in China* (Baltimore, 1942).

[39] Chang, *Ming Shih*, Chap. CCCXX, p. 7a.

[40] E. H. Parker, "The Manchu Relations with Corea," *TASJ*, XV (1887), 93. See translation in Rockhill, *China's Intercourse with Korea*, which states that only the general and ten officers were returned.

[41] Chang, *Ming Shih*, Chap. CCCXX, p. 7b.

enemy such as Chao-hsien on their flank; so in 1627, guided by Korean traitors, they invaded the peninsula. The king of Chao-hsien, In-cho, called on the Ming emperor for aid, but the Manchu chieftain in person guarded the route into Chao-hsien to prevent Chinese assistance.[42] The king fled to Kang-wha and since further resistance was useless, offered submission. Within the same year which saw the beginning of the invasion (1627), an agreement was concluded in which the relation of "elder brother" and "younger brother" was established between the Manchu nation and the kingdom of Chao-hsien.[43]

The action of the Manchus in using the "elder brother–younger brother" relation as a basis for their agreement with Chao-hsien illustrates the point of how completely Sinified the Manchus actually were. One writer has stated that the two Manchu "emperors" who ruled from Mukden before coming to China were thoroughly emperors in the Chinese manner and that "It is not too much to say that the final conquest . . . was less an alien invasion than a triumph of the strongest faction in a colossal Chinese civil war." [44] The new dynasty recognized the traditional relations between Chao-hsien and the Ming rulers, and rather than attempt to force Chao-hsien to renounce its "father" dynasty and accept the Manchus instead, they wisely selected the less exalted status of elder brother, biding their time until the elder brother should succeed to the headship of the international family through the father's demise.

The status of Chao-hsien established by the 1627 agreement differed from that accorded her under the Ming authority. For instance, though congratulatory missions were exchanged with the Manchus, the expression "honored country" (*kuei kuo*) was used reciprocally, and Chao-hsien termed

---

[42] Parker, "The Manchu Relations with Corea," *loc. cit.*, 94.
[43] *Ibid.*
[44] Owen Lattimore, *Manchuria, Cradle of Conflict* (New York, 1932), 45–46.

herself "the unworthy one" (*pu ku*) rather than the usual
more abject "humble country" (*pi kuo*). Likewise the letters
of the king to the emperor were called "respectful dispatches"
(*feng shu*) rather than "humble statements" (*piao*), and his
gifts were not "tribute" (*kung*) but an "annual subsidy" (*sui
pu*).[45] All of these usages indicate a practice more nearly approaching a status of equality than the relations which Chao-
hsien had formerly enjoyed with China.

As long as the Ming dynasty survived, however, Chao-
hsien remained faithful to it, and refused to perform even the
duties agreed upon toward the "elder brother" nation, the
Manchus. It is therefore not surprising that in 1631 an envoy
of the Manchus arrived by sea, presumably to seek the com-
pliance of Chao-hsien with the 1627 agreement and also to
secure aid against the Ming rulers. The Chao-hsien king received the envoy but refused his demands with a logic they
both understood, stating, "The Ming dynasty is as a father;
how can I be expected to help to destroy my father!"[46] In
the following year the Manchu emperor wrote to King In-cho
charging him with further violations of the 1627 agreement.
Receiving no satisfaction, he sent another mission to try to
win the king through reason, saying, "Your country looks
upon the Ming as a father, and many times you have sent
them tribute-rice. Now we are your elder brother, can you
not give it us once?" Again the king's answer was a refusal,
this time emphasized by the construction of twelve walled
cities in the northwestern provinces.[47]

In the spring of 1634 the king of Chao-hsien encouraged the
Ming forces to continue their resistance to the Manchu emperor, though the latter sought to use him as an intermediary
in concluding a peace. The following winter Chao-hsien sent
an envoy to the Manchus, but his attitude contrasted sharply

---

[45] Rockhill, *China's Intercourse with Korea,* 16; Parker, "The Manchu Relations with Corea," *loc. cit.*, 94.
[46] Rockhill, *China's Intercourse with Korea,* 14.
[47] *Ibid.*, 14–15.

to that shown toward the Ming dynasty. He not only rejected all the Manchu demands but also further indicated his lack of regard for the dynasty by using the most arrogant language and by demanding precedence over even the high ministers of the Manchu court.[48] Yet the Manchus exhibited a commendable restraint, seeking still to bring Chao-hsien to voluntary submission through reason and kindness.

The incidents which finally provoked the Manchus to arms against Chao-hsien were the imprisonment of a Manchu envoy and an insult to the Manchu emperor himself. Urged to add to his titles that of Emperor of China, the Manchu ruler had stated that "Korea is a younger brother country, with whom it is necessary to discuss the question." [49] But the envoy of the Manchu emperor, sent to Chao-hsien in 1635, was there imprisoned and would have been killed had he not made his escape.[50] To climax all the growing tension, the Chao-hsien envoys who came the following year to congratulate the Manchu emperor refused even to make obeisance to his person.[51]

4. MANCHU INVASION

Having first secured the protection of his own territory, the Manchu Emperor T'ai Tsung (1627–1644) in 1637 led his troops into Chao-hsien. When the king of Chao-hsien informed the Ming emperor of the invasion, the ruler of the fast crumbling Ming empire made a final effort to come to the aid of his loyal kingdom, only to have contrary winds prevent the arrival of the relieving fleet.[52]

The king of Chao-hsien then sent the royal family to the presumably safe island of Kang-wha and shut himself up in

[48] J. R., "The Rise and Progress of the Manjows," loc. cit., VIII, 202.
[49] Rockhill, China's Intercourse with Korea, 16.
[50] Jones, "Historical Notes on the Reigning Dynasty," loc. cit., IV, 122–23.
[51] Rockhill, China's Intercourse with Korea, 17.
[52] Ibid., 19.

the strongest fortress in his capital. But the Manchus brought boats, captured the island, and made prisoners of the queen, the crown prince, and members of the families of high Chao-hsien officers. By publicly proclaiming the courteous treatment being accorded these prisoners, an effort was made to shame the king into leaving his fortress and coming into the emperor's presence. It is noteworthy also that throughout the entire invasion the Manchu emperor made no direct accusations against his royal adversary. The first demand made by the victorious Manchus was for the surrender of the high ministers, and these men were in fact surrendered before the king submitted himself.[53]

The Manchu account gives fully the terms of submission as follows:

The Emperor then ordered the King to give him the patent of investiture and the seal which he had received from the Ming, to offer his allegiance, to give him two of his sons as hostages, to adopt the (Manchu) new year (calendar), and to send each year tribute (*kung*) with a congratulatory address (*piao*). In case of war, he would have to raise an auxiliary force and furnish supplies to the army. He was not to erect fortresses (or walled cities) at his pleasure, or give refuge to fugitives.[54]

The ceremony of submission and the re-establishment of Chao-hsien in the favored relation which it had borne toward the Ming dynasty is also recorded. The emperor, to show his esteem of the newly won inferior kingdom, remitted the tribute of Chao-hsien for two years and agreed to make additional arrangements should Chao-hsien ever be unable to meet her obligations.[55]

Nevertheless, as long as the Ming dynasty continued to

[53] *Ibid.*, 19–20.
[54] *Ibid.*, 20.
[55] J. R., "The Rise and Progress of the Manjows," *loc. cit.*, VIII, 204–205. Rockhill, *China's Intercourse with Korea*, 21; Griffis, *Corea*, 159, for tribute fixed for Chao-hsien.

exist, the Manchus could expect little aid from their new tributary kingdom. "How can these savages claim imperial power?" memorialized one Chao-hsien officer. "How can we think of casting off our allegiance to China? . . . though we live in a distant corner of the world, we have manners." [56]

In 1638 Chao-hsien troops, ordered to cooperate with the Manchus, showed so little desire to fight the Ming armies that the Manchu emperor addressed a letter of reproach to the Chao-hsien king. Yet in 1642 he paid the Chao-hsien king the compliment of asking his advice when the Ming forces sought peace. It is also significant that the dying wish of Emperor T'ai Tsung Wên was said to be for a remission of one third of the Chao-hsien annual tribute. Upon the ascension of Emperor Shih Tsu Chang and the complete establishment of the Manchus in 1644 as the rulers of China, the "elder brother" of Chao-hsien became also the head of the Far Eastern family and, as such, exercised the powers of both father and elder brother. However, instead of increasing the demands on Chao-hsien, the K'ang-hsi emperor returned the sons of the king, who had been held as hostages, and remitted one half of the year's tribute. [57]

Naturally, this generous and proper treatment of conquered Chao-hsien dispelled much of the antagonism the peninsula felt toward the Manchus. The same forms and procedure which had been set up by the Ming dynasty were followed in the relations between the two countries, and no attempt was made by the new emperors to dominate Chao-hsien by military dictatorship, direct government, or control of the Chao-hsien court through dynastic marriages. Being essentially Chinese, the relationship eventually received the approval of the Chao-hsien people. Its unusual liberality toward them is strikingly illustrated by the fact that though the Chinese themselves were forced to adopt the queue style of hair-

[56] Hulbert, *History of Korea*, II, 94–95.
[57] Rockhill, *China's Intercourse with Korea*, 22–24.

dress as a sign of submission to the Manchus, the people of Chao-hsien, as a special mark of distinction, were allowed to continue the headdress they had worn under the Ming rule.

Further marks of deference were shown by the Manchus in the matter of tribute. The agreement of 1637, by which Chao-hsien gave up the Ming seal for that of the Manchus, provided for tribute of approximately the same nature and amounts as had been sent to the vanquished dynasty. Yet, as the years passed, the amount was gradually reduced until in the eighteenth century it was only a fraction of that formerly sent to the Ming emperors.[58]

Under the rule of the Manchus, who in 1644 adopted Ch'ing as the name of their imperial dynasty, Chao-hsien enjoyed more than two hundred years of freedom from external cares. Her relations with the Japanese, who had withdrawn into seclusion, were limited to occasional congratulatory missions and to intercourse at the trading post at Fusan. Just as the Dutch were segregated at Nagasaki, so Chao-hsien segregated the Japanese at Fusan, and relegated them to an area outside the gates of the town.[59]

Aside from the diplomatic intercourse which continued regularly after the Ch'ing dynasty was established, Chao-hsien was also isolated from China. This isolation was augmented by action of the Chinese, who had constructed in the fifteenth century, about sixty miles from the Chao-hsien frontier (the Yalu River), a three-hundred-mile fortification known as the "Wall of Stakes." Between this wall and the Yalu River the population had been removed, leaving a natural barrier of waste land for any would-be invaders of China to cross. The last outpost in Chao-hsien was the city of I-Chyü (Wu-ji), and some fifty miles farther on along the

[58] *Ibid.*, 25–26.

[59] Griffis, *Corea*, 164. For the status of the Japanese at Fusan in 1870, see M. Brandt to Rehfues, *Papers Relating to the Foreign Relations of the United States. 1861–1928* (Washington, 1862–1943), 1871, pp. 74–75. Hereafter cited as *Foreign Relations.*

road to Peking was the "Border Gate" (Pien-mun) where three or four times a year a fair was held wherein goods were exchanged under the supervision of Manchu and Chao-hsien officials, who levied duty on such goods.[60]

However, since the cultures of the two nations were almost identical, little was lost in limiting intercourse. Chinese writings were well known in Chao-hsien and Chinese culture was considered native to the peninsula. In fact, the civilization of China was so completely that of Chao-hsien that the peninsula, despite isolation from the Middle Kingdom, continued to glory in its attachment to the superior country and considered the observance of its relations and the emulation of China as its proudest achievement. As a Chao-hsien writer stated it:

> Our ceremonies, our enjoyments, our laws, our usages, our dress, our literature, our goods have all followed after the models of China. The (five) great relationships shine forth from those above and the teachings pass down to those below, making the grace of our customs like to that of the Flowery Land, so that Chinese themselves praise us saying "Korea is little China." [61]

[60] Griffis, *Corea*, 84, 180–81; Longford, *Korea*, 206.
[61] Quoted in Gale, "The Influence of China Upon Korea," *loc. cit.*, 24.

CHAPTER VI

KOREA IN THE EAST ASIATIC INTER-
NATIONAL SYSTEM

1. PHILOSOPHICAL AND HISTORICAL SUMMARY

THROUGHOUT the long period of peace under the Manchus, the relations between China and Chao-hsien continued uninterrupted and according to the age-old practice. Consequently, when the Western states, toward the middle of the nineteenth century, sought to enter into relations not only with China, but with Chao-hsien as well, they found in Chao-hsien a nation which to them was neither sovereign enough to conduct independent relations nor subject enough to throw responsibility for its actions on China. Before exploring this impact of the West, however, a re-examination of the status of Chao-hsien in relation to China will be helpful in understanding the Far Eastern system of international relations, which opposed that of the West.

The peculiar character of statehood possessed by Chao-hsien at the beginning of the nineteenth century had its origin in the familistic system of control which existed from the earliest times in China. Families grew into tribes and tribes into petty kingdoms which felt themselves members of a sort of confederation based on a common civilization. This civilization, in turn, rested on genealogical ties or intermarriage relationships.[1] Each state in this small center of culture, in

[1] Marcel Granet, *Chinese Civilization* (K. E. Innes and M. R. Brailsford, trans.) (New York, 1930), 76.

its process of expansion and for protection from the surrounding barbarians, created on its vague frontiers, under the control of relatives of its rulers, barrier regions known as *fan-ch'en* (藩臣). Since *fan* literally means "hedge," it is obvious that these areas were created for the purpose of guarding the hedge or the frontier of the cultural realm. As such, they owed allegiance to the area to which they were appended.[2] As the "hedge guarding" areas became civilized they were assimilated by the kingdoms. By the time of the first emperor of the Ch'in dynasty (221–206 B.C.), such boundaries enclosed the land which is now known as China proper, and the first centralized empire, under the Son of Heaven, was established.[3]

This area came to be known as the Middle Kingdom (中國) and, presumably because distance prevented the extension of direct control, the outlying areas, when they had become Sinified, continued to remain in the *fan-ch'en* role as *shu-pang* (屬邦) or *shu-kuo* (屬國). *Shu* means "to be of," "belonging to," "connected with," "pertaining to," "depending on," or "subordinate to."[4] *Pang* means "a state," "a country," "a nation," and is synonymous with *kuo*, which is defined as "a nation," "a kingdom," "a state," "a country," "a dynasty," "a house," or "a line."[5] Thus the position of a country such as Korea can best be described as a "belonging or dependent country." This term was not a legal one, and the translation of it into such terms as "vassal kingdom" or "fief" is misleading, for the character

---

[2] The theory of this, and of the later relation of areas which surrounded the Middle Kingdom as buffers such as Chao-hsien, is found in the Chinese proverb which stated that "When the lips are gone the teeth will feel cold." In the nineteenth century this very quotation was used in a memorial protesting the loss of many of the kingdoms once dependent on China. See memorial of Chang Shu Shong, Governor of Kwangtung, Oct., 1883, in *Ch'ing Documents*, Bk. 34, p. 42, quoted in Djang Chu, Chinese Suzerainty (Unpublished Ph.D. dissertation, Johns Hopkins University, 1935), 132.

[3] See Granet, *Chinese Civilization*, Chap. III.

[4] Giles, *A Chinese-English Dictionary*, 1245.

[5] *Ibid.*, 836, 1060.

shu carries with it the idea of kinship, not that of a merely legal relation.[6]

All of this political development contributed to the Chinese theory of the nature of man, society, government, and the world. According to that theory, the preordained natural order of the world dominated the philosophy, and the five great relationships determined the action, of men in society. The province of government was to teach these five relationships through the rules of proper conduct (*li*)—that is, by example, reason, and admonition. Disorder, natural or social, was indicative of non-observance of these rules, and non-observance was sure to be followed by disorder. Within the Middle Kingdom these theories were understood; without, they fell on the ears of uncomprehending barbarians.

But the theory of the unity of all within the natural order, together with the heaven-bestowed duty of the emperor to preserve the state of things as exemplified in *li*, gave the emperor reason to be concerned with the cultural status of the bordering areas. In theory, the treatment to be accorded those outside the Middle Kingdom varied according to the degree of civilization existing. Areas which had adopted Chinese culture could be taken within the cultural family, and relations would be conducted according to the proprieties which both understood.[7] Those who had yet to advance to the stage wherein reason and shame would sway the mind, were to be dealt with on the only basis they could understand, that of force.[8] But even in relations with barbarians, the Chinese sought to conquer by converting the minds of the leaders, so that order would be maintained without the constant use of force. Tribute might be accepted over long periods as a token of submission, but only with investiture by the emperor was

[6] Rockhill, *China's Intercourse with Korea*, 3.

[7] Areas developed to the point where they considered themselves Chinese revolted if their overlord treated them as though they were barbarians. Granet, *Chinese Civilization*, 85–86.

[8] See pp. 12–13.

the stamp of legitimacy placed on the barbarian chieftain and the first step toward a civilized status achieved.

The rise of the Korean peninsula to the status of a civilized nation skipped many prescribed early steps because of the migration to the area of groups of Chinese, already civilized, who formed a controlling nucleus in the native kingdoms. Though relations with the Manchurian Kaokuli kingdom went very little beyond the payment of tribute and the reception of investiture when expedient, a higher association was accorded the more distant and more Sinified area of Hsin-lo as Chinese culture flowed in after the sixth century. By the end of the tenth century the peninsula had become united as the kingdom of Kao-li under the Wang dynasty. After this consolidation the acknowledgment of China's superiority was interrupted only by the inability of one dynasty to hold long the rulership in China, a situation presenting the inevitable dilemma of rendering allegiance to conflicting claimants of the mandate of Heaven.

The ruthless Mongol invasion, which changed the status of Kao-li from Confucian control-through-reason to control by military occupation, so definitely classed the Mongols as barbarians in the minds of the Koreans that Chao-hsien never adopted the traditional attitude toward them. With the coming of the Ming emperors, however, a new dynasty won the throne of Chao-hsien, Confucianism became the state cult, and the relationship with China reverted to the earlier accepted pattern. The same status was maintained by the Ch'ing rulers, and when the West first came in contact with the peninsula, the Confucian family of nations was operating on rules certainly as well understood and fully as meticulously followed by its members as were the rules of international law by Western nations.

The entire basis of the Confucian system of association of nations was foreign to that of any Western system. As we have seen, the relationship of Chao-hsien to China was a natural one, a family relation involving, at least in theory, an intrinsic tie between the two areas. Of the five great social relationships, that of father and son was applied and observed before the seventeenth century. When the Ming dynasty held the throne of China, the Manchus, with an eye to Confucian propriety, established the relationship of elder and younger brother with the Korean kingdom. Though they continued, as the Ch'ing dynasty, to refer to Chao-hsien as "the younger brother nation" after they had displaced the Ming rulers, the practice appears to have been no more than a mere gesture of politeness. The actual position of China remained that of a father; the elder brother had naturally succeeded to the head-ship of the Confucian family through the father's demise.[9] Therefore, although the relationship was referred to, by both Westerners and Far Easterners alike, as that of elder and younger brother, it must be remembered that in this instance the elder brother was also the head of the international house-hold and possessed the commensurate authority.[10] For this reason China is called both father and elder brother of Chao-hsien.

To those of the West, inclined to view a familial relation-ship merely as implying consanguinity rather than as a regu-larized status possessing formal power and obligations, some discussion of these two relationships may be helpful. In the first place, it should be understood that the Chinese were not given to laying down in advance definitive principles for con-duct. Instead, since example constituted the accepted mode of social control, they judged specific actions after they had happened and used them, both proper and improper actions, as guides for future conduct. Therefore, no list of prede-termined obligations and powers legally binding in the re-lationship of father and son could be given beyond that which

---

[9] T. F. Tsiang, "Sino-Japanese Diplomatic Relations, 1870–1894," in *Chinese Social and Political Science Review*, XVII (1933–34), 53.

[10] Parker, "The Manchu Relations with Corea," *loc. cit.*, 94.

imposed on the son the duty of filial piety (*hsiâo*), involving honor, obedience, and the utmost consideration for the welfare of the parent. Just as the words "filial piety" covered in the Chinese mind the entire obligation toward a father, "respectfulness" (*ti*) indicated the proper attitude toward an elder brother. This respectfulness suggested the deference by the younger to the elder in all things. But the father and elder brother were both charged with a benevolent concern for the lesser members of the family.[11]

A person occupying the position of a father was possessed of *patria potestas* over the son. At the same time Confucian ethics contained a laissez faire principle (*wu-wei*) which discouraged a parent from using this power unless it was absolutely necessary. Thus, aside from the formal courtesies, there was on the part of the son a condition of seeming independence of his father until a crisis arose. Then the father was found to have absolute power, even to the taking of his son's life. Though the elder brother, as such, possessed control to a lesser degree than a father, if he was himself the head of a family his powers embraced those of the father as well.[12]

The foregoing paragraphs should fairly well explain the relationship between China and Chao-hsien. Perhaps it may best be summed up by stating that the official attitude of China toward Chao-hsien was that of a Chinese father or elder brother, while Chao-hsien, the lesser nation, maintained the attitude of a filial son and respectful younger brother toward China, the central nation. The nature of parental control in the Confucian family serves to explain the seeming

[11] Chinese writings are replete with incidents illustrating filial piety. See the compilation of M. M. Dawson, *The Ethics of Confucius* (New York, 1915), 151–71. The virtue of brotherly respectfulness has received less attention than "filial piety," but the great encyclopedia *Tai-ping Yü-lan* (A.D. 978–983), composed of quotations from earlier literature, devotes Chap. CCCCXVI to "Fraternal Kindness and Brotherly Respectfulness."

[12] See *The Sacred Edict* (F. W. Baller, trans.) (Shanghai, 1917), 1–18; "The Doctrine of Filial Piety" in *The Sacred Books of the East*, III, 465–88.

inconsistencies in China's policy toward Korea in the nineteenth century. As with the natural son, the father nation was by Confucian theory discouraged from exercising its control except in times of crisis. Thus, a condition of ceremonial dependence sufficed between China and Chao-hsien in times of peace, while, as will be seen, the parent nation exercised an unlimited power when it judged the lesser nation to be in danger.

Though the adhesion of a lesser state to the Confucian family appears to have been to some degree optional by the nineteenth century,[13] it is to be doubted that Chinese acquiescence would have attended a breach by Chao-hsien, since she had always occupied a special and superior status among the lesser states. This is shown by the fact that only the Chao-hsien envoys were allowed an audience with the emperor or the privilege of sitting and taking tea.[14] Moreover, the imperial envoys sent to Chao-hsien were always of a higher rank than those dispatched to other countries.[15]

But being thoroughly Confucian, Chao-hsien was not likely to disrupt the Far Eastern family; she viewed dependency upon China as an honor or mark of civilization which barbarians could not attain. Though in theory her submission was abject and complete, her status cannot in fact be rightly termed "vassalage," for the Far East possessed no counterpart of the word "suzerainty" as it is understood in the West.[16] Before external pressure was felt upon the relationship, as late as the beginning of the nineteenth century, its outward evidences went little beyond formal submission and tribute, the practice of investiture being only the confirmation of the *de facto* ruler. What is more important, the in-

[13] At least outlying areas such as Siam were able to renounce their status within the system without any immediate repercussions from China. See G. Jamieson, "The Tributary Nations of China," in *China Review,* XII (1883), 94.
[14] *Ibid.,* 106–108.
[15] J. K. Fairbank and S. Y. Têng, "On the Ch'ing Tributary System," in *Harvard Journal of Asiatic Studies,* VI (1941), 170.
[16] Djang, Chinese Suzerainty, 9.

ternal fields of control and policy were left to the discretion of the king, while external relations, necessarily limited to the Far East nations, were also directed by the individual rulers. Clearly, then, the position of Chao-hsien was far from being uncomfortable.

The inferior states regularly listed as *shu-pang*, or nations dependent on China, were Korea (Chao-hsien), Liu-ch'iu, Annam, Nan-chang (Laos), Siam, Burma, and Sula.[17] There is perhaps nothing better indicative of the essential character of the Far Eastern system of international polity than the fact that the relations of China with these lesser nations were handled by the Department of Rites (Li Pu), which was concerned with *li*, the rules of proper conduct. And this was true even after the establishment, in 1861, of a Department of Foreign Affairs to deal with the Western states.

2. RULES OF FAR EASTERN INTERNATIONAL INTERCOURSE

In those fields in which China had contact with the lesser nations, the procedure was minutely prescribed.[18] In the first

[17] After 1638 a definite distinction was made between these areas, classed as nations (*pang*), and the more tribal areas to the north and west. The Li Fan Yuan, a body originally set up to handle relations with the Mongols, came to be the agency which administered areas such as Tibet, Turkestan (Hsinchiang), and Mongolia. These territories were governed like actual provinces, Chinese officers who collected taxes being in some cases in residence and Chinese penal codes in force. They were in no way comparable with the subordinate nations listed above. Manchuria, the ancestral home of the reigning dynasty, was governed separately, and certain aboriginal tribes were under the control of the Board of War. See William F. Mayers, *The Chinese Government* (Shanghai, 1886), 48–50; Fairbank and Têng, "On the Ch'ing Tributary System," *loc. cit.*, 158, 162, 174. Japan alternately acknowledged and rejected an inferior status in the East Asiatic system. During the T'ang period she sent missions continuously, but allegiance was denied during the time of the Sung and Yüan dynasties. In the fifteenth and sixteenth centuries the shoguns, *de facto* rulers of Japan, accepted investiture and acknowledged her inferiority to the Ming dynasty. China, until modern times, had always viewed Japan, however, as a recalcitrant member of the East Asiatic system. See Kuno, *Japanese Expansion*, I, 27, 29–30, 41–42, 69, 89–100, 104, 120–22.

[18] The most informative record in English of the actual practices followed in the tributary relationship between China and its surrounding dependencies

place, the missions to China bearing tribute and congratulatory messages did not appear at will. Chao-hsien, for instance, being geographically and culturally the area nearest to China, was directed to submit tribute four times a year after 1736, though actually the earlier custom of an annual presentation of all tribute due for each year continued to be practiced. Liu-ch'iu sent missions every other year, Siam every three years, Annam once in four years, Sula every five years, and Burma and Laos every ten years.[19] In addition, missions of a congratulatory nature were sent. In the case of Chao-hsien this was done upon principal anniversaries such as the emperor's birthday, the beginning of the new year, and the winter solstices. On each of these occasions the Chao-hsien king, in company with his family and officials, would perform the *San kuei chiu k'ou* ceremony of the three kneelings and the nine prostrations and also dispatch a letter of homage to the emperor.[20]

The routes which envoys to China had to take, as well as the size of the mission and the character of the gifts were definitely fixed. The Chao-hsien mission, which in no case could number more than one hundred,[21] came by way of the city of Feng-wang, thence to Mukden and through Shanhaikwan. Only twenty persons of the hundred were permitted to proceed to the imperial capital, the rest remaining at the coastal port. Articles customarily acceptable as tribute comprised generally the products of the responding countries,

---

from the seventeenth century on is the study of Fairbank and Têng, "On the Ch'ing Tributary System," *loc. cit.*, 135–246.

[19] *Ibid.*, 175; cf. Djang, Chinese Suzerainty, App., p. 182, for a varying translation of the tribute intervals.

[20] "Corea: Extracts from M. F. Scherzer's French Translation of Chao-hsien-chih" (Charles Gould, trans.), in *Journal of North China Branch of the Royal Asiatic Society*, XVIII (1884), 35–36.

[21] The 1764 edition of the *Collected Statutes of the Ch'ing Dynasty* states that the Chao-hsien missions consisted of an envoy, one attendant secretary, three chief interpreters, twenty-four tribute guards, thirty minor retainers who received gifts, and a variable number of unrewarded retainers. Fairbank and Têng, "On the Ch'ing Tributary System," *loc. cit.*, 171.

specifically elephant tusks and rhinoceros horns from Annam, and sulphur and copper from Liu-ch'iu. Chao-hsien's tribute was ordinarily two hundred pieces of grass cloth, two hundred of white silk, one hundred of red silk, one hundred of blue silk, three hundred of seal skins, ten swords, five thousand rolls of paper, and forty piculs of rice.[22]

Upon arrival, a mission followed a fixed routine of activities. If the tribute was to be presented directly to the emperor, as was the case of that from Chao-hsien, the envoys had to practice the ceremonies required in audience before him. At the audience, all the envoys were expected only to present their tribute and withdraw, except that those of Chao-hsien were allowed to seat themselves and take tea.[23] A dinner was also given before the delegates left Peking, at which function the return gifts of the emperor [24] were bestowed, gifts generally exceeding in value those brought. Each mission also received the imperial calendar for the coming year, dated according to the reign title of the ruling emperor, and was provided with an escort to the borders.[25]

Various prohibitions were placed upon these missions to China. For example, though the envoys were allowed to bring materials for trade, and though they were even given the permission for a few days to sell them in the Hall of Missions without payment of tax, the tributary ruler could have goods purchased in China only through the Chinese officials, and no contraband, weapons, or historical or geographical books could be purchased. Other rules prohibited the submission of

[22] Prior to 1727 one hundred piculs of rice were required. Jamieson, "The Tributary Nations of China," *loc. cit.*, 103. Fairbank and Têng, "On the Ch'ing Tributary System," *loc. cit.*, 175.

[23] Jamieson, "The Tributary Nations of China," *loc. cit.*, 106.

[24] The emperor's gifts were termed *Hui* (favors), while all gifts brought to Peking were termed *Kung* (tribute).

[25] Djang, Chinese Suzerainty, 182. For translation of the official ceremony prescribed for the receipt and audience of envoys, see G. Pauthier, *Histoire des relations politiques de la Chine avec les puissances occidentales* (Paris, 1859), Chap. IX.

memorials directly to the emperor or the bestowing of gifts on the viceroys.[26]

On the other hand, the Chinese envoys who were sent in return received lavish treatment from the lesser nation. The reports made by the Chinese envoy to Chao-hsien in 1843 and by Western observers in 1890 show that the ceremonies followed were identical with those observed by the Ming rulers more than 350 years earlier.[27] Of particular importance was the investiture ritual employed by the Chinese emperor in conferring on the lesser kings their patents of office. Upon the death of the monarch of a lesser kingdom, the successor would first address a petition to the Chinese emperor asking for confirmation of his accession to the throne as a guard on the frontiers of the empire.[28] If investiture was to be granted, the emperor would dispatch two envoys to perform the ceremony, whereupon the king of the lesser nation would send his ministers to the border to greet the imperial emissaries. A prescribed ceremony was carried out, whereby the casket containing the letter of the emperor received nine kowtows and his envoys themselves three. Of a highly ritualistic nature, this investiture procedure required even the investing of the queen and of the heir to the throne before they could rightfully claim their rank.[29]

Trade between China and Chao-hsien was closely supervised. Direct trade by sea was not allowed. As early as 1637 the Manchus decreed that all Chinese merchants going by sea to Korea should be sent back to China, and in 1717 the Peking Board of Rites provided that any Chinese forced by weather to land on Chao-hsien shores were to be sent back by the land route only if they possessed passports and made

[26] Djang, Chinese Suzerainty, 184–85.
[27] Rockhill, *China's Intercourse with Korea*, 35–38. See pp. 73 ff., 200 ff.
[28] See *Foreign Relations*, 1880, pp. 199–201, for investiture documents.
[29] Jamieson, "The Tributary Nations of China," *loc. cit.*, 99–100; Fairbank and Têng, "On the Ch'ing Tributary System," *loc. cit.*, 147 n.

no attempt to conduct business. Even fishing by Chinese on the coasts of Chao-hsien was forbidden.[30]

By land, trade was permitted twice a year at the island in the Yalu River near Wu-ji, and traders were also allowed to accompany the Chao-hsien missions to Peking. The Chinese trading franchise at the border was held by the soldiers of the banner troops at the frontier posts, and though efforts were made in 1736 to divert the soldiers back to their military duties, this commercial practice continued. Those Chao-hsien traders who accompanied the missions to Peking were forbidden to dispose of any of their wares on the way and were twice examined on the Wu-ji—Peking road. Restrictions on the purchase of arms, contraband, and the Chinese dynastic histories applied equally to the traders and the envoys.[31]

3. Peculiarities of Far Eastern Political Concepts

This system of international relations differed radically from anything known in the West. As already explained, the concept grew out of the rules governing the proper conduct between members of the family. Obviously, the Far Eastern view of intercourse among civilized nations was limited by their exacting idea of what constituted civilization. To the West, civilization meant the existence of enough organization and stability of government for a state to maintain its pledged word. It meant values similar to those inherited from Christian principles and provided for a similarity of treatment of the nationals of one state in the territory of another, or, lacking that, special provisions approximating this treatment. Civilization in the Far East, however, meant a knowledge of the rules of proper conduct which in that area formed the bonds for all social life, an amenability to reason rather than

[30] Rockhill, *China's Intercourse with Korea*, 32–33.
[31] *Ibid.*, 31–32.

to force or contract, and a tendency to feel shame and degradation—that is, a loss of "face"—at improper action. It involved, further, a recognition of China's supremacy and world leadership and a desire to emulate it and receive instruction from the Middle Kingdom. Thus it is apparent why the West, with some qualification, was satisfied with China's ability to maintain membership in the Western family of nations, and why it sought even to force such membership on China, while to China the Western states were not yet civilized and hence not fit subjects for international relations. To the Chinese, the Western states were rightly excluded from the East Asiatic system just as the Barbary pirates or Ethiopia were, in the nineteenth century, excluded from the Western family.

One of the main reasons why the Chinese maintained relations of any nature was to spread their culture. In the nineteenth century, however, the requests by Western nations for audience, trade, and exchange of envoys were refused by China because of the improbability that the suggested intercourse would serve to extend to an appreciable degree the culture of China. The following statements by the Chinese Emperor to George III of England illustrate the point of view:

Our ceremonies and code of laws differ so completely from your own that even if your Envoy were able to acquire the rudiments of our civilization; you could not possibly transplant our manners and customs to your alien soil. Therefore, however adept the Envoy might become, nothing could be gained thereby.[32]

Without conformance to the high requirements of the ordained system and subservience to its natural laws, inter-

[32] E. Backhouse and J. O. P. Bland, *Annals and Memoirs of the Court of Peking* (London, 1914), 324. This statement to the English indicates, however, a practical modification of the Confucian theory of the world-wide overlordship of the Chinese emperor and of his duty to extend the natural order to the barbarians. It indicates that the English were, perhaps, not just another tribe living in disorder, and that there could exist another civilization worthy of the name, though it was not Chinese.

course was impossible. Nowhere else did the theory of natural law ever approach the Confucian belief that there existed a potential and pre-established world pattern wherein all things had a definite and proper place and relation to all other things, that everything was good in its proper place, and that there was no evil as such, but only disharmony which occurred when the world order was disturbed.[33] The element which China developed in the idea of law in nature was the theory of interaction. This conceived so real a solidarity between the natural order and the social order that nonconformance to nature in the social order would cause disorders in the natural sphere, and that such natural phenomena were always indications of social disharmony.[34]

In the Confucian system, the world order was of a centrifugal nature, with the Middle Kingdom as the center and source of all culture, virtue, and rules of conduct. As a general rule, the nearer an area was to China the more nearly it conformed to the natural Confucian order. The Chinese world order was also centripetal in that it was the centrifugal flow of culture which bound the surrounding nations to China, the source of all civilization. The Chinese were confident that they had rightly solved the formula of the universe, and any alien ideas were rejected, not so much because they were alien and therefore wrong as for the far graver reason that to admit them would disturb the natural and established pattern and bring confusion and suffering to all.

The theory of Confucian international relations drew no line between the standard by which a state was judged and that applying to an individual. Just as *li* governed individual relations, those of the family, and those of the Middle Kingdom, so international relations were merely an extension of the same principles. Obviously *raison d'etat* had no standing

[33] H. G. Creel, *Sinism, A Study of the Evolution of the Chinese World-View* (Chicago, 1929), 47, 63.
[34] Jean Escarra, *Le droit chinois* (Paris, 1936), 8.

as a justification of acts which propriety did not condone, for the fundamental justification of all organized society was the pursuance of this propriety. Even the barbarians were not to be arbitrarily managed but, according to *li,* had to be treated in a definitely correct, if condescending, manner despite the fact that, being ignorant of the principles of *li,* they could not be dealt with on a basis of reason.

The Confucian international relations of the Far East lacked that concept around which the whole history of the West has revolved, the idea of "law." It is true, however, that in the third and fourth centuries B.C. a legalist school of philosophers existed in China. During the Ch'in period (221–206 B.C.) law became the basis of the government of the empire, though its very harshness and inflexibility led to the destruction of the dynasty basing its rule upon such principles and also to the repudiation of the concept of law and force as compatible with just and lasting government.[35]

The Confucian concept of a world order, of a definite unity between nature and the social order, led to the rejection of the practicality of a social order governed by rigid law as the product of individual will. In this connection M. Geny writes:

Cette entente des choses et des hommes est un souple régime d'interdependances et de solidarités qui jamais ne sourait reposer sur des *prescriptions inconditionnelles:* sur des Lois. Le prestige du concret, de sentiment de l'occasionnel sont trop puissants, l'ordre humain et l'ordre naturel paraissent trop étroitement solidaires pour que le principe de tout ordre puisse être doué d'un caractère d'obligation ou de nécessité. . . . La loi, l'abstract, l'inconditionnel sont exclus—l'Univers est un, tant de la societe que de la nature. . . . Dans l'idée de régle, on ne veut guère voir que l'idée de modele. La notion chinoise de l'Ordre exclut, sous tous ses aspects, l'idée de Loi.[36]

[35] *The Book of Lord Shang* (J. J. L. Duyvendak, trans.) (London, 1928); Fung, *A History of Chinese Philosophy,* Chap. XIII; Bodde, *China's First Unifier,* 191–99.

[36] M. Geny, *Method d'interpretation et sources en droit prive positif,* 589–90, quoted in Escarra, *Le droit chinois,* 70.

In Confucian theory the place of law was filled by *li,* the rules of proper conduct. Distinguishable from law in several respects, *li* is primarily concerned with motives and with the will actuating them. Its province does not deal with the outward acts or deeds but with the inner nature of man, and it seeks, through reason, so to regulate man's inner nature that actual laws are unnecessary. *Li* directs itself to developing in man a sense of shame which will be a more effective social control than any law. Confucius expressed this attitude toward law as contrasted to *li* by saying that,

If the people be led by laws, and uniformity sought to be given them by punishments, they will try to avoid the punishment, but have no sense of shame. If they be led by virtue, and uniformity sought to be given them by the rules of propriety, they will have the sense of shame, and moreover will become good.[37]

While law is mainly remedial in that it provides redress for those things it declares wrong, *li* is anticipatory since it seeks to instruct men so that wrong will never be committed. Law must define in minute detail what acts constitute its violation in every situation that may be anticipated, while *li* teaches general principles based on the five great relations, with illustrations of proper conformance taken from the past. Each subsequent act is judged, then, according to the general theory, rather than being regulated by minutely pre-established policy through law. *Li* is implicit in custom; law, even when customary, is made explicit by specific institutions. Law has force and punishment as its sanction, and it is enforced by the state; the observance of *li* depends solely on a moral sanction, social disapproval, and a sense of shame. In Confucianism responsibility is fixed not in terms of "who has done something," but of "what has happened." [38] The object of law is to achieve by force the condition of no apparent disobedience, whereas *li* seeks to make virtue and the

[37] *Analects* in *The Chinese Classics,* I, 10.
[38] Lattimore, *Manchuria,* 80.

observance of the rules of proper conduct second nature in men.[39]

To those reared in the tradition of the Roman law a philosophy based on the Confucian principles would seem to lead inevitably to anarchy, but the Confucians realized that

. . . the only lasting unity is one based on homogeneity of ideas and culture, and not on a forced obedience to a common body of law. . . . The result has been a remarkable evenness of civilization throughout a vast country, and continuity of culture longer than that enjoyed by any other living nation.[40]

With their concept of the natural world order, and with their doctrine that government is the centrifugal force of moral precepts, the Chinese developed no concept of the "state" or of "sovereignty." China was the center of an entire world system, a powerful core around which were grouped many weaker satellites, none able to compare with her in power, wealth, culture, and virtue. With all influence flowing outward, with no competing cultures or authority against which the barriers of definite boundaries need be raised, she had no need for the legal concept of the state or of sovereignty. Her control was through ideas which could be confined within no physical boundaries. The marking off of a certain territory within which her word was the highest law and beyond which her precepts were unrecognized, was not con-

---

[39] K. C. Wu, *Ancient Chinese Political Theories* (Shanghai, 1928), 274; Dubs, *Hsüntze, The Moulder*, 115. It is true that penal law, often barbarous by modern standards, was not entirely disregarded. For those beyond the pale of civilization or those whose natural capabilities and moral natures were such that they made no attempt to learn, laws existed and punishments were imposed. Yet the laws and punishments themselves were designed to bring these lesser persons into the observance of the rules of *li;* the principles of conduct remained, the method of conformance only modified. These codes of punishments were something apart from the Confucian theory of control through example, and were originally formed to apply in areas under military occupation outside of China, where the barbarians, lacking in civilization, could not be controlled through reason. Escarra, *Le droit chinois*, 71. For the Confucian attitude toward war, see above, pp. 11–12.

[40] Bodde, *China's First Unifier*, 199.

templated in Chinese theory. Not only was the field of Chinese influence unlimited by physical boundaries, but its field of action embraced the entire social life of man rather than merely certain fields which were deemed "public." Yet the nature of the control over the entire social life was such that other agencies might conceivably operate in some sphere of the society without raising any question of "sovereignty." [41] The Western powers were long in understanding that, in their relations with China, they were not dealing with anything comparable to a sovereign state in their sense of the expression. To be sure, there did exist an integrated hierarchy of officials whose titles, translated into Western terminology, gave the impression of a highly organized state system.[42] Yet, as a recent writer has said: "As a state, as an all-embracing control institution, the Chinese hierarchy was a pseudomorph— it looked like a state but was not really one." [43]

Inequality was a basic element found in every phase of society in the Confucian system; [44] it was necessary to preserve the natural order, for equality in any relation bred conflict and disorder and caused disharmony in the natural order of things. The rules of proper conduct knew no equality. As "all within the four seas" was viewed as a world family,[45] and as equality among the members of a family would be an absurdity, so, as well, would be equality among countries. Equality would violate the relation between the posi-

[41] Thus, though China might object to the granting of foreign concessions, to leased areas, or to outright cession because such areas presented the danger of the infiltration of "barbarian" cultures into its world, the actual loss of a small piece of territory was no blow to her national pride, because the physical occupancy of territory meant nothing to a government which controlled through ideas. China held no physical rights over the territory of Korea, of Siam, of the Liu-ch'ius, yet it considered them within its sphere of influence. Similarly, local government, exercised through the family, the village, or the guild, independent of the official hierarchy, was no threat to its control.

[42] W. C. Costin, *Great Britain and China, 1833–1860* (Oxford, 1937), 12–13.

[43] P. M. A. Linebarger, *Government in Republican China* (New York: McGraw-Hill Book Co., 1938), 21.

[44] See pp. 7 ff.

[45] *Lichi* in *The Sacred Books*, XXVII, 379.

tion of a superior and the degree of virtue which varied with that status. Equality of countries would mean an equality of virtue, an assumption no one would maintain against China and her emperor. Conversely, virtue denoted superiority, and the size of one's domain varied in direct proportion to one's virtue. Since she was the land of the sages, China had a vastly greater virtue than all others and could not possibly be thought less than their superior in every way.

The Chinese lack of any concept of the equality of nations is perhaps most strikingly presented in the early communications which the Ch'ing Throne addressed to the representatives of George III, who sought relations on their own Western terms of state equality. The following extract illustrates the nature of that correspondence:

You, O King, live beyond the confines of many seas, nevertheless, impelled by your humble desire to partake of the benefits of our civilization, you have dispatched a mission respectfully bearing your memorial. Your Envoy has crossed the seas and paid his respects at my Court on the anniversary of my birthday. To show your devotion, you have also sent offerings of your country's produce.[46]

The various proposals for intercourse and trade later urged by the English envoy were all refused with the same air of patient explanation that one would employ toward a non-understanding person, the emperor again writing:

It may be, O King, that the above proposals have been wantonly made by your Ambassador on his own responsibility, or peradventure you yourself are ignorant of our dynastic regulations and had no intention of transgressing them when you expressed these wild ideas and hopes. I have ever shown the greatest condescension to the tribute missions of all states which sincerely yearn after the blessings of civilization, so as to manifest my kindly indulgence.[47]

[46] Quoted in Backhouse and Bland, *Annals and Memoirs*, 322.
[47] *Ibid.*, 330.

Even the request by the American minister at a later date showed no alteration of the imperial attitudes in the rescript which stated:

> We have this day perused the reply of the American barbarians. . . . (It shows that) in the matter of their presentation at Court, nothing more can be done to bring them to reason. Besides, these barbarians, by their averment that their respect for His Majesty the Emperor is the same as that they feel for their Pih-li-si-tien-teh (President), just place China on a par with the barbarians of the South and East, an arrogation of greatness which is simply ridiculous.[48]

These evidences may suggest the absurdity of the Far Eastern attitude from the Occidental point of view. Yet an authority on Far Eastern affairs has written as recently as 1938 to the effect that,

> In spirit, the Chinese people have never assented to the Western concept of the family of nations, based as it is upon the idea of legal equality of states. Celestials in the majority . . . (excluding "foreign" and "modern" educated Chinese), still hold that their country is the center of the world, the hub of the universe; that theirs is the only civilization worthy of the name; that other civilizations and nations are of small import when weighed in the balance with China's civilization and objectives.[49]

The Far East had built up political ideas sharply at variance with those of the West. When intercourse was attempted between the contrasting systems, little common ground upon which such relations could be based existed. Naturally, from this basic conflict of ideas, there developed collisions of policies and institutions which found their final settlement only through war. Yet the following comment indicates that some

[48] Quoted in H. F. MacNair, *Modern Chinese History: Selected Readings* (Shanghai, 1927), No. 194, pp. 305–306.
[49] MacNair, *The Real Conflict*, 89.

Westerners were able to understand at least a part of the implications of the Confucian system. Concerning China, United States Minister Seward wrote in 1879:

It is not too much to say that it has been within the power of China for a very long period to overrun and subdue these petty states. . . . A great people filling all their territory to the limit of its sustaining power, but remaining for centuries self-contained, regardful of their own dignity and place, but regardful also of the rights of the petty powers about them, is a spectacle not very common in the history of the world. It is one upon which we may pause to raise the question whether a state capable of such conduct has not, for some reason, a poise and balance of judgment and temper greater than we have been in the habit of attributing to her, and which entitles her to a large measure of respect and esteem.[50]

[50] Seward to Evarts, Dec. 11, 1879, in *Foreign Relations*, 1880, p. 179.

KOREA IN CONFLICTING SOCIETIES OF NATIONS

CHAPTER VII

EARLIEST WESTERN CONTACTS
(TO 1876)

1. KOREA THE "HERMIT NATION"

THE early contacts of the West with Chao-hsien, which was known to the world by the older name of Korea,[1] followed the pattern found in other parts of the Far East. An opening wedge of traders and missionaries was eventually followed by government officials when, by the standards of the West, rights of these religious and commercial adventurers had been violated. In the attempt to fix responsibility for these violations the Western nations found in Korea the same views of state responsibility and of the nature of government that existed in China, all of course exotic to the West. They also found the further complicating factor of the relationship of Korea to the Middle Kingdom.

The first recorded visit of any European to Korea was that of the Spanish Jesuit, Gregorio de Cespedes, who arrived in 1593 to minister to the Japanese Christian warriors under the invading General Konshi. His contacts with natives of the peninsula were limited to the prisoners of war who were sent captive to Japan, and he himself returned after a stay of

[1] Since this name, derived from the native pronunciation of Kao-li (Ko-rai) was used by Western states, it will be employed in the following pages. The spelling "Korea" is that adopted by the Royal Geographic Society and the United States State Department. See *Korean Repository*, I (1892), 161. For discussion of the term "Chao-hsien" or "Chosen" see *Korean Repository*, IV (1897), 23, 24, 79.

only a year and a half.[2] Around the year 1627, when the Dutch ship *Ouderkress* was driven to the coast of Korea, three of her sailors who went ashore for water were captured. Two of these men were killed in the Manchu invasion, and the third, John Wetterre, was discovered a quarter of a century later by another group of sailors who survived the wreck of the Dutch ship *Sparrowhawk*. The internment and subsequent escape to Japan of seven of the *Sparrowhawk* survivors was recorded by one of their number, Hendrick Hamel.[3]

In the following century and a half, though the West was increasing its intercourse with China, no impression was made upon Korea, and the nation remained virtually unknown. European ships occasionally touched the Korean coast, as did Captain Broughton's HMS *Providence* in 1797, and in 1816 the vessels *Lyra* and *Alceste*, which had conveyed Lord Amherst's Mission to Peking. Captain Basil Hall, commanding the *Lyra*, recorded his impressions of an eleven-day survey of the southwest coast of Korea.[4] In 1832 the British East India Company's vessel *Lord Amherst* made an attempt to trade on the southern coast, and in 1845 HMS *Samarang* surveyed islands in that locality.[5]

The Western powers, particularly after the China treaties, were not content to be long excluded from the remaining Far Eastern areas. In 1845 the American Congressman Zodoc Pratt introduced in the House of Representatives a resolution

[2] See Ralph M. Cory, "Some Notes on Father Gregorio de Cespedes, Korea's First European Visitor," in *TKBRAS*, XXVII (1937), 1–55.

[3] See Hendrick Hamel, "An Account of the Shipwreck of a Dutch Vessel on the Coast of the Isle of Quelpaert, Together with a Description of the Kingdom of Corea," in *TKBRAS*, IX (1918), 91–148. See Jones, "Historical Notes on the Reigning Dynasty," *loc. cit.*, 123–24, for the Korean record of the *Sparrowhawk*'s wreck.

[4] See "Captain Basil Hall's Account of His Voyage to the West Coast of Corea in 1816," in *TKBRAS*, IX (1920), 1–37; "The Korean Record on Captain Basil Hall's Voyage of Discovery to the West Coast of Korea," in *TKBRAS*, XXIV (1935), 15–19; John M'Leod, *Narrative of a Voyage in His Majesty's Late Ship Alceste to the Yellow Sea Along the Coast of Corea* (London, 1817).

[5] Griffis, *Corea*, 359; Longford, *Korea*, 226.

to send diplomatic and commercial agents to Japan and Korea so that "the American people will be able to rejoice in the knowledge that the 'star spangled banner' is recognized as ample passport and protection for all who, of our enterprizing countrymen, may be engaged in extending American commerce. . . ." [6] Nothing came of this American proposal, but the scene was soon laid for another Western state to attempt an opening, this time not through trade but through religion.

Christianity had been slowly seeping into Korea from the Jesuits in Peking, and as early as 1777 Christian writings were winning converts.[7] The conflict of this creed with Confucianism, evidenced in the destruction by Christians of their ancestral tablets, caused the Korean literati to oppose strenuously these unorthodox beliefs.[8] The growth of the sect continued, however, particularly after three French priests were able to smuggle themselves across the border and aid actively the spread of the new religion, which by 1839 numbered 9,000 converts. In that year, when a court party in favor of extirpating Christianity came into power, persecution was renewed which culminated in the death of many converts and of the three French missionaries Imbert, Maubant, and Chastan.[9]

The news of the death of the French missionaries was slow

[6] *United States House Executive Documents*, 28 Cong., 2 Sess., No. 138, "Extensions of American Commerce—Proposed Mission to Japan and Corea" (Washington, 1845).

[7] Griffis, *Corea*, 347 ff.

[8] The following extract from a letter of the Chao-hsien king to the Chinese emperor explaining the execution of a Chinese Christian shows the general attitude:

"His Imperial Majesty knows that . . . the Little Kingdom has always been distinguished for its punctuality in fulfilling all obligations ordered by rites, justice, and loyalty. . . . This has in all ages been acknowledged by the Middle Court. . . . This kingdom, which has always preserved its purity of manners, esteems above everything the doctrine of Confucius. No books other than those . . . (of Confucius) have ever been admitted into this Kingdom by literati or mandarins; much less have they ever been studied by them. The very women and children of the streets and cottages are familiar with the five fundamental duties. . . . All other doctrine is strange to the Little Kingdom, and error has never penetrated it." Quoted in Longford, *Korea*, 256.

[9] Griffis, *Corea*, 347–67; Longford, *Korea*, 242–73.

in reaching the outside world. Not until early in 1846 did a French frigate appear at the mouth of the Han River to deliver to the local officials a letter demanding an explanation for the execution of the three men. To receive the reply, in August of the same year the frigates *Gloire* and *Victorieuse* arrived off the coast, only to meet misfortune. Grounding on uncharted shoals and left stranded by the falling tide, the unharmed crews were rescued by a passing English vessel.[10] After the rescue, however, the Korean government did forward to Peking a reply to the original demand of the French, the first record of an official dispatch by Korea to a Western power. As given by Dallet, in a translation from the version published as a Royal Proclamation in Korea, the note replied by comparing the gracious rules of Korea for the treatment of shipwrecked persons with the prescribed disposition of others, regardless of nationality, who attempted to enter Korea as the missionaries had done, secretly and in disguise. It concluded by stating that Korea was subordinate to China, to whom all questions relating to foreigners had to be referred.[11]

From the very first communication, then, the status of Korea as inferior to China was asserted. The direction that Westerners could deal with her only through China appears to have been more nearly an attempt to avoid Western contacts than a true description of her actual nineteenth century status in the Far Eastern system, for, as is shown by their dealings with Japan, the Korean governments had always been able to negotiate directly with other nations. But Korean foreign relations had always been limited to dealing with other Far Eastern governments similar in civilization and regularized in ritual. The French demands therefore presented an entirely new element, which Korea in its reply

[10] Longford, *Korea*, 226–27.
[11] Charles Dallet, *Histoire de l'église de Corée* (Paris, 1874), II, 339–41.

sought to pass on to China. If China had at the time of this incident altered the relationship so as to accept the responsibility for all of Korea's foreign affairs, a satisfactory compromise between the systems of the East and the West might have been worked out. But having troubles of her own with the Western states, and not wishing to alter the established relation in which Korea had traditionally stood, she continued to follow a policy which to the West appeared anomalous— a policy declaring Korea dependent, but refusing to accept legal responsibility for Korea's acts.

Though the Occident closed in ever nearer, thus increasing the chances for conflict between the Western state system and that of Korea, and though efforts were made to open the country through trade or through diplomatic negotiation, Korea continued to be a "hermit nation." But survey ships of such Western nations as France and Russia did chart the Korean coasts so that their shore lines became known,[12] and pressure on Korea was increased by China's cession of the Maritime Province to Russia, which put a Western nation on the northern Korean border. The barriers of the other Far Eastern nations were also giving way to the Western pressures. China herself, the superior state, beginning with the treaty of Nanking in 1842, was forced to make treaties with the Westerners, and in 1860 the Son of Heaven himself fled from his capital before their armies. Moreover, Japan, after Commodore Perry's visit, had taken over Western customs with a zeal comparable with that of her acceptance of the civilization of China in the seventh century.

It was through Japan that the Western states attempted to insert a diplomatic wedge into Korea's exclusion. In 1861 Lord Russell attempted to get Great Britain admitted to the petty trade carried on between the Japanese island of Tsushima and the Korean port of Fusan, and in the same year

12 Griffis, *Corea,* pp. 369–70 n.

Russia occupied a station on Tsushima, though she abandoned it under Japanese and British pressure. The next year the government of Napoleon III requested the aid of the Japanese envoys in Paris in opening Korea to French trade and residence [13] but to no avail since the Japanese were fully occupied with domestic matters and had themselves not dealt officially with Korea since 1763.[14] At the beginning of 1866 a Russian warship appeared at Wün san (Broughton's Bay) and demanded the right of trade, indicating that Russian troops were to cross the northern border to enforce the demands. To this, as to all other requests, Korea replied that the kingdom was a dependent country to China and could deal with no other nation without the emperor's permission.[15]

It should be mentioned that not only was Korea disturbed by these acts of the Westerners, but also by an internal dynastic crisis which occurred at the death of King Chül-chong (1849–1863). When Chül-chong died without designating an heir, the Dowager Queen Cho [16] seized the royal seals and adopted the second child of one of the royal princes as her son to occupy the throne. The father of the new king was given the title of Tai-wün-kun and made regent during his son's minority, Queen Cho trusting that his previous indifference to the exercise of power would enable her to control policy. But the Tai-wün-kun surprised the court by actively controlling matters and remained a potent figure in Korean affairs until his death in 1898. He was violently anti-Christian and opposed all contacts with the West. The following statements in his decree of 1866 describe his attitude: "The barbarians from beyond the seas have violated our borders and invaded our land. If we do not fight we must make treaties with them. Those who favor making a treaty sell their coun-

13 *Ibid.*, 372.
14 See p. 77.
15 Longford, *Korea*, 281.
16 The Dowager Queen Cho was the wife of Ik-chong who ruled only three years (1827–30) as son of Sun-cho (1800–34) and co-king with him.

try." [17] Yet his actions were largely responsible for the increased Western pressure which Korea felt after 1866.[18]

2. THE FRENCH EXPEDITION, 1866

The relations between China and Korea received their first major test at the time of the French expedition in 1866. France had done nothing to follow up her action of 1847 upon the execution of the three French priests in Korea, and without any effort at salvage, she allowed the ill-fated ships *Gloire* and *Victorieuse* to go to pieces on the Korean coast. Along with a more tolerant disposition of the national government and the arrival of new French missionaries, the number of Korean converts to Christianity was said to have risen to 18,000 in 1864.[19] The panic caused by the threatened Russian invasion of Korea in 1866 gave the Christians there an idea that they might strengthen their position by urging the government, as an offset to Russia, to make treaties with France and England, through the French bishop in Korea. But the antiforeign sentiment, which still viewed relations with any Western power as traitorous, was whipped to an antireligious frenzy by the false report, sent back from China by the Korean tribute mission, that the Chinese were putting to death all Christians in the empire. This renewed hostility, together with the lack of any reprisals for the earlier killings of the French priests in 1839 and the disappearance of the Russian threat, led to a persecution in March, 1866, which completely stamped out all organized Christianity in Korea. Only three of almost a score of French missionaries escaped with their lives. The admiral of the French Asiatic fleet and the French diplomatic representative decided immediately to demand satisfaction, and a gunboat was dispatched to

[17] G. H. Jones, "The Taiwon Kun," in *Korean Repository*, V (1898), 247.
[18] See *ibid.*, and "His Majesty, the King of Korea," in *Korean Repository*, III (1896), 423–30, for discussion of the Tai-wün-kun.
[19] Griffis, *Corea*, 372.

make preliminary surveys of the Western coast of Korea.[20]

Henri de Bellonet, French chargé, addressed a note to Prince Kung of the Chinese Foreign Office, which illustrates the previously formed Western misconceptions of the relationship between Korea and China:

July 13, 1866

SIR: I grieve to bring officially to the knowledge of your imperial highness a horrible outrage committed in the small kingdom of Corea, which formerly assumed the bonds of vassalage to the Chinese empire, but which this act of savage barbarity has forever separated from it.

Recounting the incidents of the death of the missionaries, he continued:

The government of his Majesty cannot permit so bloody an outrage to be unpunished. The same day on which the King of Corea laid his hands upon my unhappy countrymen was the last of his reign; he himself proclaimed its end, which I in my turn solemnly declare to-day. In a few days our military forces are to march to the conquest of Corea, and the Emperor, my august sovereign, alone, has now the right and the power to dispose, according to his good pleasure, of the country and of the vacant throne.

The Chinese government has declared to me many times that it has no authority or power over Corea; and it refused on this pretext to apply the treaties of Tientsin to that country, and give to our missionaries the passports which we have asked from it. We have taken note of these declarations, and we declare, now, that we do not recognise any authority whatever of the Chinese government over the kingdom of Corea.[21]

Not understanding the implications which such a reply would have in Western international law, China answered to the effect that the "out-of-the-way" country (Korea) had always "maintained its own regulations," and that China would therefore naturally be unaware of the reasons for the

[20] *Foreign Relations*, 1866, p. 536.
[21] *Ibid.*, 1867, Pt. I, pp. 420 ff.

alleged massacre. The note further urged an investigation by the French to ascertain the facts before the expedition was sent; but neither in this reply nor in the later notes did China suggest that she would assume legal responsibility for the acts of Korea. In later messages to China the French chargé saw fit to point to the Korean tributary missions to China and to the dispatch of Chinese envoys to Korea as evidence that the Middle Kingdom was not only preparing to aid Korea against the French but had even directed the policy leading to the massacre. China endeavored to explain that the practice alluded to was

of very long standing, and no recent thing. The officers who came from thence, and ours who went thither the present year, came and went on affairs of ceremonial, and in accordance with long-established usage; having no reference to the quarrel between France and Corea, they were not to be set aside or abrogated.[22]

Such diplomacy being clearly futile, a French expedition of only 600 men effected a landing on Kang-wha, the island at the mouth of the Han River, which had in the past figured so prominently as a place of refuge for the kings of Korea. Kang-wha city was captured but the French suffered a decided defeat when, of the 160 men they had detailed to capture a fortified monastery, only 80 returned uninjured, fighting as they retreated. Realizing the folly of attempting to subdue a country with such a meager force, the expedition departed. Orders from France brought disapproval of the independent action of M. de Bellonet which occasioned the impasse, and further thought of reprisals against Korea was abandoned.[23]

Records of the French expedition are not important to the examination of Korea's status but it is significant that statements made in connection with the affair show a misunder-

22 *Ibid.*, 424.
23 Longford, *Korea*, 237. See Dallet, *Histoire*, II, 572-86, for accounts of this expedition.

standing, on the part of the West, of the ties between China and Korea. The Western states had long known that some relationship had existed, one which they loosely translated as "vassalage." Yet, to the French, and to others later, it appeared that China had, of her own will, altered that status by refusing to sanction any of the legal implications which the Western states attached to this presumed relation. For instance, M. de Bellonet, in his note to the Chinese Foreign Office, referred to the previous disavowals by China of control over the governmental affairs of Korea. Moreover, China had refused to extend the treaties of Tientsin to Korea or to provide the French missionaries with passports for their protection in the peninsula. All of this indicated to France that China no longer considered Korea in a state of vassalage, and that she had acknowledged that renunciation by her own refusal to accept the customary responsibility which the West attached to such a status.

In this light the references to the "former" status of vassalage were made, and the French impression was formed, that Korea could be dealt with as "independent" and "sovereign"—that is, she could be forced to an acceptance of legal responsibility for acts against Western nationals. Thus, if one of the two nations was no longer controlled by the other, the tributary missions to China and the return visits of the Chinese envoy appeared to Western eyes as unfriendly acts whereby China was intervening beyond the limits of "good offices" in the affairs of two other separate entities.

It must be admitted that China did little to correct this initial impression that Korea was only a former vassal. In the first place, she presumably did not realize the implications which Westerners would draw from her reply to the French which asserted no legal rights over Korea and merely urged caution and a pacific settlement of the dispute. China did not understand her statement, that Korea "maintained its own regulations" for which China could not be responsible, to be

in effect her renunciation of any special interest in the peninsula. Apparently she was attempting to avoid the further conflicts with the West which would result from her acceptance
of responsibility for Korea. This assumption is supported by
the dispatches to M. de Bellonet in which no mention was
made of what obligations and relations did exist between the
two Far Eastern nations until the French themselves referred
to the tribute missions and return envoys as evidence of Chinese aid to Korea. Even then the only defense of the Chinese
government was the statement that the custom was of long
standing and bore no relation to the current quarrel between
France and Korea.

It is entirely possible that China at this time was too greatly
concerned with her own affairs to care much whether the
special status over Korea was preserved or not. Certainly the
Chinese rulers made no effort to assert it at this first opportunity. Yet it may be, as one writer has stated,[24] that China
thought her superior position over Korea secure as long as
the Korean government itself did not repudiate it. "As to the
loyalty of Korea, there was no question; indeed with foreign
pressure increasing, Korea drew closer to her suzerain. Under
such conditions, it was natural that the Yamen (Foreign Office) should take up a laissez-faire attitude." [25]

3. THE AMERICAN EXPEDITION, 1871

The United States was placed in a position similar to that
of the French by an incident involving the murder of the
crew of the American ship *General Sherman*. When the
French expedition returned from Korea, they brought confirmation of the rumor [26] that the *General Sherman,* a vessel
presumably on a trading expedition, had grounded in the Ta-
tung River, and that after an altercation between the Amer-

---

[24] Tsiang, "Sino-Japanese Diplomatic Relations, 1870–1894," *loc. cit.,* 55.
[25] *Ibid.*
[26] *See Foreign Relations,* 1867, Pt. I, p. 415.

ican seamen on one hand and Korean officials and natives on the other, the ship had been set afire and the crew killed as they came ashore.[27] Though Secretary of State Seward had in 1866 proposed to the French a joint expedition when he thought their venture heralded the inevitable partition of Korea,[28] the United States proceeded more circumspectly concerning the *General Sherman* than had the French on the murder of their missionaries. As with the French, however, the status of Korea was confused in American thinking. The Minister of the United States to China, Anson Burlingame, brought the affair to the attention of the Chinese Foreign Office and received an immediate disavowal of China's control over the internal regulations of the Chao-hsien government, the reply stating that the "only connection between the two countries was one of ceremonial." [29] Accordingly, Burlingame informed the admiral of the American Asiatic squadron that ". . . the Chinese government disavows any responsibility for that of Corea, and all jurisdiction over its people." "Consequently," the minister added, "the occurrences there relating to the General Sherman are beyond my jurisdiction." [30] The request of Admiral Bell, the American squadron commander, for a mission backed with 1,500 to 2,000 troops was not honored, but Commander Shufeldt of the vessel *Wachusett* and, later, Commander John C. Febiger of the *Shenandoah*, conducted inquiries and charted the rivers leading to the Korean capital.[31]

The dispatches of Anson Burlingame indicate that he, like

[27] See *ibid.*, 427–28; M. W. Oh, "The Two Visits of the Rev. R. J. Thomas to Korea," in *TKBRAS*, XXII (1933), 95–123; J. S. Gale, "The Fate of the General Sherman: From an Eye Witness," in *Korean Repository*, II (1895), 252–54; and E. M. Cable, "United States–Korean Relations, 1866–1871," in *TKBRAS*, XXVIII (1938), 1–54, for accounts of this incident.

[28] Tyler Dennett, *Americans in Eastern Asia* (New York, 1922), 418–20.

[29] *Foreign Relations*, 1867, Pt. I, p. 426.

[30] *Ibid.*, 428.

[31] C. O. Paullin, *Diplomatic Negotiations of American Naval Officers, 1778–1883* (Baltimore, 1912), 284–86.

the French, also viewed the Chinese statements disavowing control over the internal regulations of Korea as a renunciation of a previously held status of "vassalage." In his communication of December, 1866, to the State Department, he classed Korea as "formerly tributary to China," the only connection then existing being "one of ceremonial." [32] But the first part of his statement imputes a recent change of condition which neither China nor Korea would admit. Perhaps the different views as to the part played by "ceremonial" in Eastern and Western thinking was at the very base of the misunderstanding, for ceremony (rites or *li*) in the Far Eastern scheme of governmental control indicates something far different from anything Westerners would expect and also much more extensive.

Though these earlier investigations had secured fairly satisfactory explanations of the *General Sherman* incident, the unsettled affair was to serve as a cause for further attempts to deal with Korea. In 1868 the American consul-general at Shanghai, George F. Seward (nephew of the then Secretary of State), hearing that Korea was anxious to conclude a treaty of friendship, sought and received permission to proceed there accompanied by a naval force. But by the time the authorization arrived it had been discovered that actually there was little promise of success of the effort, and plans for the expedition were dropped.[33]

By 1870 some of the Western states were conscious that, despite China's disavowal of control, a connection still existed between that country and Korea. Therefore, when the United States decided in 1870 to attempt the conclusion of a treaty for the protection of sailors shipwrecked on the Korean coasts, the negotiations were entrusted to a diplomatic officer rather than to a naval officer "because the political relations between China and Corea are such as to make it desirable to

32 *Foreign Relations*, 1867, Pt. I, p. 426.
33 *Ibid.*, 1870, pp. 336–39.

first obtain the good will and possibly the good offices of the Chinese government." [34] That the exact nature of these relations was still not known to the United States, however, is illustrated by the following suggestion sent to Minister Frederick P. Low, who was to undertake the expedition: "Some political connection exists between China and Corea, which may make it advisable for you to secure, in advance, the good will and, possibly, the good offices of the Pekin government." [35]

The actual accomplishments of the expedition, which reached Korea at the end of May, 1871, were little greater than those of the French five years earlier. When the Americans were fired upon, they attacked, after waiting in vain for proper apologies, and subdued several forts with thoroughness. Yet, seeing that any attempt to secure a treaty would fail, the expedition withdrew, leaving the government and people of Korea with the impression that another Western nation had been forced to retreat under the pressure of Korean arms.[36]

Just one year before the American experiment, in the summer of 1870, the Prussian Minister to Japan had attempted to open relations with Korea by sailing to Fusan with a Japanese official and using the Japanese there to transmit his letters. The Korean authorities, however, considered the Japanese aid in this instance an extreme impudence, and even refused to have any dealings with them until the German vessel had left the harbor.[37] The American expedition confirmed the existence of this policy of strict isolation and proved false the early impression of Consul-General Seward that Korea

[34] *Ibid.*, 1870, p. 333.
[35] *Ibid.*, 335.
[36] *Ibid.*, 1871, p. 145. For accounts of the expedition, see *ibid.*, 116–49; Griffis, *Corea*, Chap. XLVI; Cable, "United States–Korean Relations, 1866–1871," *loc. cit.*, 63–230; "Our Little Battle in Corean Waters," in *Overland Monthly*, VIII, 2d series (1886), 125–28.
[37] *Foreign Relations*, 1871, pp. 74–75.

was now eager to enter relations with the West.[38] Through exchanges of documents it also served to throw light on the relationship of Korea to China as well as on her attitude toward the nations of the Occident.

It should here be pointed out that Korea's refusal to negotiate was not due as much to mere stubbornness on her part as to the nature of her relationship to China, which was that of a "protector on the hedges" of the empire, a guard of the outposts of civilization. This made the king of Korea a trusted minister of the emperor, and even at the time of the American expedition the king quoted the old admonition "A minister of the Emperor must not have relations with a foreign state." [39] To Minister Low the Kang-wha high magistrate wrote:

The non-intercourse of Corea with foreign states is a settled principle, established by our ancestors five centuries ago; a principle of which the whole world has heard, and of which the Emperor of China also is graciously aware. It is precisely because we must not break through the ancient policy that we cannot discuss and cannot settle that which the honorable envoy desires . . . , whatever it may be.[40]

The attitude of Korea toward exposing her civilization and customs to relations with Westerners is brought out in the first communication delivered to Mr. Low upon his arrival in that country. The impossibility of intercourse between the two nations was the theme of the message, which stated:

Our respective dispositions are mutually dissimilar; our guiding principles are not alike. . . .
If you are going to want us to gi e away land and people, then let me ask how can 3000 li of river, hill, city, and country be lightly thrown away? If you will desire us t agree to negotiate and carry out friendly relations, then let me ask how can 4000 years' cere-

[38] *Ibid.*, 1870, pp. 336 ff.
[39] *Ibid.*, 1871, p. 134.
[40] *Ibid.*, 132.

monies, music, literature, and all things, be, without sufficient reason, broken up and cast away? It does not consist with right, it cannot be spoken of.[41]

The American desire for a treaty of amity was, of course, incomprehensible to Korea. Since propriety alone dictated the conduct of friends, the only type of contractual agreement necessary or known in the Far East was a "peace-compact," though the two characters forming this expression were loosely translated as "treaty." [42] But as separation and non-intercourse meant noninterference "with each other's tranquility; then," the Korean note logically argued, "without waiting to lay it down in a definitive compact peace exists already in the very fact." [43] The Korean policy of kindly treatment of shipwrecked sailors was reiterated in the several notes exchanged with Minister Low, and documents not only in Korea but also in Peking, reported such action in regard to American sailors in the years 1855, 1865, and 1866.[44] Therefore, Korea could easily question the sincerity of a mission which sought an arrangement as to shipwrecked sailors, and her suspicions were correct when she wrote to China that "although this letter of the American envoy has not spoken out fully . . . it most likely alludes to this sort of thing [viz., commercial intercourse]." [45] As this was a matter upon which the Koreans refused to consult, their king wrote the Board of Rites in Peking hoping that

the honorable board will lay before the throne all the facts connected with this matter, and that the Emperor will send forth a special edict to exhort and instruct the envoy of the nation in question so as to overcome the doubts and dispel his anxiety, and thus each of us be left to himself without trouble.[46]

[41] *Ibid.*, 130–31.
[42] *Ibid.*, 137, 137 n.
[43] *Ibid.*, 136–37.
[44] *Ibid.*, 133.
[45] *Ibid.*, 134.
[46] *Ibid.*

In connection with this episode China did little to enlighten the Western powers as to her relationship with Korea. For the first time, however, the dispatches show an admission that Korea was her subordinate, though the customary assertion of the autonomy of Korea as to government and religion was also made.[47] China was thus maintaining the relationship exactly as it had existed before contacts with Western civilization. The Western states, on the other hand, considered a nation which was autonomous as to its government, religion, and laws to be completely free and sovereign, and they therefore had no real comprehension of the actual situation. Yet it should have enlightened the Westerners to discover that it was possible, despite the irregular nature of the request, to get a message from the American minister to the king of Korea through the Chinese government, after all other attempts by all other means of communication had failed. The letter of the Korean king to the Chinese Foreign Office in answer to that of Mr. Low should also have indicated that a nation which kept another officially informed about all its Western contacts, even to details, was something more than a "former vassal."

The American minister continued to assume erroneously that China had recently renounced control over the government and foreign affairs of Korea in an attempt to avoid the responsibility for the lesser country's acts in collisions with Westerners.[48] But China was actually pursuing a policy established at least as early as the fourteenth century. The notion that she at this time began an entirely new policy gives the Chinese credit for much more knowledge of state responsibility under Western international law than they could possibly have had. Yet Minister Low missed the essence of the Confucian relationship when he wrote: "Corea is substantially an independent nation. To be sure, it sends tribute to

[47] *Ibid.*, 112.
[48] *Ibid.*, 111.

China annually, but from the best information I am able to obtain, the tribute is sent rather as a *quid pro quo* for the privilege of trading with the Chinese, than as governmental tribute." [49]

After his failure in Korea, Mr. Low wrote that "It now becomes the duty of all civilized and Christian governments to carefully consider what their rights are, and their duty to their citizens and subjects when these rights are trampled upon by countries which reject and set at defiance the law of nations as well as the laws of humanity." [50] Nevertheless, the Western nations made no attempts for another decade to establish direct relations with Korea.

4. THE JAPANESE-KOREAN TREATY, 1876

Where the West had failed, Japan, by using a combination of Eastern and Western techniques, succeeded in negotiating the first treaty with Korea on the basis of Western international law. The Japanese efforts furnished the first instance of a conflict between the Eastern and Western systems of international relations in which the party advancing the claims of the Western system also appreciated to some degree the system of the East. To the Japanese, who could not but be aware of the ancient relationship between the Middle Kingdom and the peninsula, the Western idea of sovereign statehood was a convenient tool with which to start the process of breaking the bonds uniting Korea and China.

It also appears that this action of Japan in securing a Western-style treaty moved China from the policy of attempting to maintain the same relations with Korea which had existed before the intervention of the West. The Chinese realized that if Korea was any longer to be connected with China, this connection must exist through a greater degree of control and

[49] *Ibid.*, 1870, p. 362.
[50] *Ibid.*, 1871, p. 146.

domination than had hitherto been exercised through the exchange of complimentary missions and envoys. This led China to modify her policies in order to compete with Western techniques. The traditional Confucian base of the relationship was, however, unaffected. The elder brother or father nation was merely asserting its control in times of stress.

The Japanese had sought to re-open relations with Korea as early as 1868 when they sent a mission to announce the reorganization of their government, in the expectation of a congratulatory mission in return. But the Tai-wün-kun, scornful of Japan's acceptance of Western ideas, refused to have anything to do with the envoys, and subsequent missions in 1869 and 1871 received the same curt treatment. The Japanese were highly insulted, and the war faction of their government demanded an invasion of Korea. Only the imperial will and fear of the Western nations enabled the policy of the peace group to prevail, whereupon the disgruntled members of the Japanese cabinet resigned to head later the Satsuma Rebellion.[51]

Following accepted Western practice, the Japanese waited for a more definite pretext for securing satisfaction from Korea. This occurred in September, 1875, when the Japanese gunboat *Unyo Kwan*, engaged in surveying the Korean coast, was fired upon. The Japanese retaliated by storming the attacking fort, destroying both the bastion and its defenders.[52] Amid popular clamor for war, the Japanese government decided to use this incident as a means of forcing Korea into a treaty relationship.

While the Japanese made preparations to dispatch a military expedition to Korea in emulation of Perry's expedition to their own country, they also took the precaution of sending simultaneously a diplomat, Mori Yurei, to China to secure

[51] H. B. Morse and H. F. MacNair, *Far Eastern International Relations* (Boston, 1931), 387–88.
[52] Longford, *Korea*, 299 ff.

Chinese sanction and aid. Mori arrived in Peking on January 5, 1876, and on the tenth presented a memorandum to the Chinese Foreign Office. This note reviewed Korea's persistent refusal to enter into official intercourse with Japan, and recounted the recent incident of the attack on the surveying ship. The Japanese envoy indicated that his country was, in consequence, sending a mission "with guards." If the mission was not courteously received and if its demands for a treaty were refused, Korea, he stated, would "draw to itself an incalculable calamity." [53]

Mori's task was not merely to issue threats. He hoped to secure from China a more definite declaration of Korea's independence than that which had satisfied the Western states, or, failing that, to demand China's aid. Even though she was now operating under the rules of Western international law, Japan, being well aware of the traditional relationship between China and Korea, realized that China's assurance of Korean freedom with respect to government, laws, and foreign affairs did not mean actual independence as long as China still maintained that Korea was a dependent nation. Mori, therefore, through argument based on Western principles, sought to force China to abandon the Confucian connection under which the legal freedom of Korea could mean little.

The Chinese Foreign Office in its conversations with Mori continued to maintain the traditional status which had fixed the relationship of China and Korea for centuries. In these negotiations a much greater effort was made by China to explain and to stress the strength of the connection than was undertaken in dealing with France and the United States, because the Japanese were Far Easterners and therefore presumably able to understand the relation, though it appeared of little importance to Western states. The reply to Mori's memorandum stated that the threatened Japanese action was in violation of the previously concluded Chinese-Japanese

[53] Tsiang, "Sino-Japanese Relations, 1870–1894," *loc. cit.*, 57.

treaty of September 13, 1871, wherein each party had agreed not to interfere in the other's "domain," the term reciprocally used being *Pang t'u* (nations and lands).[54] The Chinese further asserted that negotiations could settle this affair over which China had no control, although, it was added, Korea was a dependent nation with respect to China. Mori seized upon this usual declaration of "dependence yet lack of control" and asserted in Western fashion, "It is quite obvious now that China's claim of suzerain rights over Korea is only a nominal one." [55] Further notes were exchanged, each side standing its ground, Mori interpreting the Foreign Office's statement of no control over the actual territory of Korea as a renunciation of any control, the Foreign Office countering as follows:

Whereas Korea has always been a dependent state of China and whereas the word "dependent" is synonymous with the word "subordinate" it is hard to conceive that a state can be dependent to another without being subordinate. Furthermore, in replying to you we have never made the statement "the territory is not subordinate to China." [56]

[54] From the Chinese text of this agreement, the abstract printed January 15, 1872, in the *Journal de St. Pétersbourg* and reprinted in *Foreign Relations,* 1872, pp. 484–86, was the first translation made of the treaty. "Article I establishes that there shall henceforth reign between the two states, and between the countries which are subject to them, a perfect friendship and agreement. (Corea being in a certain degree a vassal of China, this article seems intended to guarantee it against Japan.)" *Ibid.,* 485. The text, printed in *ibid.,* 1873, pp. 602–605, is a translation from the Japanese text and omits any reference to reciprocal respect for the "nations and lands." The translation in the *British and Foreign State Papers* (London, 1841–1938), LXII, 321–24, erroneously dates the treaty as of 1872, and likewise omits this phrase. However, the Chinese and Japanese texts must have contained this statement as Li Hung-chang and Mori discussed the point and, furthermore, it was referred to by Li in his preliminary report to the court of August 31, 1871, and again upon the exchange of ratifications of the treaty. See T. C. Lin, "Li Hung-chang: His Korea Policies, 1870–1885," in *Chinese Social and Political Science Review,* XIX (1935–36), 209–12.

[55] Quoted in Djang, Chinese Suzerainty, 145.
[56] *Ibid.*

With negotiations at this impasse, Mori left for Paotingfu to consult with Li Hung-chang, the Viceroy who was to carry the burden of China's foreign relations for years to come.[57]

In the conversations at Paotingfu, Mori, assuming the Western attitude, again declared that Korea was not a Chinese dependency because China levied no taxes upon her and did not interfere with her local administration. Li endeavored to explain to Mori the difference between what he termed China's interior dominion, like that over the provinces, and the exterior dominion over the inferior states such as Korea. Referring to the treaty of 1871 between China and Japan in which each agreed to respect the nations and territories of the other,[58] he stated:

The word *territories* (lands) refers to the provinces, which are our inner domains or inner possessions subject to Imperial taxation and administration. The word *nations* refers to Korea and other similar countries, which are our outer dominions or outer possessions and whose administration and taxation have always been carried on by the natives themselves.[59]

Mori, by his visit to China and his attempts to secure Korea's acceptance of a Japanese mission through Chinese aid, indicated his recognition of the special position of China. And Li Hung-chang, by agreeing to use his influence to get a courteous reception for the Japanese, did not, as it is generally supposed,[60] renounce China's claims to Korea; rather by instructing the king of Korea to receive the mission, he gave concrete illustration of the strength of the time-honored connection.[61]

[57] For an account of the life of Li Hung-chang, see *Memoirs of Li Hung Chang* (W. F. Mannix, ed.) (Boston, 1913), and Robert K. Douglas, *Li Hungchang* (New York, 1895).

[58] See pp. 128–29.

[59] Quoted in Lin, "Li Hung-chang: . . . ," *loc. cit.*, 209; Djang, Chinese Suzerainty, 144.

[60] Griffis, *Corea*, 422.

[61] Tsiang, "Sino-Japanese Relations, 1870–1894," *loc. cit.*, 58.

When the Japanese mission arrived in Korea on February 6, 1876, they were able to arrange with little trouble for a treaty of peace and friendship. The agreement, signed February 26, 1876, and known as the Treaty of Kang-wha, provided for Japan three open Korean ports for trade, diplomatic relations, the privilege of coastal survey, and other such matters.[62] The treaty in two instances also endeavored to affect the relationship between China and Korea: Article I, in the English translation, stated that "Chosen, being an independent State (*tzŭ chu*),[63] enjoys the same sovereign rights as does Japan," [64] and the document was dated, not according to the Chinese reign year, but by the Japanese reign year and that of the Li dynasty of Korea. Korea had thus finally entered into relations with a nation in the Western manner and ended her reign of isolation.

One writer has stated [65] that the Japanese treaty not only ended Korea's national isolation but that it "terminated forever . . . theoretically at least, her dependence on China." That the treaty ended the isolation may be true, but that it altered to any great degree the pre-existing relationship with China does not appear to be the case. Certainly as far as China was concerned, there had been no definite change of status. She had consistently upheld to the Japanese, as to the Americans and French, the Far Eastern principle of the Confucian relationship in which the inferior not only was sub-

[62] See text of treaty, *British and Foreign State Papers*, LXVII, 530–33.

[63] *Tzŭ chu* means "self-governing" or "autonomous" (literally "master of himself"), not "sovereign" or "independent" as understood in the Western state system and as here translated.

[64] *British and Foreign State Papers*, LXVII, 531. Shuhsi Hsü translated this Article in a manner more favorable to China as follows: "Chao-hsien, being an autonomous (*tzŭ chu*) state, shall enjoy the rights of equality with Japan." This was, he says, ". . . nothing more than a declaration of historical facts, for Korea had been an autonomous state ever since she came into existence, with the possible exception of a short period during the Yüan dynasty, and had always enjoyed the rights of equality with Japan, not excluding the days of the Hideyoshi invasion." *China*, 109.

[65] Longford, *Korea*, 302–303.

ordinate but acknowledged it, while the superior made no effort directly to control and administer the inferior nation. And obviously, the suggestion for a courteous reception of the Japanese mission could come well within the benevolent attitude a father and elder brother nation might exercise and also within the province of *li*, the rules of propriety. The new treaty also served as a demonstration that beneath the ritualistic homage and submission there was still concealed an avenue of successful approach to the East, which the Western nations could have used in earlier dealings with Korea had they known of it.

Statements which hold that China, in sanctioning the Japanese negotiations with Korea, thereby renounced her former relationship with that country are based on the doubtful assumption that the relation was one of "suzerainty" as known in the West. One of the features of "suzerainty" is the control of the foreign relations of the lesser nation by the superior. It is obvious, however, that a disclaimer of control over foreign relations can affect only a status which possesses the element of such control; and China had consistently acknowledged her lack of control of Korea's relations with the West, and had made no attempt to assert that hers was a suzerain's control over a vassal. A like misapprehension was shown in the statements of the Japanese negotiator, Mori, when he pointed to the absence of Chinese control over the collection of taxes in Korea as an indication that China was not suzerain. Clearly, the inability of the status to fit the concepts of an alien standard would not exclude relations on some other basis.

In 1878 when the Japanese questioned China's designation of herself as the "superior nation" with respect to Korea and proposed its incompatibility with Article I of the Japanese-Korean treaty, China replied that ". . . Korea has long been subordinate to China and has always been self-governing in its administration and laws. That it is a self-governing (*tzŭ*

chu) nation is a fact long known to all under Heaven." [66] In
other words, to the Chinese, Korean autonomy (*tzŭ chu*) and
Chinese superiority (*tsung kuo*) were not incompatible. On
the contrary, they were bound together as the announced
policy of China.[67]

The Japanese, for their part, made every effort to have
their treaty with Korea appear as one between equal and completely independent entities. Equality was demanded by
Western custom and without doubt by Korea as well, for she
had never since her unification acknowledged inferiority to
Japan.[68] Independence was emphasized so that the stipulated
equality would not automatically place Japan, along with
Korea, in a position inferior to China. Therefore, by variant
methods—one, the legal statement of Article I, understood in
the West, and the other, the dating of the document in terms
of the Korean dynasty rather than that of the Chinese—
Japan endeavored to alter Korea's international status. But
the mere declaration of independence in the treaty could in
no way force recognition of that status by other nations, and
it was to Japan alone that Korea was an "independent state"
enjoying the same sovereign rights as herself. Indeed, in the
years following the treaty, when Westerners were in trouble
in Korea, it was to the Chinese Foreign Office that their states
appealed, and it was the Chinese Foreign Office which effected
the release of the Westerners detained in Korea.[69]

Korea herself attached no weight to the assertion of independence, as preceding events show. In the first place, it was
at China's suggestion that the treaty had been made, and exchange of goods and envoys with Japan on a basis of equality
had long been known. Moreover, that an intention to renounce the relationship with China was not present in the
minds of the Korean representatives is shown by their refusal

[66] Quoted in Lin, "Li Hung-chang: . . . ," *loc. cit.*, 217.
[67] *Ibid.*
[68] Shuhsi Hsü, *China*, 109.
[69] Morse and MacNair, *Far Eastern Relations*, 389.

134   KOREA AND THE OLD ORDERS

to acknowledge in the treaty that the Japanese envoy was acting for the Japanese "Emperor." Such an admission would have been tantamount to an unthinkable arrogation of equality of the latter with their overlord, the one and only Son of Heaven. Since the Japanese refused to credit themselves as acting for the Japanese "King" (Wang), the treaty omitted all reference to the titles of the rulers and was made in the names of the two governments only.[70] Further proof that the treaty meant no alteration of the Confucian relationship is Korea's continued practice of reporting regularly to Peking all events in her relations with Japan.[71]

In summarizing the status of Korea from the time of the French expedition through that of the Japanese treaty, one must insist that, in spite of contrary alien influences, Korea remained, in relation to China and the Far East, in the position she had occupied for thousands of years before the appearance of the Western states. A bond of culture and a common recognition of reasonable and proper action continued to supersede legal ties and controls. The true situation, from the very first an enigma to the Occidental mind, was adroitly exploited by the Japanese, who, by a tactful appeal to Peking, were successful in securing with the Koreans the first Western-type treaty. Thus, where Japan succeeded, France, Germany, and America failed; and to the West in general, Korea was apparently still as much of an anomaly in 1876 as she had been fifty years earlier.

[70] See Griffis, *Corea*, 423 n.
[71] Tsiang, "Sino-Japanese Relations, 1870–1894," *loc. cit.*, 61.

CHAPTER VIII

KOREAN-WESTERN TREATY SETTLE-MENTS 1876–1882

1. CHINESE POLICIES

CHINA did not at first realize how seriously her relations with Korea would be affected by the Japanese-Korean treaty of 1876 [1] since she was convinced of Korea's loyalty and presumably read the "independence" clause of Article I in a light more favorable than that of the English translation.[2] Yet in the next two or three years she awoke to the realization that the dependencies which had long paid tribute and acted as the wardens of her borders were gradually being lost. The kingdom of Annam, whose dependent status with respect to China dated back to Han times, was yielding its southern extremities to the French. The British had seized lower Burma; and the Japanese, in the process of destroying China's influence over Liu-ch'iu and Formosa, had now made their first move in Korea.[3]

Whether the Chinese realized it or not, this was the inevitable result of the intrusion into their world of other nations each as powerful as China herself. The Far Eastern system of international relations was held together by the fact that, with no competing bodies to exert their gravitational pull, the satellites naturally revolved around the greater body without any special inducement. But the appearance of na-

---

[1] Tsiang, "Sino-Japanese Relations, 1870–1894," *loc. cit.*, 61.
[2] See p. 131.
[3] For a summary of the loss of the Chinese dependencies, see M. J. Bau, *The Foreign Relations of China* (New York, 1921), Chap. II.

tions each of which viewed itself as the equal of China interrupted the normal flow of allegiance to her as the Far Eastern nucleus. The East Asiatic area, therefore, became one of conflicting attractions wherein each satellite was urged, or forced, to revolve around a new center, or to become itself, not a satellite, but a planet.

The rulers of China began to see that their disavowal of control over the laws, governments, and foreign relations of the lesser nations did much more than to relieve them of responsibility for the acts of these nations. It soon became clear that this disavowal also allowed others to feel free to enter into the affairs of the satellite nations and to influence those very spheres which China had disavowed. Moreover, the ingress of foreigners was greatly abetted by the fact that the Western states considered of no consequence the symbolical, ceremonial connection which Korea and China claimed.

In the absence of those attributes which in their own legal system denoted the control of one state by another, the Western states saw full liberty for each to attempt by diplomacy or force to strengthen its own position in the Far Eastern area. China, therefore, could no longer remain passive and rely upon the traditional loyalty of Korea to keep that nation subordinate. Not only were the Western states attempting to force the Middle Kingdom into a relationship with Korea conformable to Western practice, but Japan, aided by her knowledge of both the Eastern and Western systems, was cleverly using Western international law to break up the traditional association of China and Korea. After the loss of the Liuch'iu Islands to Japan, Korea's dangerous position became so clear that Li Hung-chang wrote to the Chinese Foreign Office that "we can no longer refrain from devising ways and means for the security of Korea." [4] China therefore decided to take a more active interest in Korean affairs.

Despite the weight of tradition which forbade any altera-

[4] Lin, "Li Hung-Chang: . . . ," *loc. cit.*, 219.

tion in established procedures, the very principle behind the existence of the frontier-guarding nations (*fan-ch'en*) lent sufficient precedent for an increased interest in their welfare. The Confucian principle of a father's or elder brother's active control over a lesser member of the family in times of crisis provided the theoretical basis. In regard to Korea, therefore, after about 1879 China embarked on three new policies. The first was the immediate development of an army with which the two nations, finding Confucian reasoning of little use against foreign aggression, could some day answer force with force. Korea was urged to strengthen her army and to prepare for other similar reforms. The second policy was to strengthen the diplomatic ties between China and Korea, not by altering any of the forms of intercourse, but by a more active use of the right of the elder nation to advise and instruct the younger nation. Li Hung-chang, who was becoming more and more the director of China's foreign policies, was officially given the control of her relations with Korea when the Foreign Office in 1881 petitioned the throne to take the direction of all Korean relations, except the customary ceremonials, out of the hands of the reactionary, tradition-bound Board of Rites.[5]

The third new Chinese policy was designed to protect Korea until the military might of China should be sufficient to deal with all encroachments upon her. Li Hung-chang, who had been corresponding with Li Yu-wün, the Korean minister, since 1876, sought in 1878 to explain to him the virtue of making treaties with those commercial nations having no territorial designs, as a balance to the ambitions of Japan and Russia in the peninsula. About the same time Sir Thomas Wade, British minister to Peking, also suggested this policy for Korea, and the Chinese Foreign Office memorialized the throne to have Li Hung-chang officially pursue this line of

---

[5] Tsiang, "Sino-Japanese Relations, 1870–1894," *loc. cit.*, 63; Shuhsi Hsü, *China,* 107 n.

action. The director of Chinese foreign affairs accordingly redoubled his efforts, writing to Korea that unless this advice of China was accepted, Korea would become a second Liuch'iu. On the other hand, he argued, by treaties with the Western states Korea would be protected from aggression just as the smaller states of Europe, such as Belgium and Denmark, existed despite their inferior power. His writings were also interspersed with examples from Chinese history showing the traditional policy of seeking friends before meeting a foe.[6]

It should be noted that these three policies in no way affected the base of the Sino-Korean relationship, the Confucian elder brother–younger brother status. A nonlegal, natural relationship, there were no limits as to what policies could or could not be carried out as long as China sought to protect and preserve the lesser nation as a natural brother would do. That is, China, unlike Japan and the Western powers, was not dealing with Korea on the basis of legal contracts accurately defining her position. This fact must be kept in mind when judging her actions on the Korean peninsula and when comparing them with Occidental methods.

2. TREATIES AND KOREA'S STATUS

The Chinese government was, of course, not to lack cooperation from the Western states in its policy of encouraging Korea to enter into treaty relations with the "commercial" nations. Though no move had been made by a Western power to open relations with the peninsula since that of Minister Low in 1871, the success of the Japanese in 1876 led to a resolution in the United States Senate on April 8, 1878, to appoint a commission to negotiate a treaty with Korea through the friendly offices of Japan.[7] While the resolution

[6] *Ibid.*, 62–63.
[7] *Congressional Record*, (Washington, 1873———), VII, 2324, 2600–2601.

never emerged from the Committee on Foreign Affairs, in that same year the Navy Department decided to send Commodore Shufeldt with the USS *Ticonderoga* to Korea and certain other Eastern countries. The Navy Department instructed the commodore to explain to the Koreans the reasons for the American attack on their forts in 1871 and to negotiate for the opening of their country to commerce. Having approved these orders, the State Department directed the American minister in Japan to seek letters from the Japanese government facilitating Shufeldt's project.[8]

But the Japanese hesitated to give their aid, Inouye Kaoru, their foreign minister, pleading Korean reluctance to open the country and Japanese fear of complications in the execution of their own treaty of 1876 with Korea. Nevertheless, Shufeldt was given letters to the Japanese officials at Fusan, though the local Korean governor rejected his request, made upon his arrival there, to have a letter sent to the Korean king.[9] He returned to Japan, and pressure on the Japanese government led to the inclusion of a letter from him in a dispatch of the Japanese foreign minister to the Korean king. The Korean Minister of Ceremony, however, rejected the commodore's missive because it was addressed to "Corai" (Korea) instead of "Chosen" (Chao-hsien) and also because, he argued, "it was well known that our foreign relations are only with Japan, neighboring to us, which have been maintained since three hundred years, and that other foreign nations are not only situated far from us, but there has never been any intercourse with them." [10] This rebuff caused Shufeldt to suspect the Japanese of desiring to monopolize the commerce of Korea; [11] and the reports of Italian visitors and

---

[8] Paullin, *Diplomatic Negotiations*, 294–96.
[9] *Ibid.*, 296–97; Tsiang, "Sino-Japanese Relations, 1870–1894," *loc. cit.*, 64.
[10] Quoted in Paullin, *Diplomatic Negotiations*, 298.
[11] Payson J. Treat, *Diplomatic Relations Between the United States and Japan, 1853–1895* (Stanford, 1932), 124. Cf. Minister Bingham's views, *ibid.*, 138–39.

of Minister Angell in Peking appeared to justify his fears.

Before his return to the United States was forced by the expiration of the time allotted for his cruise, Shufeldt made the acquaintance of the Chinese consul at Nagasaki and received through him an invitation from Li Hung-chang to come to China for a personal interview. At the conversations in China, Li agreed to use his influence to induce Korea to undertake negotiations with the United States. Back in the United States, Shufeldt persuaded Secretary of State Blaine to send him again to China to complete his mission, this time under cover of an appointment as attaché to the American legation. Upon his return to China he found that Li was now less enthusiastic over the proposed American-Korean treaty, presumably because fear of Russia had been lessened by the treaty of St. Petersburg, which was signed in 1881.[12] Li had, however, written to the Korean government and he had also discussed the matter with a Korean official in China. Finally, near the end of the year 1881, word was received from Korea indicating a willingness to sign the treaty.

Fear of offending the strong antiforeign party in his kingdom caused the Korean king to be reluctant in dealing with the Americans, but by March, 1882, he felt secure enough to request that Li undertake the negotiations for his government.[13] Though a Korean representative was at Tientsin,[14] Li and Shufeldt themselves agreed upon a treaty dealing with peace, amity, commerce, and navigation. The only stumbling block was Li's insistence on a clause acknowledging Korea as a dependent state of China while Shufeldt contended that such a clause was not necessary to a treaty which Korea was sovereign enough to sign on her own authority.[15] The dispute was compromised through the exclusion of the clause from the treaty and the sending of a supplementary letter

[12] Text in MacNair, *Modern Chinese History*, 475–77.
[13] Tsiang, "Sino-Japanese Relations, 1870–1894," *loc. cit.*, 66, 68.
[14] *Ibid.*, 66.
[15] Paullin, *Diplomatic Negotiations*, 315–18.

from the king of Korea to the President of the United States acknowledging Korea's inferior status.[16]

The treaty provided for "perpetual peace and friendship" and stated that "If other Powers deal unjustly or oppressively with either Government, the other will exert their good offices, on being informed of the case, to bring about an amicable arrangement, thus showing their friendly feelings." Other clauses provided for the exchange of diplomatic and consular representatives, protection of navigation and United States citizens, extraterritoriality, trade, and most-favored-nation treatment.[17]

It was America, as Shufeldt said, who accomplished "the feat of bringing the last of the exclusive countries within the pale of Western Civilization." [18] But the future would have been less complicated if Korea at the same time had been free of the ties which bound her to the contrasting status of a nation subordinate to China. The discussions during, and subsequent to, the treaty negotiations with the United States, and the trend of later events, all show clearly the conflict and misunderstanding caused by China's attempt to perpetuate and strengthen a traditional and natural relationship with Korea. The Western nations viewed these actions as mere opportunistic diplomacy based upon a nebulous ceremonial overlordship and without any legal effect in the Occidental system of international relations.

The new policy of encouraging Korea to negotiate treaties with the Western states was not viewed by China as having any effect upon the traditional relations of the two countries.[19] Actually, it was designed to protect and continue that relationship in the face of threats from Japan and Russia. Though

16 *Ibid.*, 322.
17 For text see *United States Statutes at Large* (Washington, 1850–1943), XXIII, 720–25.
18 H. G. Appenzeller, "The Opening of Korea: Admiral Shufeldt's Account of It," in *Korean Repository*, I (1892), 62.
19 Tsiang, "Sino-Japanese Relations, 1870–1894," *loc. cit.*, 65.

Li Hung-chang wrote to Shufeldt that Korea had from time immemorial been a dependent country in the Chinese Empire, and that her government would consequently act according to the instructions of China,[20] his actions in securing Korea's consent did not go beyond the appeals to reason necessary to convince the Korean king of the wisdom of the proposed policy. He deliberately refrained from anything approaching direct coercion or interference in the internal affairs of the peninsula, a caution illustrated by his refusal to use the imperial name to silence the opposition party in Korea.[21] Though such action in the name of the emperor would have given the Americans an advantage in negotiations, Li opposed it as being incompatible with the relationship between the two countries, preferring delay and risk of failure to such direct interference. That such a move was possible, and that it would have been viewed in Korea as a command not to be disregarded, shows conclusively that Korea was still bound to China by definite ties despite the contrary statement in the Japanese treaty and Shufeldt's opinion that such an assertion of dependency was "inadmissible and not even justified by the facts. . . ."[22]

It was to lay at rest such rash statements that Li insisted, though vainly, on a mention of Korea's subordination to China in the proposed treaty with the United States. He presumably realized that the opinion of the Western countries as to the status of Korea could have some effect upon that

[20] Shufeldt to Freylinghuysen, enc. 2, March 11, 1882, in China: Dispatches, United States Department of State, Vol. LIX, no. 2.

[21] The secret agent of the Korean king had brought a pathetic letter to China revealing that the opposition of many groups, including the followers of the Tai-wün-kun, had caused the king to hesitate to agree to negotiations. Through his agent he stated that "The only way out is for the Emperor to issue an open Decree to be given to the next tribute mission in the spring, commanding Korea to send negotiators to take up the treaty with America. In that case my King, relying upon Imperial influence, can manage the affair." Tsiang, "Sino-Japanese Relations, 1870–1894," loc. cit., 66.

[22] Shufeldt to Freylinghuysen, March 11, 1882, in China: Dispatches, Vol. LIX, no. 2.

status, and that in spite of Korea's loyalty to the relationship and the perfect understanding of its nature by both China and Korea, its preservation no longer depended merely upon the two nations involved. The Western states, he rightly divined, would henceforth govern their actions by the legal evidence which, under their concepts of international law, indicated Korea's status to them. Since China had already observed the results of one such mistake—that of phrasing the first article of the Japanese-Korean treaty so the English translation suggested Korean independence—she tried to have incorporated in the treaty with the United States a clause, after the Western fashion, definitely setting forth Korea's true status. Li Hung-chang's insistence upon the inclusion of this dependency clause was due to a better understanding of Western law than China possessed when she made the treaty of 1876 and also to the influence of Ma Chien-chung, who had studied political science in France.[23] This was not, however, an attempt to alter Korea's status, but instead to proclaim it in such a manner that the Western legalists would accept it.

Shufeldt and the new American minister to China, John Russell Young,[24] were both inclined to ignore any validity in the Chinese claim of some special relation with Korea. They appear to have viewed Chinese encouragement of Korea to sign the American treaty as China's scheme to safeguard her own borders and especially Manchuria, the homeland of her dynasty, from Russia or Japan through the moral protection of an American-Korean treaty. The Americans thus correctly suspected that part of Li's policy was to use the Western treaties to offset territorial designs on Korea, and, with warranted precaution, John Russell Young asked, "How far should we commit ourselves to a convention which China

[23] Tsiang, "Sino-Japanese Relations, 1870–1894," loc. cit., 68.
[24] For background of John Russell Young, see Tyler Dennett, "Documents, American Choices in the Far East in 1882," in American Historical Review, XXX (1924–25), 84–86.

would regard as protecting her frontiers . . . ?" [25] But in stating, as Shufeldt did, that China's claim of Korea's dependence was "inadmissible and not even justified by the facts," [26] the United States was ignoring a situation which continued to perplex the Western governments until force decided the issue in 1894.

In exchange, however, for the commercial and other benefits expected from the treaty with Korea, the Americans were willing for its moral implications to be used to thwart the territorial aggressions of Russia and Japan.[27] But Li's demand that a clause attesting Korea's inferior position be included was viewed as an attempt to induce the United States to become joint guarantor of a status which did not then exist and which China was merely trying to initiate. Shufeldt termed this an unfounded proposition to which China sought to gain the support of his government because she herself had "not the courage authoritatively to assert it to the world." [28] In his conversations with Li Hung-chang, he argued that if Korea were sovereign with respect to her own foreign relations, as China had repeatedly asserted, the Americans could properly treat with her without reference to China and thus avoid involving the United States as a joint protector of the peninsula.[29] This logic was incontestable from the Western point of view, yet Shufeldt failed to see its incongruities when he was at the very time negotiating a treaty with Korea through China's minister—not Korea's—and had already admitted to his superiors that it was only through the aid of China that he saw the possibility of success.[30] As a matter of fact, though the treaty was finally signed in Korea, it had been

[25] Young to Freylinghuysen, May 1, 1882, in China: Dispatches, Vol. LIX, no. 1.

[26] Shufeldt to *id.*, March 11, 1882, *ibid.*, no. 2.

[27] Young to *id.*, May 1, 1882, *ibid.*

[28] Shufeldt to *id.*, March 11, 1882, *ibid.*

[29] Paullin, *Diplomatic Negotiations*, 316.

[30] Shufeldt to Freylinghuysen, March 11, 1882, in China: Dispatches, Vol. LIX, no. 2.

completely formulated and agreed upon by Li Hung-chang and Shufeldt in Tientsin.[31] The name of the Chinese negotiators did not appear on the document, but the signing ceremony was under the supervision of two Chinese officials, Ma Chien-chung and Admiral Ting Ju-ch'ang, who had by arrangement preceded Shufeldt to Korea.[32]

Throughout the negotiations Shufeldt had maintained his position that no acknowledgment of Korea's inferiority should be included in the treaty itself. He was successful in securing a compromise whereby he was to forward to the President of the United States a separate letter from the Korean king which asserted the inferior status of Korea with respect to China. This letter was duly sent and was before the American Senate at the time the treaty was approved. According to the translation sent by Shufeldt to the Department of State and placed before the Senate, it ran as follows:

The Chose Hsien country (Corea) is a dependency of China, but the management of her governmental affairs, home and foreign, has always been vested in the sovereign.

Now, as the Government of the United States and Corea are about to enter into treaty relations, the intercourse between the two nations shall be carried on in every respect on terms of equality and courtesy, and the King of Corea clearly asserts that all the articles of the treaty shall be acknowledged and carried into effect according to the laws of independent States.

In the matter of Corea being a dependency of China (in) any question that may arise between them in consequence of such dependency the United States shall in no way interfere.

The King has accordingly deputed commissioners for the purpose of negotiating the treaty, and now, as in duty bound, addresses this communication for the information of the President of the United States.[33]

[31] Paullin, *Diplomatic Negotiations*, 322.
[32] For an account of the signing ceremony, see Shufeldt to Freylinghuysen, and encs., June 8, 1882, in China: Dispatches, Vol. LX, no. 8.
[33] *Foreign Relations*, 1888, Pt. II, pp. 255–56.

The translation accepted as official by China, however, was that sent by Mr. Holcomb in his communication of June 26, 1882, to Secretary of State Frelinghuysen, which read:

> Cho-sen has been from ancient times a State tributary to China. Yet hitherto full sovereignty has been exercised by the Kings of Cho-sen in all matters of internal administration and foreign relations. Cho-sen and the United States, in establishing now by mutual consent a treaty, are dealing with each other upon a basis of equality. The King of Cho-sen distinctly pledges his own sovereign powers for the complete enforcement in good faith of all the stipulations of the treaty in accordance with international law.
>
> As regards the various duties which devolve upon Cho-sen as a tributary state to China, with these the United States has no concern whatever.
>
> Having appointed envoys to negotiate a treaty it appears to be my duty, in addition thereto, to make this preliminary declaration.[34]

Both of these translations involve words such as "sovereign," "independent," and "international law" which, for the Western reader, contain implications that the Koreans and Chinese did not get from their text of the document. For example, the statements that the king of Korea is "independent" and "equal" and possessed of sovereign powers enabling him to carry out the treaty in every detail, appear to contradict the subsequent statement of his "dependency" and tributary position. On the basis of the above translations, however, and in view of the fact that Korea had actually signed a Western-style treaty with the United States, it is understandable that the American government chose to accept the averments of independence and sovereignty as possessing more weight than the statement of dependency.

To the Chinese and Koreans, in whose language the letter was written, a much different meaning was conveyed by the document. The following translation, with the note appended

[34] Holcomb to Freylinghuysen, enc. 1, in China: Dispatches, Vol. LX, no. 133.

by the translator,[35] gives the impression the document would make on an educated Chinese or Korean of that time, and presumably the meaning which it was the writers' intention to convey.

The Prince and Lord (*chün-chu* 君主) of Chao-hsien, in the matter of a communication, begs to give information that Chao-

[35] Translation for the author from photostat of the original by Professor H. H. Dubs, who adds the following comment:

"Both Shufeldt and Holcomb really paraphrase this letter, instead of translating it exactly, thus securing a more literary effect, which is at the same time more readable and gives an impression that is misleading. In my translation I have tried to be literal and to give the impression the letter would make upon an educated Corean of that date.

"This letter contains three phrases that were very likely invented by those who drafted it for the purpose of conveying certain occidental ideas. These phrases were not used in the Chinese of that day, hence their meanings would be quite vague to Coreans or Chinese who were not familiar with occidental concepts.

"The first is the curios phrase for President—*po-li-hsi-t'ien-te* 白理璽天德 —evidently a transliteration, and quite different from the Chinese phrase used today for that concept. An educated Chinese or Corean could probably guess that this long barbaric phrase is the title of some barbarian chieftain or ruler. In themselves, the words of this phrase form a quite meaningless combination.

"The second is the phrase *chün-chu* 君主 , used as the title of the Corean ruler. It is curious that he was not entitled 'king,' *wang* 王 . The drafters of this letter evidently thought that the title, *wang,* would not do for the purposes of the letter. *Chün-chu* was anciently quite uncommon in Chinese literature; in the *Shih-chi* (written about 100 B.C.) it was used rarely to denote a princess in the state of Ch'in. Today this phrase is used as the equivalent of the English words 'monarch' and 'monarchical,' and is the antonym of the phrase for 'democratic,' *min-chu* 民主 . This term, *chün-chu,* is found in the Chinese text of the commercial treaty of 1861 between China and Prussia, where it is used to denote the Kings of Prussia. Hence the term had probably become recognized in diplomatic usage of the period, for a ruler with a status below that of an emperor. To an educated Corean or Chinese of that period, it probably meant something like 'prince and lord.'

"The third phrase is *tzu-chu kung-li* 自主公例 , which is likewise un-Chinese. The drafters of the letter probably intended it to be the equivalent of the English phrase 'international law.' But it is not the phrase used at present in Chinese to mean international law, which is *kung-fa* 公法 . That phrase has probably come into use subsequent to the writing of this letter. To educated Coreans or Chinese of that date, except for a few persons who knew occidental ideas, the phrase *tzu-chu kung-li* must have been quite puzzling and needed explanation, for nothing was known in China or Corea about 'autonomous universal rules.'

hsien has long been a country subordinate (*shu-pang* 屬邦) to China, yet both her internal government and her foreign intercourse have always been under the autonomous (*tzu-chu* 自主 [literally "master of himself"]) [power of] the Prince and Lord (*chün-chu*) of Chao-hsien.

Now that the countries of Chao-hsien and the United States are mutually entering into a compact, both will treat each other on equal terms. The Prince and Lord (*chün-chu*) of Chao-hsien explicitly promises that every article in this treaty shall be acknowledged and put into effect in accordance with autonomous universal rules (*tzu-chu kung-li* 自主公例) .

With regard to all the duties which must be performed by the state of Chao-hsien because the latter is subordinate (*shu*) to

---

"In addition to these three phrases, the phrase *tzu-chu,* which I have translated 'autonomous,' is also ambiguous. Shufeldt translates it once as 'independent' and in the phrase *chün-chu tzu-chu* as 'sovereign.' Holcomb translates it as 'sovereignty.' Yet it does not have the occidental meaning of sovereignty, which did not exist in Chinese thought of the time. There is no word or phrase in the letter that means 'sovereignty' or 'sovereign,' although both translators use that term. *Tzu-chu* means literally, 'master of himself,' which English phrase, like autonomy, is itself ambiguous. An adult Chinese son can make contracts at will, without consulting his father, providing he does not pledge the family property or interfere with his duties to his father. Hence he may be said to be autonomous. Yet, in a crisis, the father has complete control of his son, and may demand absolute obedience, on the ground that the son's acts have or will interfere with his duties to his father. This control may, in unusual cases, rightfully demand the life of the son. Hence the son is autonomous and may nevertheless be rather completely controlled by the head of the family. Probably the Coreans and Chinese were thinking in such terms, whereas the Americans were thinking in terms of sovereignty and independence, and so misunderstood this phrase completely.

"I would guess that some of the important persons among the drafters of this letter had been to occidental countries, for the letter shows unmistakable evidence of having been drafted by someone who knew occidental ideas fairly well, but not exactly enough for legal purposes.

"The phrase *shu-pang* 屬邦 is quite Chinese and has long had a definite meaning in Chinese, quite different from anything in occidental international law. To an educated Chinese, this phrase exactly defined the relationship borne by Corea to China, and, since it was used, no further explanation was needed.

"The dating of the letter is itself significant. An educated Chinese or Corean would see immediately that the use of a Chinese year-period to date the letter indicates that the sender (the Corean monarch) considers himself, not as independent, but as subordinate to the Chinese ruler whose year-period was used."

China, the United States shall have absolutely no concern with any item [of such duties].

In addition to having appointed persons to negotiate a detailed treaty, in making communications, it is necessary to transmit the foregoing communication for the information of the President (*Po-li-hsi-t'ien-te*) of the United States.

Transmitted in the 448th year of the founding of Chao-hsien, which is the eighth year of [the Chinese year-period] *Kuang-hsü*, the third month, the twenty-eighth day [May 15, 1882].

It is readily seen that this translation does not indicate an assertion of sovereignty and independence as was later claimed by Western interpretations. Korea's dependence upon China is in fact the main theme; the assertion of her equality with the United States is in no way a declaration of her independence from China. Yet, evidently little attention was given to this letter.[36]

Other Western countries were quick to follow the lead of the United States in the conclusion of treaties with Korea. Some British ships under Admiral Willis were already in the harbor of Chemulpo when the Chinese officials Ma and Ting returned there from a visit which they made to the king of Korea at Seoul directly after the signing of the American agreement. Upon the arrival of Ma and Ting, the admiral immediately produced the draft of a treaty similar to the American one, and a letter from Li Hung-chang instructing the Chinese officials to aid the British as they had the Americans.[37] On June 6 a treaty with England was signed, and later in the month Ma Chien-chung again came to Korea to negotiate with M. von Brandt for an agreement with Germany.[38] Other states were to follow, and in every instance the

---

[36] Cf. letter to the *London Times,* August 19, 1882, protesting the recognitions in the American and British treaties of Korea's dependency to China.

[37] Tsiang, "Sino-Japanese Relations, 1870–1894," *loc. cit.,* 69.

[38] Holcomb to Freylinghuysen, June 12, July 13, 1882, in China: Dispatches, Vol. LX, nos. 124, 146.

treaty was accompanied by a letter which formally acknowledged the superior position of China to Korea.[39]

From the date of the conclusion of the Japanese treaty
through the period of early treaties with the Western states,
the status of Korea in the Far Eastern system underwent
little alteration. It should be reiterated that the policy of
China in encouraging her to deal with the Occidental powers
was not an attempt to alter in any way the position of Korea
in her relationship to China, but rather an effort to strengthen
and insure that position by stopping the designs of Japan and
Russia. It also hoped to put, if possible, a definition of the
status of Korea into a legal form acceptable to the Western
states. Though the attempt to include such a definition in the
treaties themselves was unsuccessful, the device of accompanying each document with a letter attesting the true Sino-
Korean relationship was used as a substitute.[40]

China's actions in pursuing the policy of urging treaty relations for Korea did not go beyond the traditional form and
nature of advice to the king of Korea necessary to convince
him through reason of the efficacy of the proposed policy.
While the device of an imperial decree could have been used
to insure immediate success, Li Hung-chang kept the traditional attitude of noninterference in internal affairs and preferred to wait until the king himself agreed to favor the policy.

[39] Wilkinson, *The Corean Government Constitutional Changes*, 12. Both
England and Germany concluded superseding treaties on November 26, 1883.
British and Foreign State Papers, LXXIV, 86–93, 633–40. Treaties of other
Western powers, as follows: Italy, June 26, 1884, *ibid.*, LXXV, 308–16; Russia,
June 25 (July 7), 1884, *ibid.*, 510–18; France, June 4, 1886, *ibid.*, LXXVII,
500–517.

[40] As far as is known no situation ever arose in which an effort was made
to determine the exact legal significance of these letters. At best such a letter
would constitute a sort of reservation to the document it accompanied, which
when considered with the treaty, as was the case in the United States Senate,
would infer an acceptance of the letter's interpretation along with the approval
of the treaty. At least the letter was evidence of the negotiators' intent, which
is valid as to the interpretation of the document. See Charles G. Fenwick,
International Law (New York, 1934), 336 and note. L. Oppenheim, *International Law* (London, 1937), secs. 517–517a.

Thus, the relation of Korea and China still conformed to the Confucian pattern which it had respected before the coming of the West. China merely became more interested in the relationship, now that it seemed to be in danger.

The American and European states, on the other hand, assumed that any Far Eastern relationship existing between China and Korea had no bearing on their Western legal system and that Korea, by stepping into this new realm of international law, would henceforth be governed, under all circumstances, by it alone. The letter accompanying each treaty, in which Korea's inferior status to China was asserted, was viewed by the Western states as of no legal import and effect on the treaty terms themselves.[41] In fact, by the United States the letter was apparently interpreted as a renunciation of a former status.[42] The very action of China in encouraging Korea to enter into treaty relations added to this impression, for to the Western states such action indicated that China no longer cared to exercise her suzerainty, which, according to their way of thinking and as has been explained in preceding pages, involved a control of the foreign relations of the vassal state. Therefore, though Korea remained actually in the same relation as always with respect to China, the Western governments considered her independent in all spheres necessary for full statehood.

[41] Tyler Dennett, "Early American Policy in Korea, 1883-1887," in *Political Science Quarterly*, XXXVIII (1923), 87 n. Li Hung-chang, however, in his letter of September 24, 1883, to the Korean king stating that British and Germans would arrive in Korea to proceed in making treaties as the Americans had done, showed in the following words the importance he attached to the king's declaration to the American president: "You must not permit any precipitate discussion with these Plenipotentiaries, which shall nullify the purport of your former notice that Chosen is a dependency of China, particularly so, since for two hundred years your country has been obedient. . . ." Foote to Freylinghuysen, enc., November 10, 1883, in Korea: Dispatches, United States Department of State, Vol. I.

[42] See p. 162.

3. INDICIA OF STATUS—THE EMEUTE OF 1882

In the same year of the signing of the first treaties, two incidents forcibly indicated the real strength of the Sino-Korean relationship, viewed hitherto as ceremonial, and reopened the discussion among Western diplomats as to Korea's actual status with respect to China. These two incidents were the attempted seizure of power in Korea by the Tai-wün-kun, with the subsequent Chinese intervention and restoration of the king to power, and the conclusion of a commercial agreement between China and Korea wherein the Confucian superior-inferior relationship was openly asserted.

The father of the king of Korea, though shorn of official power since 1873,[43] continued to exert a rallying influence over the antiforeign element which he had led at the time of the French and the American expeditions. He was particularly bitter toward the family of the queen, whose members, occupying many governmental posts, favored contacts with outside nations. The growth of Japanese influence in Korea, and the recent signing of the American, English, and German treaties furnished the materials for an explosion. After these resentments were strengthened by the significant omen of drought and poor crops, and by a reduction in the wages of the troops, an uprising occurred on July 23, 1882, in which mobs attacked and burned the Japanese legation. The Japanese officials, however, fought their way to the coast and, putting to sea, were rescued by a British surveying ship. A futile attempt was made at the same time to kill the queen, and many of the members of her family were put to death. Though the king himself was unharmed, the Tai-wün-kun assumed the authority to control affairs in his name.[44]

Upon hearing of the incident, and upon learning also that

---

[43] Jones, "The Taiwon Kun," loc. cit., 248.
[44] For accounts of the uprising, see Longford, Korea, 308 ff., and Griffis, Corea, 437 ff.

Japan was sending an expedition to Korea under the personal command of the Japanese foreign minister, Inouye,[45] the Chinese Viceregal office assumed the initiative. They ordered Admiral Ting Ju-ch'ang to prepare his ships to sail, and General Wu Ch'ang-ch'ing, with an army on the Northern Coast of Shantung, to be ready to move. They then wrote the Foreign Office for the requisite authorization, and on August 9 dispatched Messrs. Ting Ju-ch'ang and Ma Chien-chung with a Korean official, Yu Yung-ching, to Chemulpo to investigate. On August 12 the Japanese minister to Korea and 700 soldiers arrived in Korea.[46] Li Hung-chang was recalled from his temporary retirement, Messrs. Ting and Ma returned to speed the sending of ships and men, and on August 18 a Chinese expedition embarked at Chefoo. Setting up a camp outside the Korean capital, General Wu, Admiral Ting, and the Tao-tai Ma, with part of their forces, entered Seoul on August 26. At noon the three officials called formally on the Tai-wün-kun, and at four o'clock the Tai-wün-kun came to return the call. In the meantime, Chinese forces had been strategically placed throughout the city, and during the formal preliminaries of the visit the Tai-wün-kun's bodyguard was removed.[47] Toward evening the Chinese executed their *coup*. Conversing through written Chinese, the Tao-tai Ma questioned the Tai-wün-kun: "Do you understand that the King of Korea is invested by the Emperor of China?" The answer was "I do." The Tao-tai Ma continued:

Since the King is invested by the Emperor, he is the one who has power to issue commands. Your plot has enabled you to get in power, to kill your political enemies and to use your personal friends. It is an act against the King. Hence, it is also an act against

[45] See telegrams of Li Hsu-chang, Chinese minister in Tokyo, quoted in Tsiang, "Sino-Japanese Relations, 1870–1894," *loc. cit.*, 70–71.
[46] Tsiang, "Sino-Japanese Relations, 1870–1894," *loc. cit.*, 71–73.
[47] The person who distinguished himself by overcoming all resistance by the soldiers of the Tai-wün-kun was Yüan Shih-k'ai, later Chinese Resident in Korea and still later President of the Chinese Republic.

the Emperor. Your sin is unpardonable. Considering the fact that you are the father of the King we will not press hard on you. Please go to Tientsin to receive whatever punishment is to be bestowed upon you.

The Tai-wün-kun was then escorted aboard a Chinese warship and carried to Tientsin.[48]

Upon the completion of this move the Tao-tai Ma issued a proclamation explaining his action to the Koreans. "Korea, a dependency of China," he stated, "has always acted in accordance with established customs, but of late powerful functionaries have abused the administration for the promotion of personal interests." [49] He referred to the Imperial Decree in which the Chinese emperor declared that "Corea is a state tributary to Our Empire. For centuries, as a feudatory state, her rulers have been confirmed by us, and we have always esteemed her as loyal and respectful. The Throne has always looked upon her happiness and her sorrow with the same interest as upon those of Our own family." [50] The Tao-tai Ma's proclamation further mentioned the emperor's rage at the evil deeds of the Tai-wün-kun and his order to bring the culprit to China.

The king of Korea now reassumed the direction of his country's affairs. He sent his thanks to General Wu for removing the Tai-wün-kun and requested lenient treatment of his father.[51] Meanwhile the Japanese had presented their demands and Ma Chien-chung told the Korean negotiators, Li Yu-wün and Kim Hung-chi, what concessions to make.[52] The resulting formal agreement between Japan and Korea pro-

[48] Wang Yün-shen, *Sixty Years of Sino-Japanese Relations*, 168–69, quoted in Djang, Chinese Suzerainty, 152.

[49] Young to Freylinghuysen, enc. 2, October 2, 1882, in China: Dispatches, Vol. LXI, no. 27.

[50] Imperial Decree, *ibid.*

[51] Tsiang, "Sino-Japanese Relations, 1870–1894," *loc. cit.*, 74. By imperial decree, the Tai-wün-kun was to be kept in China for life at the city of Paoting. See *London Times*, September 26, 1882, 7b.

[52] Tsiang, "Sino-Japanese Relations, 1870–1894," *loc. cit.*, 74–75.

vided for indemnity and apologies by Korea, the right of Japan to maintain a guard for their legation in Seoul, and the privilege of limited travel in the interior by the Japanese.[53] The Tao-tai Ma thought that the terms were on the whole reasonable.[54]

To those nations who had signed treaties with Korea in the month previous to this uprising, the actions of Korea and of both Japan and China during the incident were somewhat mystifying. Here was a nation they viewed as independent, yet into which another nation could intervene, restore order, issue proclamations of control, force a member of the royal family to go to China to be judged for his acts, and receive for all such action the thanks of the monarch. United States Minister Young wrote from Peking that the amazing thing in the proclamation of Ma Chien-chung upon removing the Tai-wün-kun was "the assertion by the Emperor of China of his sovereignty over Corea. And yet," he continued, "in the treaty made by Commodore Shufeldt, the independence of Corea is acknowledged." [55] That Japan made no objection to China's intervention and yet sought to place no responsibility on her for the Korean attacks on the Japanese legation added further confusion and prompted the following comment by Young:

> Notwithstanding this clear avowal of sovereign power over Corea by the Emperor, an avowal that according to western ideas would have justified Japan in asking the Peking Government for explanations in reference to the massacre, the Japanese ignored the Chinese and dealt directly with the Coreans.[56]

This single action of China, in terms less subtle than the traditional Chinese controls, was sufficient to cause the specu-

[53] Text of agreement, Young to Freylinghuysen, enc. 8, October 2, 1882, in China: Dispatches, Vol. LXI, no. 27.
[54] Tsiang, "Sino-Japanese Relations, 1870–1894," loc. cit., 75.
[55] Young to Freylinghuysen, October 2, 1882, in China: Dispatches, Vol. LXI, no. 27.
[56] Ibid.

lation that perhaps Korea was not as independent as the Westerners had thought. The American minister hinted at a status like that of Bavaria in the German Empire, a view which he said was that of the French minister as well.[57] Yet it was difficult, he stated,

. . . to understand the shadowy, shifting, elastic, evanescent relations between these great Asiatic Empires and their subordinate States. One would think from our point of view that if China were mistress of Corea, she would govern the country and make treaties with foreign powers, just as she suppressed a rebellion and banished a royal prince.[58]

The question was also raised, whether a treaty with Korea would be valid without the approval of the Chinese emperor. Young, however, with the concurrence of the German minister, held the point of no consequence, for, as he stated, if Korea ". . . is satisfied with the convention as it is, is sound and honest, with a responsible government behind it, a government with which we can deal, it is not of our concern as to what mysterious, religious attitude its King may choose to hold toward another sovereign." [59]

The American Secretary of State, however, was not impressed either by the reports that China's actions were evidence of Korea's lack of legal independence, or by the suggestions of the American minister that such a possibility was "worthy of serious consideration." [60] Cognizant of all those occasions since 1866 in which China refused to accept legal responsibility for Korea, he regarded "the administrative independence of Corea as a pre-established fact, abundantly recognized by the events of the past few years, and not created by or recognized by the conclusion of our treaty." The fact that it was through China that the treaty was made caused

[57] *Ibid.*
[58] *Ibid.*
[59] *Ibid.*
[60] *Ibid.*

the Secretary to instruct the minister to say to the Chinese authorities that

. . . we have not regarded the aid lent to us by Chinese officials in bringing about this treaty as in any way an assertion of China's administrative rights over Corea, to the waiver of which we became a party; but that we regard Corea as *de facto* independent, and that our acceptance of the friendly aid found in China was in no sense a recognition of China's suzerain power. For if we had regarded or were constrained by any action of China to regard Corea as dependent upon the Empire, we should look to it for the execution of the rights of our citizens on the Corean Peninsula.[61]

The proposition that treaties with Korea would be valid only with the imperial Chinese approval was also rejected by the American Secretary of State. To his minister in China he wrote:

Nowhere in the treaty or elsewhere have we admitted that the relations of Corea and China are such as to require the ratification of the latter government to add force to any treaty concluded with the former. . . . That China claims some right of suzerainty over Corea is understood, but when the Corean King expressly states that full sovereignty has been exercised by the Kings of Chosen in all matters of internal administration and foreign relations, the effect of that claim is not apparent.[62]

Thus the confusion was continued. If China were suzerain she would be handling Korea's foreign relations. Since she was not, Korea, to the Western states, was independent.

It remains to be considered whether the action of China in intervening and removing the Tai-wün-kun had altered the traditional relationship between herself and Korea. To be sure, Chinese interference in the internal quarrels of the ruling house of an inferior state was very infrequent. Regardless of the local struggles for power, it had always been obvious

[61] Freylinghuysen to Young, August 4, 1882, in China: Instructions, Vol. III, no. 30.
[62] Davis to *id.*, January 22, 1883, *ibid.*, no. 81.

that any victor in such an affair would, as a matter of course, pay homage and receive investiture from the Middle Kingdom. Therefore, China concerned herself only slightly with the intra-family quarrels of the ruling houses of the lesser nations. Still, though the exercise of the rights implied by the power of investiture had been long in abeyance, the amount of control which the Middle Kingdom could exercise under this power was almost indefinitely expansive. This is illustrated by the complete control exercised by the Mongols while still operating within the framework of the traditional forms and ritual.[63]

Since China, the father and elder brother, had taken an active interest in the preservation of the status of Korea after 1876, and since the usurper of the kingship in the peninsula through the *coup* of 1882 was opposed to the policies China favored, it was no strain on the relationship for the Middle Kingdom to intervene to keep the duly invested ruler on his throne. The action, as Ma Chien-chung's conversation with the Tai-wün-kun indicated, was taken on this Confucian basis; the restoration of order and of the legitimate ruler had the full sanction of the Classics.[64] Although the action was unprecedented in recent practice, it was certainly within the limits of the succor a father and elder brother should render an inferior. It was not, despite its approximation to a practice understood in the West, an attempt to follow the Western system. At the most, it was an opportunistic move within the framework accepted by both China and Korea to preserve the Confucian status and prevent Western-style intervention and advancement of hegemony by Japan. The act of removing the instigator of the anti-Japanese riots left Japan no practical grounds for protest, and none was made.[65]

---

[63] See pp. 59 ff.
[64] See *Doctrine of the Mean* in *The Sacred Books of the East*, Vol. XXVIII.
[65] Tsiang, "Sino-Japanese Relations, 1870–1894," *loc. cit.*, 76.

4. INDICIA OF STATUS—THE TRADE REGULATIONS

The second incident in the year 1882 which disquieted believers in the complete independence of Korea was a commercial agreement between China and Korea, signed in September.[66] The first paragraph of the text of this agreement contained the assertion that no change was contemplated in Korea's standing "as a boundary state of China," but that the new Korean treaties for sea-borne trade with the Western states made it necessary to remove the still existing Chinese and Korean prohibitions upon such trade between themselves.[67] Li Hung-chang, as Superintendent of Trade at the Northern (Chinese) Ports, was instructed to appoint Commissioners of Trade to reside in the Korean coastal cities, and the Korean king was likewise to delegate similar officers for the Chinese seaports (Article I). The Chinese commissioners were to have jurisdiction over all disputes in which Chinese were involved, while Koreans in Chinese ports were to enjoy no form of extraterritoriality (Article II). Intercourse was opened through the northern frontier as well (Article V), and the prohibition denying Chinese fishermen access to the Korean coast was removed.

These regulations gave the Chinese a decided advantage over other foreigners living, traveling, and trading in the interior of Korea, with respect both to the facility of transferring native goods from one open port to another and to certain import duties.[68] The positions of the only Western states that had signed trade agreements with Korea at the time—the United States, England, and Germany—were identical in that the treaties of the latter two nations contained the same terms

[66] English translation of the text in *Foreign Relations*, 1883, pp. 173–76, and Carnegie Endowment for International Peace, *Korea: Treaties and Agreements* (Washington, 1921), 1–6.
[67] See pp. 96–97.
[68] See Holcomb's memorandum, *Foreign Relations*, 1883, p. 179.

as their model, the Shufeldt treaty.[69] To these Western powers, however, the most disturbing clause of the competitive agreement was one stating that these new regulations "are understood to apply to the relations between China and Korea only, the former country granting to the latter certain advantages as a tributary Kingdom, and treaty nations are not to participate therein." [70]

The American minister viewed this commercial agreement and its averment of Korea's inferior status as violating what he thought had been a recognition by China of the independence of Korea. Still applying Western concepts of suzerainty, Minister Young viewed China's suggestions that Korea enter treaty relations on equal terms with the West as an acknowledgment by China of Korea's independence. This conclusion he deduced from the Western view that the power to make treaties was the hallmark of independence. In this light, then, the recent negotiations between China and Korea, he stated, reopened the whole subject and gave "color to the averment of the Japanese that China never meant in sincerity to accept the independence of Corea. . . ." [71]

Mr. Chester Holcomb, in a memorandum included in the American minister's dispatch to his government, indicated several other perplexing problems which the signing of the Sino-Korean treaty presented. He referred to the fact that the preamble of the contract contained no assertion that the king of Korea was acting in his sovereign right or even at his own option, and that no provision was made for any subsequent rejection or ratification of the efforts of the negotiators by the monarch. A provision which further increased Western confusion was that which provided that the king of

[69] *Foreign Relations*, 1883, p. 176. The English and German treaties were not ratified and were superseded by others in 1883. The American treaty was not ratified until May 19, 1883.

[70] *Korea: Treaties and Agreements*, 1.

[71] Young to Freylinghuysen, December 26, 1882, in China: Dispatches, Vol. LXIII, no. 85.

Korea and Li Hung-chang, the Superintendent of Trade, were to correspond on a basis of equality (Article I). In the light of the Western treaties, in which the heads of the Western states dealt with the Korean king on a basis of equality, this placing of the Korean king on a level with a mere appointee of the Chinese emperor confused the basis of the diplomatic relations between the heads of foreign states and the Korean king, between the Korean commercial agents in China and those of other nations, and between the Chinese and other foreign representatives in Korea.[72]

Westerners, nevertheless, still viewed the relation between China and Korea as too "vague and indeterminable" to have any legal effect. Ignoring the Korean king's letter which accompanied each treaty, their attitude was illustrated by Holcomb's statement that "The right of suzerainty is neither recognized nor referred to in any of the three treaties made between Corea and Western Powers, and . . . the best way to deal with this question would be to ignore it altogether. . . ."[73]

But such an optimistic view was not held by the Japanese, who realized that the relation of Korea to China was much stronger and more effective than the Western states believed. They knew, on the other hand, that if no evidences existed which the West would accept as legally binding, the Western view would prevail. Hence, their efforts were directed toward combating the growing consciousness in the minds of the foreign ministers in Peking that Korea's status might be something other than independence. To this end the Japanese diplomats urged that the American representative soon to be sent to Korea should induce the Korean king to withdraw his letter acknowledging his country's status as tributary to China.[74] In a letter to the American minister in China, Mr.

[72] Holcomb memorandum, *Foreign Relations*, 1883, p. 177.
[73] Young to Freylinghuysen, Holcomb memorandum, December 26, 1882, in China: Dispatches, Vol. LXIII, no. 85.
[74] *Id.* to *id.*, January 28, 1883, *ibid.*, no. 112.

Yoshida wrote: "Not only did China gratuitously interfere in an unwarranted manner at the outset in a matter which concerned only Japan and Corea and between which two powers she was fully aware a solemn treaty existed, but her agents volunteered the opinion that our demands were exorbitant." [75] He termed the Chinese claim of a status superior to that of Korea "that mysterious but accommodating suzerainty which may at pleasure be denied . . . ," [76] and, to settle the Korean question once and for all, further proposed a congress in Tokyo of England, Germany, Russia, France, the United States, and Japan to neutralize Korea after the manner of Belgium.[77]

But the American minister refused to respond to the Japanese suggestion, pointing out that England, Germany, and the United States had all treated with and regarded Korea as an autonomous and independent country and that his legation did not attach much consequence to the letter of the king of Korea. "There would be no end of trouble," the minister wrote, "if we ventured into the atmosphere of romance and hyperbole which surrounds these Oriental claims to sovereignty. The letter of the Corean sovereign," he concluded, "was simply a concession to the pride of the Chinese Emperor." [78]

Thus far it is clear that China had been unsuccessful in getting any effective elements of the traditional relationship between Korea and herself recognized by the Western system of international relations. The real position that Korea occupied in the Far Eastern order was simply ignored, the Western states being cognizant only of the superficial evidences of that status, which had long prevailed and which, subjected to no strain, had exhibited little but the outward ceremonies

---

[75] Young to Freylinghuysen, enc. 1, January 18, 1883, *ibid.*, no. 104.
[76] *Ibid.*
[77] Young to Freylinghuysen, December 28, 1882, *ibid.*, no. 87.
[78] *Id.* to *id.*, January 28, 1883, *ibid.*, no. 112.

of subservience. These they rejected as having no legal effect. The further acts of China disclaiming those controls which to the West indicated the dependence of one nation on another, were viewed as a renunciation of all other connections with Korea, whatever their nature, that may have once existed.

It was China's seeming lack of knowledge of the Western system, and perhaps a desire to avoid responsibility as well, that allowed such a confused situation to come about. Her repeated assertions that she exercised no control over either the internal administration or the foreign affairs of Korea—definitive indicia to Western minds—completely overbalanced her always concomitant assertion, much less definitive, that Korea was a nation dependent on China. After the Japanese-Korean treaty, attempts were made by the Chinese to perpetuate the Far Eastern system by getting it recognized in the first Korean treaties with Western powers. Failing in this, they instituted the custom of having the king of Korea write supplementing letters acknowledging his inferiority. Inasmuch as the Western states understood, however, that along with this acknowledgement he also claimed equality and sovereignty, they viewed the letter more as an assertion of independence than as an announcement of inferiority.

CHAPTER IX

DEVELOPMENT OF THE SINO-KOREAN
RELATIONSHIP 1882–1888

1. CHINESE ADVISORY CONTROL

LI HUNG-CHANG, after the events of 1882, decided to approximate in his future relations with Korea a degree of control which Western practice would recognize. He may have been encouraged in this policy by the impression made on the Western nations by China's positive assertions of influence over Korea in the Tai-wün-kun affair, and by her promulgation of the subsequent commercial regulations, for it appeared that the Occidentals would accept outward evidences of control more readily than a claimed power virtually never used. In some measure this new policy was also the result of pressure within China from those individuals who wanted full advantage taken of the recent Chinese successes in Korea. For example, Chang-Ch'ien, quartermaster for the general who had commanded the Chinese troops in Korea in 1882, wrote a memorandum to Li Hung-chang advocating the annexation of Korea and war on Japan. Li gave this suggestion no consideration, though similar views were later taken up by the Censorate and the Hanlin Academy, and though a political group called the "Party of the Pure" also memorialized the throne in much the same vein, advocating at least a Chinese Resident in Korea.[1]

Instead, Li concentrated on preparedness, preferring to retain the traditional forms of the relationship and to control

[1] Tsiang, "Sino-Japanese Diplomatic Relations, 1870–1894," *loc. cit.*, 76–77.

affairs in Korea by the Confucian methods of advice and admonition. Thus far the policy showed no deviation from its previous course. But the new element which Li added after 1882 was the use of the commercial agents to be appointed under the recent trade regulations as vehicles for his intended control. These agents, who were Chinese subjects, could mask their functions under their office. Westerners formerly employed by China, or known to be favorable to her, also were to be employed as Korean officers to aid in the administration of the government. In pursuance of this policy, early in 1883 Li Hung-chang sent to Korea, P. G. von Möllendorff, formerly of the Chinese customs service, and Chen Shu-tang, former Chinese consul at San Francisco. Von Möllendorff was created Inspector General of Korean Customs and appointed a member of the Korean Foreign Office.[2] Chen Shu-tang, taking up his duties as commercial agent in October, posted a notice in Seoul which read in part as follows:

I wish to inform the people that I have received the appointment of Commissioner for China to manage the Commerce of Korea. . . . Whereas Korea has been dependent upon China since the time Kinchi [3] was appointed King of Chosen, several thousand years ago, and the people . . . have been wonderfully obedient to our existing dynasty. . . .

Therefore, the Chinese Government has issued trade regulations benefiting Korea; and I hope the merchants and citizens will appreciate this fact, and obey and adhere to these regulations, that harmonious feelings may exist between China and Korea, especially as Korea is a dependency of China. . . .[4]

---

[2] Young to Freylinghuysen, enc. F. D. Cheshire, Vice-Consul General in Charge, to John Russell Young, March 20, 1883, in China: Dispatches, Vol. LXIV, no. 162.

[3] *Chi-tzŭ*.

[4] Foote to Freylinghuysen, enc. 1, November 8, 1883, in Korea: Dispatches, Vol. I, no. 39.

Von Möllendorff, on his part, organized the customs service and was active in introducing reforms in communication and for the industrial, commercial, and financial improvement of the country.[5]

Among the Western powers this new move in Chinese diplomacy was of concern mainly to the United States, the only country that had ratified the treaties made the previous summer.[6] Furthermore, it was only the United States that had appointed to Korea an Envoy Extraordinary and Minister Plenipotentiary, making the post independent of and equal to the American legations at Peking and Tokyo. The other powers, when they established relations, avoided the issue of Korea's status by making their Korean representative an appendage of or inferior to their officials in China.[7] Thus, there was little disposition on the part of most Western representatives to do other than observe the interesting phases of Li Hung-chang's moves in Korea.

But to some American observers Li's action in sending the commercial agent and von Möllendorff to Korea served only to "strengthen the feelings of uneasiness and suspicion . . . as to the candor of China, in recognizing the King of Corea as an independent prince."[8] The American legation in China, however, had no doubt that the treaty of the United States with Korea constituted a full assertion of Korean independence, and, aside from China's ceremonial, historical associations with Korea, they were of the opinion that the Middle Kingdom occupied a no more favored relative position than

[5] H. B. Morse, *The International Relations of the Chinese Empire* (London, 1918), III, 10–11.

[6] Ratifications were exchanged at Seoul, May 19, 1883. Foote to Freylinghuysen, May 24, 1883, in *Foreign Relations*, 1883, pp. 241–42. Text of the treaty, *United States Statutes at Large* (Washington, 1850–1943), XXIII, 720–25. Germany and England concluded new treaties on November 26, 1883. See p. 150, n. 39.

[7] Morse, *International Relations*, III, 9. Dennett, *Americans in Eastern Asia*, 475.

[8] Young to Freylinghuysen, March 20, 1883, in China: Dispatches, Vol. LXV, no. 162.

any other nation. Though the legation viewed the attempt of China to interfere now in Korea in the same unfavorable light and as lacking the same degree of legality as a similar attempt by a Western state would occasion, and though they admitted that certain ceremonial relations might exist, that these ceremonies were the outward evidences of a status under which China could take positive action in Korea was not accepted. Thus, they believed that Li's actions in 1882 and 1883 rested upon no valid grounds.[9] To Minister Young, Li Hung-chang's policies appeared merely an attempt to establish "a kind of 'Monroe Doctrine' so far as Corea is concerned." [10]

The letter of the Korean king to the President, the only legal evidence of the perplexing relationship, was again examined. This time its declarations of inferiority and its naming of various duties of Korea as a dependent nation to China were observed, but their importance was discounted as seeming to come within that ceremony and ritual which were of no concern to the West. With reference to the express statements in the king's letter, not only of Korea's inferiority but of her "various duties" toward China as well, John Russell Young observed:

> While nothing could be clearer than this concession, the Legation has never laid much stress upon it, being disposed to believe that in all the essential points of government, in laws, customs, and religion, Corea was as independent as Japan. All that remained was a sentimental, ceremonial suzerainty, never going beyond gifts and compliments, embassies of courtesy now and then, with no practical interference by China in Corean affairs. . . .
>
> The Legation has always felt that with these Oriental relations of stately intercourse . . . we had no concern. The true questions were these:—Could the King carry out his Convention? Was he a sovereign so far as the engagements of this treaty were concerned? [11]

[9] See *id.* to *id.*, March 21, 1883, *ibid.*, Vol. LXIV, no. 166.
[10] *Id.* to *id.*, August 6, 1883, *ibid.*, Vol. LXV, no. 228.
[11] *Id.* to *id.*, March 21, 1883, *ibid.*, Vol. LXIV, no. 166.

The Japanese, gratified that the United States had seen fit to recognize definitely Korea's independènce by accrediting to the post a full minister,[12] were also opposed to the new policy of Li Hung-chang, and they viewed the United States as a possible ally in their efforts to stop the growing Chinese control. Even echoing the American willingness to permit "the ceremonial intercourse which has been so long observed," Inouye Kaoru, in a letter to John Russell Young,[13] held that:

Whatever may have been the relations between China and Corea . . . , since the latter has made an independent treaty with Japan, which was made without the intervention of China and solemnly declared herself free in her internal administration and foreign intercourse, which declaration was made with the knowledge advice and consent of China to the United States, England and Germany, it appears to me, we are bound to cause her to abide by those acts and declarations.

While the United States concurred in this attitude toward Korean independence, the suggestion went unheeded that America, with Japan, should advance this view by backing the Japanese-sponsored "progressive" party in Korea.[14]

The two contrasting conceptions of the status of Korea— in fact the two contrasting systems of international relations —were brought face to face in a conversation which took place in the summer of 1883 between Li Hung-chang and Minister Young. In response to Li's assertion that China had no real friends in the world, a lament substantiated by the inroads upon her outlying tributary nations, Minister Young asserted that the nation's troubles were of her own making. China, he said, refused to set up legal definitions of the extent of her territory, claiming certain areas as dependencies and yet denying international responsibility for them. The

[12] *Foreign Relations*, 1883, pp. 603–604.
[13] Young to Freylinghuysen, enc., February 2, March 24, 1883, in China: Dispatches, Vol. LXIV, no. 170.
[14] *Ibid.*

American expedition into Korea in 1871 was cited as an example wherein China refused this responsibility. According to the minister's dispatch, Li replied

. . . that the limits of the empire were well defined. There was China, and there were the tributaries of China. These tributaries were self governing, except in the fact that they owed the emperor an allegiance, which was satisfied by acts of tribute and ceremony. These offices done, the emperor never interfered in the internal affairs. At the same time their independence concerned China, and he could not be insensible to any attack upon it! [15]

The American official in turn maintained

. . . that in modern times and under the form of organization which now prevail, there were no such institutions as tributary states. A colony was as much a part of the empire as the capital. . . . This is the rule of civilized nations.[16]

Li Hung-chang answered this argument by placing his finger on the crux of the entire controversy over Korea: whether or not the Western states could rightly assume that their international law was the only system to be recognized and applied, particularly to a part of the world whose divergent system antedated that of the West by thousands of years and whose record of maintaining international peace among the nations in its sphere surpassed that of the West. Because there existed in Western practice no relation such as that which China claimed for herself and Korea, Li stated that he could see "no reason why the outside nations should destroy relations that had existed between China and their outlying nations for ages. They had gone on well together, doing each other good. . . ." [17]

This Chinese agent, to be sure, was no longer allowing the relationship between his country and Korea to disintegrate.

[15] *Id.* to *id.*, August 8, 1883, *ibid.*, Vol. LXV, no. 230.
[16] *Ibid.*
[17] *Ibid.*

His former policy of mere assertions of China's superiority over Korea was now being implemented by concrete control through von Möllendorff as Inspector General of Customs and Vice-President of the Foreign Office, and through the Chinese commercial agent, Chen Shu-tang. Despite denials of the existence of a superior-inferior relationship, in 1883 Li was able to assert with a smile: "I am King of Corea whenever I think the interests of China require me to assert that prerogative." [18]

2. The Thwarting of Japanese and Russian Advances

The Japanese, however, had not been idle in the affairs of the peninsula. Opportunity for their participation was offered by the progressive or reform party, which sought their sponsorship in opposition to the conservatives, who followed the lead of China. Count Inouye had admitted that Japan favored and in a crisis would aid this progressive group; [19] and, according to Professor Ariga,[20] sums of money were advanced by the Yokohama Specie Bank for the founding of newspapers and the training of Korean soldiers. Agents were dispatched, and Takezoye was sent as minister to give his support to the reform party. Luckily for the Japanese, by the middle of 1884 the number of Chinese troops in Korea, because of the war with France over Tongking, had been reduced to 1500 plus two Korean companies instructed by Yüan Shih-k'ai.[21] After October, Takezoye dared to speak freely of the approaching destruction of China and of Korean independence, and in November, at an audience with the king, he talked of the injustice of the present Chinese policies and stated that the Japanese government would be

[18] *Ibid.*
[19] Inouye to Young, enc., Young to Freylinghuysen, March 24, 1883, *ibid.*, Vol. LXIV, no. 170.
[20] Quoted in *Japan by the Japanese* (Alfred Stead, ed.) (London, 1904), 189.
[21] Tsiang, "Sino-Japanese Relations, 1870–1894," *loc. cit.*, 80.

very glad to see Korea assert her real independence according to international law.[22]

Finally, on December 4 a Japanese-inspired *coup* occurred,
in which members of the progressive party seized the king's
person and forced him to ask for the protection of the Japanese minister. The minister came with Japanese troops and
surrounded the palace, from which place the conspirators issued orders in the king's name, calling the conservative ministers thither. When they arrived there, six were summarily
executed. Learning immediately of the affair, Yüan Shih-k'ai,
after being refused entrance to the palace, by force expelled
the Japanese and released the king. Beset by Korean mobs
who had heard of the *coup,* the Japanese made their way,
together with the remaining Korean rebels, to the coast and
safety. The king then resumed control, issued a proclamation
condemning the traitorous action, and thanked the Chinese
for their aid.[23] Japan sent Inouye to Korea to settle the incident between the two countries, a very mild treaty resulting
wherein, though indemnity was paid to Japan, her position
in Korea was not strengthened.[24]

In dealing with China over the armed clash in Korea, Japan
was in no position to act arbitrarily, for the war between
China and France, which had diverted Chinese troops from
Korea, had ended not too unfavorably for the emperor's
forces only two days after the opening of the negotiations.
Count Ito, who was sent to China as a special ambassador to
protect Japanese interests in the peninsula, therefore con-
tented himself with a treaty which fell short of his earlier

[22] *Japan by the Japanese,* 190–91, quoting Ariga.
[23] Young to Freylinghuysen, enc. 7, April 2, 1885, in China: Dispatches,
Vol. LXXV, no. 701. For accounts of this affair, see F. H. Mörsel, "Events
Leading to the Emeute of 1884," in *Korean Repository,* IV (1897), 95–98,
135–40, 212–19; Longford, *Korea,* 321–25; Tsiang, "Sino-Japanese Relations,
1870–1894," *loc. cit.,* 81–84; *Foreign Relations,* 1885, pp. 331–41; *London
Times,* December 18, 1884, 3a, 3e, December 22, 5c, December 27, 3a, and
December 29, 3c.
[24] Text of Treaty, *Foreign Relations,* 1885, p. 343.

objective of securing recognition of Korean independence by China, though he did gain substantial advantages.[25] This treaty, signed at Tientsin [26] on April 18, 1885, provided that both the Middle Kingdom and Japan should withdraw their troops from Korea. Korea was to be encouraged to maintain sufficient forces of her own and to invite foreign military instructors from a power other than China or Japan, these two powers binding themselves not to send any of their own officers to assist in giving the proposed instruction. Should grave disturbances necessitate their sending troops to the peninsula, they were to take such action only after prior notification of the other foreign power in writing, and the troops were to be withdrawn upon settlement of the difficulty.

This treaty, which placed Japan and China on equal terms in Korea as regards military intervention and control over the Korean armed forces, constituted a victory for Japan. But thereafter, barring "grave disturbances," Japanese advances in the peninsula had to rely on diplomacy alone. In this field China had the advantage through her relations with the Korean throne, Foreign Office, customs service, and, above all, through Korea's acceptance of a dependent position toward the Middle Kingdom. Thus far, then Li Hung-chang's policy had been successful; the Japanese influence began to decline.[27] The American minister to Japan believed, however, that under this treaty neither China nor Japan could thereafter "claim any colorable authority over the rightful sovereignty of the Corean Government." [28]

But the growing power of the Chinese influence was shown in an incident in 1885 wherein China had to face Russia in Korea, rather than Japan. Von Möllendorff, though sent to Korea in China's interest, soon identified himself with local cliques and, in his position as Vice-President of the Korean

[25] Dennett, *Americans in Eastern Asia*, 479–80.
[26] Text, *British and Foreign State Papers*, LXXVI, 297–98.
[27] Longford, *Korea*, 326.
[28] *Foreign Relations*, 1885, p. 563.

Foreign Office, intrigued over the heads of his superiors to control policy with the palace eunuchs. Li Hung-chang recalled him to China to explain his actions, but the two parted still in disagreement.[29] The incident which led to the downfall of von Möllendorff and a diplomatic victory by Li Hung-chang over Russia was von Möllendorff's attempt to displace Chinese influence in Korea and substitute Russian. Being in touch with the Russian legation in Japan, he suggested that Korea would like Russian officers to instruct her army.[30] To further the project, a Korean agent, Kim Yong-wün, was promptly dispatched to Russia, where he signed a secret agreement putting the Korean army and gendarmery under Russian control, giving Russia the "loan" of Port Lazareff on the eastern coast of Korea for an ice-free winter harbor, and in general placing the peninsula under Russian protection.[31]

The news leaked out when the Russian agent de Speyer appeared in Korea to secure confirmation of the agreement. The king of Korea, having earlier requested that American military instructors be sent,[32] disclaimed any knowledge of the agreement and, acting on Li Hung-chang's advice, disavowed the secret agreement despite threats from Russia [33] and von

[29] Tsiang, "Sino-Japanese Relations, 1870–1894," loc. cit., 88.

[30] Foulk to Bayard, July 5, 1885, in Korea: Dispatches, Vol. II, no. 192.

[31] Id. to id., June 23, 1885, ibid., no. 186. Smithers to id., enc. from China Mail, dated July 17, 1885, entitled "History of the Russo-Corean Treaty," August 21, 1885, in China: Dispatches, Vol. LXXVI, no. 52. It appears to have been this news which caused Great Britain to seize Port Hamilton, an island off the southern Korean coast. Dennett, "Early American Policy in Korea, 1883–1887," loc. cit., 94. For the Port Hamilton correspondence, see British and Foreign State Papers, LXXVIII, 143–69.

[32] President Arthur had asked Congress on January 30, 1885, for a joint resolution authorizing such instructors to be sent. United States House Executive Documents, 48 Cong., 2 Sess., No. 163, "Military Instructors for Corea: Message from the President of the United States" (Washington, 1885). After much inaction and a change of administration, arrangement was made without legislative action, and the officers finally arrived in April, 1888. See Congressional Record, XVII, 604–605, 1080, 1721.

[33] See Dennett, "Early American Policy, 1883–1887," loc. cit., 95; Tsiang, "Sino-Japanese Relations, 1870–1894," loc. cit., 90–91. For a memorandum of

Möllendorff's complicity in the scheme as indicated by his support of the Russian agent.[34] At the same time, Li Hung-chang had the American minister to China telegraph the United States government asking prompt action upon the king's request for the American military instructors.[35] Li also ordered the immediate discharge of von Möllendorff and looked about for a man to replace him.[36]

By this incident Chinese power and prestige in Korea were further augmented. In fact, by the end of 1885, under the policies of Ito and Inouye, Japan was bent only on increasing her own economic resources and was steadily losing ground diplomatically in Korea.[37] Moreover, the Russian attempt had been successfully thwarted by China, and the practical policy of directing Korean affairs through Chinese agents in the peninsula was impressing the Western nations with the actual strength of the Confucian relationship. While Japan and Russia could make their advances only on the legal bases of their treaties with Korea, China had the non-legal Confucian status within which any policy deemed expedient could be pursued.

The non-legal nature of this relationship is illustrated by a letter from Li Hung-chang to the Korean king, a letter which, despite its appearances to Western observers, also shows that Li Hung-chang was still basing the Chinese rela-

---

the de Speyer-Foreign Office conversations of June 24, 1885, see George C. Foulk Papers, New York Public Library, or Foulk to Bayard, enc., June 29, 1885, in Korea: Dispatches, Vol. II, no. 189.

[34] Smithers to Bayard, August 21, 1885, in China: Dispatches, Vol. LXXVI, no. 52. See *London Times*, August 3, 1887, 4a, for comment on Chinese influence in Korea and the story of the von Möllendorff incident.

[35] Smithers to Bayard, July 22, 1882, in China: Dispatches, Vol. LXXVI, no. 37.

[36] Tsiang, "Sino-Japanese Relations, 1870–1894," *loc. cit.*, 91. For Foulk's comments on von Möllendorff, see Foulk to Bayard, August 4, 1885, in Korea: Dispatches, Vol. II, no. 211. Though relieved of his Foreign Office position, von Möllendorff was retained in his control of the Korean customs until September 4, 1885.

[37] Tsiang, "Sino-Japanese Relations, 1870–1894," *loc. cit.*, 105.

tionship with Korea on Confucian principles rather than trying to create the Western concept of a protectorate. "Matters
between the Chinese government and your country," he wrote
to the king, "are just like those of one family." [38] Earlier in
the letter he had said:

> In her relations with the vassal states, China is guided by the
> 'rites.' [*li*, rules of propriety.] She seeks to be considerate with-
> out once encroaching upon their rights, and yet goes to their rescue
> whenever there is need, as if they were under her direct rule. Take
> your country . . . : in the troubles of 1882 and 1884 she came
> to your rescue without any thought of the hardship, but the duties
> which the relation has imposed upon her and from which she cannot
> escape. In the West such is not the rule. Nations that are under
> the protection of others can never stand on the same plane. No,
> under power and oppression they would not remain feudatory
> states even if they were willing to, for the protector would not only
> interfere with their national policies but would also count their
> people, control their military forces, tamper with their power of
> appointment and collect their taxes, and, worse still, even pension
> their kings off as private citizens with empty titles to live the lives
> of exiles. I do not need to cite to you the distant examples of Egypt
> and India: Annam has afforded one.[39]

3. A CHINESE RESIDENT IN KOREA

With the growth of Chinese power in the Korean peninsula
other nations which had earlier rejected China's claim to a
special position there, now came to recognize the fact that
China was fast becoming master of the area. Being themselves unable to compete with a non-legal Confucian personal
relationship, these states sought by agreement with China to
halt her advance short of annexation. In September, 1884,
the Russian Minister Ladygensky had proposed to Li Hung-

[38] Shuhsi Hsü, *China*, 133.
[39] *Ibid.*, 131.

chang a guarantee of the status quo in Korea.[40] In July, 1885, Count Inouye, through his Peking minister, Enomoto, presented a memorandum proposing what amounted to a condominium of China and Japan over Korea. The German chargé at Seoul, in a memorial to the Korean king, which was forwarded to Li, also suggested the neutralization of the area.[41]

Li Hung-chang, however, favored none of these moves. In view of the ascendancy of China in Korea since 1882, he decided in the fall of 1885 on a further modification of his government's Korean policy, aiming eventually to establish exclusive Chinese control of the peninsula, a situation analogous in many of its aspects to the position of Korea under the Yüan dynasty.[42] Li had already dropped his policy of preserving the status quo in Korea through encouraging the activities of the commercial nations in order to foil those with territorial designs. He now visualized a Korea dominated by China. Japan had been unsuccessful in advancing herself there by nonforceful means, and Russia could be checked by British surveillance. Moreover, exclusion of all foreign influence from the peninsula except that of China would be more understandable to other nations than the earlier Chinese policy which theoretically allowed Korea complete autonomy.

The main reason, however, why Li Hung-chang wished to tighten his control over Korea at this particular time was the native monarch's growing indifference to a firm observance and acceptance of the Confucian relationship. Obviously, Korea's respect for this traditional association with China was fundamental to the preservation of the Far Eastern status of the peninsula kingdom. It must be remembered here that everything China had been able to do in Korea rested not on a treaty-contract basis, as it would have done in West-

[40] Djang, Chinese Suzerainty, 165.
[41] Tsiang, "Sino-Japanese Relations, 1870–1894," *loc. cit.*, 89–90.
[42] See Chap. IV.

ern practice, but upon the personal adherence of the ruler of Korea to the time-honored relationship. For, aside from the commercial regulations, no legal document, no pledged word, bound the two nations together. Through their common belief in the Confucian principles and Korea's consequent attitude toward the Middle Kingdom, China had enjoyed a much greater degree of participation in the affairs of the peninsula than would have been possible for a nation whose field of action was defined by the terms of a treaty. But the entire relationship would have crumbled if the personal allegiance of the lesser ruler had been appreciably weakened.

With the Western nations viewing Korea as sovereign and independent and with Japan also adhering to that opinion, the king of Korea, since the signing of the first treaties between these nations and his government, had naturally been affected by pressure which sought to make his adherence to the Confucian relationship less secure. The Japanese, for instance, had urged an open declaration of independent status, while the Western states in making their treaties, and the Western diplomats, particularly the Americans, had dealt with Korea as an independent and equal nation. Some of the foreigners employed by the Korean government were also not subservient to China, even though she was their sponsor. It was to strengthen Chinese control, therefore, and to combat the above-named influences that Li modified his policy toward Korea. Having no desire to continue the encouragement of foreign interests, the Tai-wün-kun, who had been removed previously because of his anti-foreign and pro-Chinese policies, was to be returned. The control of affairs through foreigners in the employ of the Korean government and through the Chinese commercial agents was to be supplemented by a Chinese "resident" who was to act through the king. China was to control matters still further by dealing with foreign states on purely Korean questions directly through the Chinese Foreign Office. Thus, between 1885 and 1894, before force changed events, Li Hung-chang could truly say, "I am King of Korea."

As has been mentioned, the Tai-wün-kun was deposed and removed to China in 1882 because he had obstructed Li's earlier policy of encouraging Korea to have intercourse with the outside world. Now that this policy had been superseded by that of strengthening Korea's allegiance to China, the Tai-wün-kun would be of use in the peninsula, especially in view of the fact that during his enforced residence in China he had informed Li Hung-chang of his loyalty and had urged for Korea the appointment of a Chinese resident whose advice the ruler would be compelled to follow.[43] This was precisely what Li Hung-chang proposed to do.

The subsequent imperial decree releasing the Tai-wün-kun from his exile in China is significant for its accent upon the virtue of filial piety, not only as between the Korean king and his father whose return was asked, but also as an element in Far Eastern governmental theory. The decree read in part as follows:

> The Court considers filial piety as a prominent essential in the administration of Government and its compassionate concern for its border tributaries is specially profound . . . , it feels that it is meet that special bounty should be exercised towards them, that the yearnings of filial affection may be indulged.[44]

Along with the Tai-wün-kun, Li Hung-chang sent Yüan Shih-k'ai back to Korea to be the first Chinese resident there since the Mongol times 500 years earlier. Having been connected with Korean affairs since the uprising of 1882, Yüan now received the official title of "Director-General Resident

[43] Djang, Chinese Suzerainty, 163.
[44] Smithers to Bayard, enc., September 28, 1885, in China: Dispatches, Vol. LXXVI, no. 65.

in Korea of Diplomatic and Commercial Relations," [45] and his status was henceforth never comparable with that of a mere diplomatic representative of a friendly power.[46] As to the matter of ceremony, only the Chinese resident held the privilege of being carried through the palace gates to the audience hall and of remaining seated in the presence of the Korean king. Other representatives had to dismount at the palace gates, proceed on foot, and stand when the king was present.[47] Further evidence of Yüan's unusual authority was revealed during a banquet given at the Chinese legation in Seoul when he explained his seating the president of the Korean Foreign Office below all the foreign representatives by saying that the Korean official was not a guest but a member of the family of China.[48] Even as interpreted by Western state etiquette, such procedure could not fail to indicate a special status for him above that possessed by a mere diplomatic representative. Though his actions were limited technically to the giving of advice, Yüan soon had control of the Foreign Office and was presenting memorials directly to the king.[49]

Coincident with the return of the Tai-wün-kun and the installation of Yüan Shih-k'ai as resident, the Korean customs service was drawn closer to that of China through the gradual drafting of men from the Chinese customs organization to fill the higher positions in the Korean establishment.

[45] W. H. Wilkinson, "The Corean Government," in *Korean Repository*, IV (1897), 12.

[46] Yüan's status caused much confusion among the representatives of the other powers in Korea. He viewed himself as "resident" and not "minister," which latter title would have been an admission of Korea's independence. He refused to attend the conferences of the foreign diplomats, indicating he would consult with them only at the Korean Foreign Office, and refused to be considered as the *doyen* of the diplomatic corps in Seoul. Foulk to Bayard, November 25, 1885, in Korea: Dispatches, Vol. III, no. 255; Heard to Blaine, January 22, 1891, *ibid.*, Vol. VII, no. 114.

[47] Dinsmore to Bayard, May 27, 1887, *ibid.*, Vol. IV, no. 20.

[48] Foulk to *id.*, August 16, 1885, *ibid.*, Vol. II, no. 214.

[49] See *Foreign Relations*, 1887, pp. 256–58, for Yüan's memorial on governmental reforms.

Sir Robert Hart, Inspector General of Chinese Customs, nominated Mr. Henry F. Merrill, an American in the Chinese Service, to be Inspector General of Korean Customs instead of von Möllendorff, who was recalled for his Russian intrigues. The new appointee assumed control in October, 1885.[50] Simultaneously, the position of Vice-President of the Foreign Office, which had also been held by von Möllendorff, was conferred on Mr. O. N. Denny, formerly American consul at Tientsin.[51] Li Hung-chang, it is said, divided these functions in order to prevent the extension to Korea of the strong influence which Sir Robert Hart had on foreign affairs in China.[52] Though the dispatch of such experienced men to Korea presaged a more efficient operation of the Korean customs, their appointment also indicated that the peninsula nation's connection with China was viewed as even more important than a mere increase of efficiency and, further, that it was a move toward the eventual union of the Chinese and Korean customs services. "Take care," wrote Sir Robert to the newly appointed Korean customs head, "that I am well informed and quickly of all that goes on, as you will find in the long run that the best holding ground is in this office—so do not be tempted to hook on, or drop your moorings elsewhere." [53]

4. The Weakening of Korea's Western Status

One of Li Hung-chang's first moves in his policy of increased dominance over Korea was the attempt to end the fiction of the kingdom's complete sovereignty which was indicated by the presence there of separate ministers of the

[50] *Ibid.*, 1885, pp. 358–59.

[51] Foulk to Bayard, August 16, December 9, 1885, April 2, 1886, concerning Denny's appointment, in Korea: Dispatches, Vol. II, no. 214, Vol. III, nos. 260, 290.

[52] Morse, *International Relations*, III, 14.

[53] Sir Robert Hart to H. F. Merrill, quoted *ibid.*, III, 13, 13 n.

foreign powers. Through the American minister to China, Charles Denby, who had succeeded John Russell Young,[54] Li requested that the United States follow the lead of the other European powers in handling Korean affairs through their Chinese legations. The American post in Korea had already been reduced by the Diplomatic and Consular Act of July 7, 1884, from equality with those at Peking and Tokyo to that of Minister Resident and Consul General.[55] Minister Foote had resigned in protest, and since December, 1884, affairs were being conducted by a naval attaché and chargé, George C. Foulk.[56] Minister Denby, who favored Li's plan, pointed out that "There is at Corea a Chinese Minister and a Japanese Minister, but no other nation has a Minister there." He continued by stating:

Corea has always had a King who has been invested as such by China. But, though she has made independent treaties with foreign countries, yet she is still practically tributary to China, and Li Hung-chang, representing the Chinese Government, exercises the controlling influence over the public and foreign affairs of Corea and is in constant communication with the King and his Government.[57]

This move to bring the United States into line indicated the new Chinese policy of directing Korea's foreign relations through Peking as well as Seoul, and, though the American legation in Korea was maintained, it was not until June 6, 1886, that a minister arrived.[58]

The length to which China was prepared to go after 1885 was shown in her action of 1886 when the Korean government

[54] See Young's resignation, January 27, 1885, in China: Dispatches, Vol. LXXIV, no. 635.
[55] *United States Statutes at Large*, XXIII, 227–36.
[56] Foote to Freylinghuysen, September 17, 1884, in Korea: Dispatches, Vol. I, no. 112.
[57] Denby to Bayard, October 12, 1885, in China: Dispatches, Vol. LXXVI, no. 12.
[58] Dennett, "Early American Policy in Korea, 1883–1887," *loc. cit.*, 97.

was accused of again soliciting Russian aid.[59] The inferences are that the American, O. N. Denny, whose loyalty was to Korea rather than to China from whom he received his position, had encouraged the Russian involvement as an aid to Korean independence.[60] Yüan Shih-k'ai convinced Li Hung-chang of the seriousness of the situation by producing the· note of Sim Shun Taik, the Korean prime minister, to the Russian representative Waeber. In this note statements were made that previously Korea, though self-ruling, had always been dependent upon China, that henceforth she was determined to be independent, and that she desired Russian aid if anyone objected—"anyone" of course referring to China.[61] Li thereupon stated that if this was the true situation, he would depose the king and return the Tai-wün-kun to the throne.[62] The Chinese minister in St. Petersburg was instructed to request the Russian government not to receive the proposal of Sim Shun Taik,[63] and, though the Russian Foreign Office denied the receipt of it, Russia threatened war if the matter was not dropped.[64] The Korean king confessed that the note had been sent, but without his authority. On Yüan's advice the Korean Foreign Office was obliged to send a circular announcing to all foreign governments that any document it henceforth communicated to them would be valid only if countersigned by the Minister of Foreign Affairs.[65]

Whether or not this complicity with Russia was as real as the Chinese made it appear,[66] its speedy termination illus-

[59] Shuhsi Hsü, *China*, 128–29.

[60] Dennett, *Americans in Eastern Asia*, 482–83; Morse, *International Relations*, III, 15.

[61] Tsiang, "Sino-Japanese Relations, 1870–1894," *loc. cit.*, 96.

[62] *Ibid.*, 97.

[63] Shuhsi Hsü, *China*, 129.

[64] Tsiang, "Sino-Japanese Relations, 1870–1894," *loc. cit.*, 97.

[65] Shuhsi Hsü, *China*, 129.

[66] Dennett, *Americans in Eastern Asia*, 483, citing only O. N. Denny who was urging Korean independence, terms the note a forgery and the entire affair a Chinese plot to dethrone the king, which was exposed by Denny and

trated the firmer policy now taken by China and revealed a willingness even to depose the Korean king if necssary to maintain Korea in her position. Later in 1886 Li Hung-chang, in conversation with Ladygensky, the Russian minister, even refused an agreement for preservation of the status quo in Korea, not because he was dissatisfied with the status quo, which was favorable to China, but because he did not want to rule out the possibility of a change in the internal regime of Korea.[67]

Before the year was out another incident occurred which may be considered a test case of China's control over Korea and which served to advance the Chinese government another step in the weeding out of all influences likely to move the Korean king to thoughts of independence and renunciation of his relationship to China. The present instance was that of the American naval attaché, George C. Foulk, who had been in Korea since 1884. Foulk had ingratiated himself with the king and the progressive, anti-Chinese party, and he appeared to have had a rather intimate advance knowledge of the *coup* of 1884 in which the king was seized and the conservative ministers assassinated.[68] Since he was convinced that Korea should free herself from Chinese influence, he naturally opposed the growing Chinese control as evidenced in the establishment of the Chinese resident.[69] This attitude, together with the fact that he enjoyed the highest personal

others. George C. Foulk also concurs in this view. See Foulk to Bayard, September 8, 1886, in Korea: Dispatches, Vol. III, no. 3.

[67] Tsiang, "Sino-Japanese Relations, 1870–1894," *loc. cit.*, 98.

[68] See Foulk's report on the émeute. *Foreign Relations*, 1885, pp. 335–41, and Mörsel, "Events Leading to the Emeute of 1884," *loc. cit.*, 136. His influence was not measured by his position as mere naval attaché, for he was in charge of the affairs of the United States for much of the time between 1884 and 1887. From December, 1884, to June, 1886, he was in sole charge of the legation. Minister Parker, arriving in June, 1886, was removed on a warship in disgrace on September 3, 1886. On Foulk's request for relief, W. W. Rockhill came from China in December, 1886. Foulk took up his duties again as attaché in March, 1887. On March 31, 1887, H. A. Dinsmore arrived as American minister.

[69] Dennett, "Early American Policy in Korea, 1883–1887," *loc. cit.*, 97.

favor of the Korean king, caused Foulk to be viewed as a stumbling block to the increased influence China desired to exercise after the arrival of Yüan Shih-k'ai. Though Yüan never came out in open opposition to the American attaché, Foulk's advice to the king and to foreign officers in Korean employ, based as it was on the assumption of Korean independence, made him anathema to the Chinese.[70]

After the new American minister arrived in 1887 and after the king of Korea had prepared to appoint Foulk his adviser in foreign affairs, moves were made to secure the latter's withdrawal from the country. A number of his dispatches in which there was praise of men later stigmatized officially as traitors, and his disparagement of certain high officials, including the president of the Foreign Office, had been published by the American Department of State and reprinted in part in the *North China Daily News*.[71] These expressions aroused suspicion about him, and his intimate connection with those who had attempted to seize power in 1884 served to link him with that affair also. The president of the Korean Foreign Office therefore demanded that Minister Dinsmore recall him.[72] The Chinese government, through its chargé in Washington, pressed Secretary of State Bayard to achieve the same end.[73] On June 18, 1887, Foulk received peremptory orders to report for duty on board an American vessel then in the port of Chemulpo.[74] When the Korean king and other officials appealed to the American minister for Foulk's retention, Minister Dinsmore complied, informing the Secretary

[70] H. J. Noble, "The United States and Sino-Korean Relations, 1885–1887," in *Pacific Historical Review*, II (1933), 292–96. This paper is based on the archives of the former legation at Seoul, Korea. See also Dennett, "Early American Policy in Korea, 1883–1887," *loc. cit.*, 82–103, for Foulk's services. See Foulk Papers,

[71] Rockhill to Bayard, encs., January 3, 1887, in Korea: Dispatches, Vol. IV, no. 46.

[72] Dinsmore to *id.*, and encs., May 3, 1887, *ibid.*, no. 14.

[73] Bayard to Dinsmore, June 17, 1887, in Korea: Instructions, 2 vols., United States Department of State, Vol. I, no. 21.

[74] Dinsmore to Bayard, June 20, 1887, in Korea: Dispatches, Vol. IV, no. 29.

of State that the affair was actually a test case on the power of China's suzerainty.[75] Secretary of State Bayard refused to alter his decision, however, replying to Dinsmore:

Ensign Foulk's presence in Corea is by reason of his being an officer of the United States Navy, detailed to perform the duties assigned him by his own Government. The opposition manifested officially by the Korean Foreign Office to the continued presence of Mr. Foulk must seriously impair his utility in that capacity, and his appointment as Naval Attaché has accordingly been cancelled. To authorize him to remain in Corea, without representative employment, and occupying what your dispatches indicate to be an equivocal position as respects the relation of Corea to China, is believed to be inexpedient.[76]

The removal of Foulk as *persona non grata* to China and to the Chinese-controlled Foreign Office of Korea, was a distinct triumph for Li Hung-chang. It was a recognition of the existence of Chinese hegemony over Korea by the very country which, aside from Japan, had been consistently the most ardent supporter of Korean independence. Viewed as a test case on China's power in the peninsula, it further increased the prestige and influence that China had developed since Li Hung-chang began directing Korean policy.

5. The Korean Mission to Washington

That the removal of Foulk was viewed by the United States, however, more as a matter of expediency than as a recognition of China's domination over Korea is indicated by the stand taken in 1887 when Korea sent a legation to Washington. The reluctance of the American government upon this occasion to treat the Korean representatives as inferiors to and under the sponsorship of the Chinese minister at the Capital was in itself the significant aspect of another test case

[75] *Ibid.*
[76] Bayard to Dinsmore, June 23, 1887, in Korea: Instructions, Vol. I, no. 23.

in which the United States reaffirmed her determination to consider Korea as an independent state.

It is likely that Korea's action in sending representatives to the United States and Europe did not at first appear to Li Hung-chang as a threat to China's interest in the peninsula.[77] But Yüan Shih-k'ai's disturbing reports that the foreign representatives in Seoul, particularly the British,[78] had indicated the motives behind the move and its probable effect on China caused Li to reconsider the project. On September 18, 1888, he wired the Korean government to the effect that such a step should not be taken before consultation with him, and five days later he sent an imperial order for the throne to be memorialized and permission secured before the representatives were sent.[79] Resident Yüan in the meantime had dissuaded the Korean envoy from proceeding on his way, and the American minister had written Yüan asking for explanations.[80] The king of Korea, however, in the customary terms used by a nation inferior to the Middle Kingdom, forwarded the required memorial to the emperor and received permission to dispatch the envoys under regulations laid down by Li Hung-chang. In addition to Li's instructions that Korea must send only ministers *resident* and in no event ministers *plenipotentiary*—"to show by this means the difference between Corea and China"—the instructions ran as follows:

First. After arrival at his post, the Corean minister must go first to the Chinese legation and ask the Chinese minister's assistance, and call together at the foreign office. After which, he may call at his pleasure and convenience.

Second. If there should be any reception, or official assembly or dinner, or toasts drunk, or any mutual meeting, the Corean representative must take a lower place than the Chinese representative.

[77] Shuhsi Hsü, *China,* 133–34.
[78] Tsiang, "Sino-Japanese Relations, 1870–1894," *loc. cit.,* 100.
[79] *Foreign Relations,* 1888, p. 434.
[80] Dinsmore to Bayard, September 30, 1887, in Korea: Dispatches, Vol. IV, no. 53.

Third. If there happens to be any serious question, the Corean representative must consult secretly with the Chinese representative, and discuss the affair with him. This rule is absolutely required according to the rules of a vassal State. It does not concern the other Governments, and they will not be able to know of it.[81]

In return for the imperial approval, the Korean king sent a letter of thanks; then through a separate memorandum he secured special permission to allow his representatives to the Western powers to go as ministers *plenipotentiary,* provided he would replace them with mere *chargés* as soon as the formalities were ended.[82] The king's letter of thanks contained a full acknowledgment of Korea's inferior status, his acceptance of Li's regulations governing the proposed legation, and assurance that the chosen emissaries had been duly instructed. "Henceforth," it stated, "both our position toward China and our international relations will be maintained, the gods of our country will enjoy perpetual peace, and a stop will be put to troublesome remarks." [83]

Upon their arrival in the United States, the envoys promptly ignored these instructions. Indeed, the American member of the delegation, Dr. H. N. Allen, threatened to resign if the group had any contact with the Chinese legation.[84] Then after the American government had intimated that they could not be received as vassal envoys,[85] their visit to the Secretary of State and their presentation to the President were made without the presence of the Chinese minister.[86] When the slighted official reported that Li's instructions were being flouted, the king of Korea pleaded a disregard of his orders,[87] and, though Dr. Allen signed a document accepting all responsibility for

[81] *Foreign Relations,* 1888, pp. 237–38, 441–42.
[82] Shuhsi Hsü, *China,* 134; *Foreign Relations,* 1888, pp. 249–50.
[83] *Foreign Relations,* 1888, pp. 249–50.
[84] H. N. Allen Papers, New York Public Library.
[85] H. N. Allen, *Things Korean* (New York, 1908), 164.
[86] See *ibid.,* Chap. X; *Foreign Relations,* 1888, pp. 443, 453–54.
[87] Tsiang, "Sino-Japanese Relations, 1870–1894," *loc. cit.,* 100.

the infraction, upon the insistence of Yüan Shih-k'ai the Korean minister was banished when he returned home.[88] No minister was ever sent to Europe, though Li had received approval of his rules of presentation from both London and St. Petersburg.[89]

This incident reopened for the United States the subject of China's relationship to Korea; the growing Chinese influence in the peninsula could no longer be overlooked. Minister Dinsmore complained that

> . . . it is now but a very few years since Chinese intercourse with Korea was limited to the observance of their ancient mutual rites and ceremonies as "brother countries" . . . but now China, the "elder brother," avails herself of the excuse that it is necessary for him to have officials on the ground with a view of protecting his "younger brother" from the dangers of association with foreign powers. . . .[90]

That China was then in Korea by virtue of any properly established relationship Dinsmore would not admit. He held this view despite the fact that in a conversation with the president of the Korean Foreign Office he was told that China "is our elder brother and, because we are weak and a small country, we ask China to advise and assist us." [91] At the same time, however, the Korean official denied any desire to be ruled by the Middle Kingdom. To Dinsmore's protest against Chinese interference with the sending of the Korean mission to the United States, and against Chinese claims of suzerainty, Yüan Shih-k'ai replied by referring to the letter of the Korean king to the President of the United States supplementing the treaty between the two countries. This letter, he said, was "of greatest importance and it alone must be

---

[88] Allen, *Things Korean*, 164. Dinsmore to Bayard, December 10, 24, 1889, in Korea: Dispatches, Vol. VI, nos. 212, 213.

[89] Tsiang, "Sino-Japanese Relations, 1870–1894," *loc. cit.*, 101.

[90] Dinsmore to Bayard, May 27, 1887, in Korea: Dispatches, Vol. IV, no. 20.

[91] *Id.* to *id.*, May 30, 1887, *ibid.*, no. 23.

looked to [to] ascertain the views held by my Government toward Korea." [92]

Though the American minister in Korea concluded that China's pretended seriousness about the dependent status of Korea was not authorized by the history of the two countries and that it was designed only "to assist in bringing about a relation which has never before existed," [93] Denby, the American minister to China, was inclined to a more realistic view. "The suzerainty of China," he stated, "over the great territories surrounding the Empire is one of the most difficult and shadowy questions arising in Eastern affairs." [94] While admitting that the relationship was a present and existing one and not a claim based merely on some former status, he was yet uncertain about what its legal elements were and what restrictions the superior state could impose on its inferior's dealings with Western countries. There was, he continued, color in Yüan Shih-k'ai's reply to Dinsmore [95] that the treaty with the United States had recognized Korea's dependent status, since the letter of the Korean king to the President referred to Korea's inferior position and obligations to China. On the other hand, he pointed out the letter's apparently contradictory assertion that the treaty was between equal states, and contended that China, in consenting to its terms, was thereby estopped from objecting to the sending of ministers *plenipotentiary* under it. Nevertheless, the situation, he admitted, was peculiar and worthy of consideration.[96]

Secretary Bayard, however, was not impressed by Minister Denby's statements. He had wired Denby an order "to express to the Chinese Government the surprise and regret with which the United States learns of obstructions being placed by Chinese officials in the way of Corea's diplomatic repre-

[92] *Id.* to *id.*, enc., October 15, 1887, *ibid.*, no. 63.
[93] *Foreign Relations*, 1888, p. 437.
[94] Denby to Bayard, October 13, 1887, *ibid.*, 222.
[95] See Yüan to Dinsmore, September 30, 1887, *ibid.*, 435–36.
[96] Denby to Bayard, October 13, 1887, *ibid.*, 223.

sentation in the United States as stipulated in existing treaty." [97] Upon the minister's reply referring to China's claims and Korea's acknowledgment, Bayard laid down the American policy in instructions which refused to go beyond the legal stipulations of the American-Korean treaty, and held that the United States, seeking only a responsible party with which to deal, interpreted the treaty to mean that Korea was responsible for her acts. The following paragraphs from Bayard's instructions are pertinent:

The essential thing is to fix the responsibility of execution of treaty stipulations, and to determine wherein lies the discretion which guides the acts of independent and sovereign states in their mutual relations. Whether the act performed is obligatory or permissive is not material, so long as it is done by the one contracting party in pursuance of a treaty compact with the other.

The reciprocal sending and receiving of diplomatic and consular officers is provided for in the treaty between the United States and Corea. No act of national sovereignty is more express and decided than this, and it is necessarily an attribute of the power to manage her own affairs, domestic and foreign, which, as the United States were assured when the treaty with Corea was negotiated, belonged to Corea, notwithstanding her tributary relation to China. That treaty sprang, logically, from the announcement of the Chinese Government that its treaties with foreign powers did not extend to Corea, and that it was in no way internationally responsible for any acts of Corea toward foreigners. By treaty Corea assumes that responsibility.

It seems, now, from your telegram, that the accepted sovereignty of Corea in her foreign relations is not absolute. It seems to be claimed by China that one of the simplest and most ordinary provisions of the treaty can not be executed without the King of Corea memorializing the Emperor of China and being accorded permission to do so.

The right to accord permission necessarily involves the right to refuse it, but the exercise of the latter right suggests a responsibil-

[97] Bayard to Denby, October 6, 1887, *ibid.*, 220.

ity which has not heretofore been admitted and is expressly disclaimed. What would have been the consequence if the Emperor of China, in the exercise of a sovereign claim of right, had refused to allow Corea to maintain a diplomatic mission in the United States?

I do not think the advisors of His Majesty the Emperor have considered the necessary inferences from the premises on which they act. For if the treaties of Corea with sovereign States can not be executed without the authority and consent of China, they can not be violated without the responsibility of China.

The Department's instructions to your legation, during the past few years, show the concern felt here at the indeterminateness of the question of China's relation to Corea. The object of this instruction is to impress like solicitude upon you, so that in any discussion affecting this question you may ascertain the real position of China, and avoid any admission that might be construed as approving China's singular claim of ultimate control without ultimate responsibility.[98]

Denby in reply disclaimed any attempt to fix Korea's relation to the society of nations, but in the following words he indicated that the rules of Western legalists should not be too literally applied in determining that relation:

Vattel discusses . . . the status of dependent states with reference to foreign powers. This discussion furnishes little information applicable to the peculiar relations existing between China and her dependent states. The text has little application to countries which, in their history, antedate international law, of which, also, they never had any knowledge. What unwritten law or tradition controls the relations of China with her dependencies remains unknown.[99]

He acknowledged, however, that the position of the United States was to regard the independence of Korea as established; and from the point of view of expediency he suggested

98 *Id.* to *id.*, November 4, 1887, *ibid.*, 266.
99 *Ibid.*, 236.

that if the independence thus recognized was to be preserved, the United States should consider such factors as the disorganized state of the country, its geographical position, and the possible acts of Japan, Russia, England, and China.[100]

Bayard replied, again defining the government's position. He referred to the king's letter sent to the President at the time the treaty was made as "the only official statement ever received by this Government as to Corea's relation to China," and stated that according to Admiral Shufeldt the treaty "was agreed to without any political consideration whatever." [101] He therefore concluded:

The position of the United States is that of simply requiring the observance of treaty obligations, and it is not thought expedient to pursue any controversy as to the relations of China and Corea, further than may be necessary to enable us to secure such observance. The interest of this Government is not political. It seeks merely the protection of American citizens and their commerce, and is not disposed to go beyond the point where such protection can be obtained.[102]

[100] *Ibid.*, 237.
[101] *Ibid.*, 255–56.
[102] *Ibid.*

CHAPTER X

DEVELOPMENT OF THE SINO-KOREAN RELATIONSHIP 1888-1895

1. KOREA'S STATUS TO THE WEST AND EAST

SECRETARY BAYARD had set in a strictly non-political atmosphere the American policy of dealing with Korea. This meant that the United States was disposed to go no further into the relationship of China and Korea than necessary to secure observance of the American-Korean treaty. Accordingly, with the political question of the acceleration of Chinese influence over Korean affairs, the United States was not concerned. Writing to his minister in Korea, Secretary Bayard stated:

If, contrary to the expectations of this Government, the progress of Chinese interference at Seoul should result in the destruction of the autonomy of Corea as a sovereign state with which the United States maintain independent treaty relations, it will be time then to consider whether this Government is to look to that of China to enforce treaty obligations for the protection of the persons and interests of citizens of the United States. . . .[1]

The political question of the growing *de facto* power of China in Korea, and the broader question of the whole nature of the Confucian relationship between the two countries, were projected into at least momentary discussion by O. N. Denny, the remaining Western opponent of Yüan Shih-k'ai in Korea and the king's American adviser. The policies of Li Hung-

[1] *Foreign Relations*, 1888, p. 237.

chang and the practice of attempting to make Denny subject to Yüan's orders influenced the adviser to ally himself with the cause of Korean independence in opposition to his Chinese rival, whom he termed a "smuggler, conspirator and diplomatic outlaw." [2]

Through Senator Mitchell, Denny had his views presented on the floor of the United States Senate on August 31, 1888.[3] In the course of his talk the Oregon senator, apparently anxious to stir up further antagonism toward China in connection with the discussion of the Chinese immigration question,[4] stated that

. . . if ever the Government of the United States was under obligation, either morally or by virtue of treaty stipulation with any foreign power, to exert its good offices in favor of any struggling people or government being unjustly, arbitrarily, and oppressively dealt with, then it is now called upon by each of the considerations to extend such good offices in a considerate and proper manner to the Government and people of Corea.[5]

For the most part, the senator's remarks consisted of the incorporation into the Senate records [6] of Denny's pamphlet *China and Korea,* a document significant not only for the vituperation heaped upon Yüan Shih-k'ai and the Chinese policies in general, but also for its attempt to argue into existence an independent sovereign Korea through the use of the tools of Western legalism.

Being a wholehearted acceptance of those concepts which existed in Western international law, and ignoring completely the existence of any *de facto* condition which Western publicists had not set up and defined, Denny's pamphlet is a rep-

[2] O. N. Denny, *China and Korea* (Shanghai, 1888). A copy of this pamphlet was enclosed, Dinsmore to Bayard, August 24, 1888, in Korea: Dispatches, Vol. V, no. 127; and it was reprinted in *Congressional Record,* XIX, 8136–40.

[3] *Congressional Record,* XIX, 8135–40.

[4] Dennett, "Early American Policy in Korea, 1883–1887," *loc. cit.,* 98 n.

[5] *Congressional Record,* XIX, 8135.

[6] *Ibid.,* 8136–40.

resentative summary of the attitude which the Western powers had rather consistently maintained toward the status of Korea since their first contacts were made with the peninsula. Its arguments completely failed to recognize the possibility that there could be a system of international relations not based, like that of the West, on legal concepts and the idea of the sovereign independence and equality of states, nor did it provide for any connection which did not fit into one of the categories prescribed by Western "international law." The most effective way the pamphlet had of disposing of the Chinese arguments concerning the status of Korea appears to have been the assertion that should such claims be admitted, "a new chapter will have been added to international jurisprudence, the principles of which such well-known expounders as Grotius, Vattel and Wheaton never comprehended." [7]

According to Denny, China's claim to the vassalage of Korea was false because, as judged by Western international law, Korea possessed certain definite characteristics of an independent and sovereign state. After quoting Wheaton's definition of a sovereign state,[8] Denny commented that "A nation which has always managed its internal as well as external concerns in its own way . . . is juridically independent and must be ranked in the category of sovereign states." [9] Among the reasons demanding that Korea be held independent and sovereign by the "law and the facts," he offered the following argument:

Corea has the right of negotiation; a vassal has not. Corea has concluded treaties . . . without reference to China, which a vassal can not do; and in virtue of those treaties has dispatched public ministers to the courts of her respective treaty powers, while vassal states can not even appoint consuls-general, but only consuls and commercial agents. Corea has the right to declare war or

[7] *Ibid.*, 8138.
[8] See Henry Wheaton, *Elements of International Law* (Boston, 1866), sec. 20.
[9] *Congressional Record,* XIX, 8137.

peace, which a vassal can not do except through its suzerain. China under her treaty is represented at the Corean court by a diplomatic officer, and by consuls at all the open ports. . . .[10]

Since Korea could not, under the Western concept, be a vassal of China and at the same time possess those attributes which the West held indicative of independence, her sovereign position was further confirmed, according to Denny. International law, he insisted, recognized a vassal status as springing from international agreement or conquest, and neither basis existed for the Chinese-Korean relationship. Furthermore, in a vassalage status, he continued, that "which disturbs the heart of the sovereign affects the pulse of the vassal, and so far as is known neither the wars which have been waged against China by foreign states, nor her rebellions, nor internal dissensions have apparently disturbed or concerned Corea. . . ." [11]

The obvious evidences that Korea had confessed her inferiority, Denny attacked in an ingenious way. Admitting that the nation had at times followed the commands of China, he again cited Wheaton, and Austin as well, to establish the principle that occasional obedience to a superior state does not affect the sovereignty or independence of the submissive power. Wheaton states his position in these words:

The sovereignty of a particular state is not impaired by its occasional obedience to the commands of other states, or even the habitual influence exercised by them over its councils. It is only when this obedience or this influence assumes the form of express compact that the sovereignty of the state inferior in power is legally affected by its connection with the other.[12]

The king's American adviser held also that Korea's inferiority to China as indicated by the payment of tribute did not constitute vassalage. That Korea was a tributary nation

10 *Ibid.*, 8138.
11 *Ibid.*
12 Wheaton, *International Law*, sec. 33.

he admitted, but that the paying of tribute constituted vassalage he denied. Here again Denny resorts to Wheaton for support of his assertion that Korea admitted vassalage by this act no more than did the European powers in their payment of tribute to the Barbary states.[13] The commercial regulations between China and Korea [14] in which Korea acknowledged her inferior status, were held by Denny to be no proof of her vassalage, but rather of her independence, for under them China secured extraterritorial privileges and the establishment of Chinese consuls in the open peninsula ports. Suzerains, according to Denny, did not send diplomatic representatives to their vassals, nor did they need to secure an extraterritorial status. He also took the position that the memorials of the Korean king to the Chinese emperor admitted only a tributary position, not one of vassalage.

Thus the fallacies of the Western reasoning in regard to the actual relationship between China and Korea are thrown into sharp relief. The West, through its diplomats, applied its own criteria of independence. Korea fitted the framework and hence was independent, even though her relations with China had always been maintained without reference to "international law" and despite the fact that both countries recognized the ties of their common system. The West likewise applied its own determinant of vassalage. Here Korea did not fit the category; therefore Korea was not subject to China, though both still maintained relations on a Confucian basis and recognized the inferior status of Korea. Denny tried to make a legal distinction between vassalage, which to him meant subservience and control, and a tributary position, which he held did not, in order to show why, though Korea made gifts to China and occasionally followed her wishes, the West held her independence unaffected.

13 *Ibid.*, sec. 37.
14 See pp. 159 ff.

This construction, however, could not in fact affect a status that was neither definable in Western words nor governable by Western law. Korea's position was actually that of a *shu-pang*, and the mere translation of these oriental characters into "tributary" or "vassal" certainly could not affect the living institutional relationship. To pronounce *shu-pang* and "vassal" synonymous and then to cite the Western qualities of a vassal as proof that Korea was not one appears to be shadow-boxing which completely failed to touch the relationship that existed. The whole misunderstanding about Korea's status was based on putting the *shu-pang* relation on the rack of Western categories and then trying to determine a non-Western status by Western rules.

Denny's attempt to bring the United States to Korea's aid was frustrated when Senator Mitchell's favorable resolution concerning the American adviser's views failed to emerge from the Committee on Foreign Affairs.[15] Moreover, Denny and Yüan Shih-k'ai had long been at odds, and as early as 1887 it was reported that the Korean king, presumably through Yüan's influence, had asked the American to resign and that Li Hung-chang had offered to send a new adviser to replace him.[16] After the publication of Denny's pamphlet in February, 1888, the issue between its author and Yüan became drawn. Each demanded the dismissal of the other. Before the year was out Denny was forced to resign,[17] and Chinese influence, as represented by Yüan Shih-k'ai, had removed another person who sought to turn the Korean king from dependence on China.

2. MATERIAL AND IDEOLOGICAL CONTROLS

Li Hung-chang's policy of increasing China's control over Korean affairs to prevent the growth of foreign influence in

[15] Dennett, "Early American Policy in Korea, 1883–1887," *loc. cit.*, 98 n.
[16] Rockhill to Bayard, January 22, 1887, in Korea: Dispatches, Vol. VI, no. 49.
[17] Morse, *International Relations*, III, 17–18.

the peninsula, and thus to preserve, by the use of Western techniques, the Confucian basis of Chinese-Korean relations, gained momentum as the persons opposed to Chinese hegemony fell by the way. But this objective demanded that China undertake to control the material progress of Korea as well as her diplomacy, in order to eliminate industrial developments motivated by political considerations. Looking to that end, the Chinese obtained the monopoly of Korean telegraphs on July 17, 1885, and completed a line from Peking to Seoul in November of the same year.[18] Attempts by Japan to get permission to build a line from Fusan to Seoul, thus providing a Japanese-controlled line from the capital to Tokyo, were refused; and the Korean government, with Chinese direction and capital, built the line itself, completing it in July, 1887.[19] When Korea tried to regain control of the telegraph system in 1889 by paying off the loan made for its construction, China evaded the issue by stating that an earlier unsecured loan to the China Steamship Company, on which the payment of interest had lapsed, must first be liquidated.[20]

Fearing that Korea's need for money would bring up the problem of loans to her by Western states, China moved to keep this sphere of activity also under her supervision. The initiative was taken by Sir Robert Hart, the controller of Chinese customs, who proposed to Li Hung-chang that China formally notify the foreign powers that future loans to Korea could be made only with Chinese approval. Though Li hesitated to follow this suggestion—since such a policy would not only cause Korea to ask his government for more financial aid, but would also encourage old creditors of Korea to turn to China with their claims [21]—still, as China's advisers

[18] H. N. Allen, *A Chronological Index: Some of the Chief Events in the Foreign Intercourse of Korea from the Beginning of the Christian Era to the Twentieth Century,* Supplement for 1901-1902 (Seoul, 1901), 18-19.

[19] *Ibid.,* 22; Dennett, *Americans in Eastern Asia,* 484.

[20] Tsiang, "Sino-Japanese Diplomatic Relations, 1870-1894," *loc. cit.,* 102.

[21] *Ibid.*

saw it, the monopoly of loans and the matter of getting Western recognition of the Chinese position in Korea were inseparably related. In August, 1889, Sir Robert's memorandum on Korean loans insisted that China's acceptance of the responsibility for Korea's debts would be conclusive evidence of the relationship desired and claimed. Since loans by other states would lead to foreign political influence, China, Hart argued, should stop such a threat by immediate notification of the powers feared.[22]

Though Li Hung-chang was still not inclined to take over Korea's financial obligations completely, he did virtually the same thing by making her two loans of 100,000 taels each through the Chinese Merchants Steamship Company at a comparatively low rate of interest.[23] In return, the steamship company received certain concessions, while China took over the Korean telegraphs and customs as securities for the loan.

While Li Hung-chang may have followed Western techniques in securing in Korea control of those spheres where foreign states might insert an economic wedge as a prelude to political action, he succeeded in maintaining the ancient relationship between the two countries. And China knew that Korean cooperation and nonresistance was not due to weakness alone, although it appeared to the Western states that her growing influence in Korea was similar to that which any aggressive state could achieve against a weak and disorganized country. What the Chinese had been able to accomplish in the peninsula rested upon the existence of the Confucian superior-inferior relation.

To those who had many times proved conclusively by Western international law that Korea was sovereign and independent, the mission from China in 1890 upon the occasion of the Korean dowager queen's death proved a startling dis-

[22] *Ibid.*, 103.
[23] See Heard to Foster, November 13, December 13, 1892, in Korea: Dispatches, Vol. IX, nos. 323, 344.

closure. Here, at the very end of the nineteenth century, Korea made the same humble acknowledgments of China's superiority that she had regularly offered in the most ancient times. The Korean king, according to custom, had dispatched an officer of the second rank to inform the Chinese emperor of the death of the queen dowager,[24] and in November of 1890 the return mission of condolence arrived bearing the imperial letter. Thereupon the king sent an officer of special rank to welcome the Chinese at Chemulpo, another was directed to meet them at the midway station on the road to Seoul, a third at the river suburb of the capital, and a fourth at the city palace which was constructed for and used only by imperial envoys.[25] As of old, the king went outside the city to greet the mission. The envoys were preceded by three small palanquins, one containing funeral presents, another vases, and the third, hung in imperial yellow, the imperial decree,

. . . conferring on the deceased Queen the first grade of the second class and the Imperial invocation . . . to be read before the tablet of the deceased and afterward burned. As the palanquin was borne before the King, the yellow curtains were drawn aside, and he is supposed to have prostrated himself in the interior of his tent.[26]

[24] Letter of the Korean king to the Chinese Emperor, *Notes on the Imperial Chinese Mission to Corea in 1890* (Shanghai, 1892), quoted by G. N. Curzon, *Problems of the Far East* (London, 1894), 211. The body of the letter follows:

"Our country is a small kingdom and a vassal State of China, to which the Emperor has shown his graciousness from time immemorial. Our Government was enabled to survive the political troubles of 1882 and 1884 through the assistance received from the Throne, which secured for our country peace and tranquillity. Since His Majesty has been good enough to confer these favors upon us, we should make known to him whatever we desire; and whatever we wish we trust that he may allow, as to an infant confiding in the tender mercies of its parents."

For a French version of this letter, see Henri Cordier, *Histoire générale de la Chine* (Paris, 1920), III, 223.

[25] Heard to Blaine, enc., November 17, 1890, in Korea: Dispatches, Vol. VII, no. 86.

[26] *Ibid.*

Ceremonial visits were then made and on November 11 the king returned to the same spot outside the city to bid the Chinese mission farewell.[27]

This incident, which was to be followed the next year by a congratulatory mission to China in observance of the emperor's twentieth birthday,[28] imparted, for the Western observers, a *de jure* status to China's *de facto* position in Korea. It served as a fitting climax to the efforts China had been making since the first Western contacts, to secure recognition of her claimed relationship with Korea and to give notice to the world of its actual existence. With other political influences almost wholly excluded, China had achieved, against much competition, a position which, even though the ceremonial evidence be disregarded, could not now be denied. The Western powers were beginning to attribute more force to the familial relationship which for two decades they had rejected as purely ceremonial. Concerning it the American representative at Seoul wrote:

> The feeling of the Corean toward the Emperor of China is not wholly, or mostly, one of political subserviency: it is rather one of religious deference. The head of a family in the East has a far higher position than he has in the West, and the elder brother has a real authority over the younger, a claim for service and devotion, which we can never recognize or understand.[29]

Li Hung-chang's policy was thus a success. Even Japan turned to China in 1892 to secure satisfaction for loss suffered because of the Korean embargo on her importation of beans from the peninsula.[30] The *Chinese Times* of November 3, 1890, in an article titled "Suzerainty," justly lauded the Middle Kingdom's control which had been maintained against even the Western invasion.

[27] *Ibid.*
[28] Allen to Blaine, May 22, 1891, *ibid.*, no. 163.
[29] Heard to *id.*, November 19, 1890, *ibid.*, no. 89.
[30] *Id.* to Gresham, May 6, 20, 1893, *ibid.*, Vol. X, nos. 396, 399.

To establish such relations with their outlying neighbors as that the latter should almost feel proud of owning an allegiênce to the Great Emperor, which cost nothing, yet which on the one side secured the empire from attack and on the other supplied the stable force which kept chieftains in their seats and kings on their thrones, was not the work of children, but of statesmen of the first class. To make policy accomplish the purposes of marching armies is the triumph of mind over matter which is the crown of state craft, and probably no government ever attained such perfect results in this direction as that of China has done. . . .[31]

3. THE SINO-JAPANESE WAR

It is probable that had war not intervened, the foreign powers would have soon felt constrained to remove their legations from Korea.[32] But Li Hung-chang was not seeking to make Korea again a "hermit nation" or even, despite the presence of the Chinese resident, to control her as a Chinese province. In an interview with Minister Dinsmore, Li stated that he had never contemplated any change in the relative position of China and Korea, that he was quite willing that foreign powers should treat Korea as if she were independent, but that his government would interfere if the king were to attempt to emancipate himself and to assert his independence.[33] By the spring of 1894 China's control of Korea, under a relation nominally the same as that which existed in 1882, was complete.[34] Within a year, however, it was all to be overthrown by force of arms.

After the failure of the Japanese-inspired *coup* of December 4, 1884,[35] the influence of Japan in Korea had noticeably declined. It appears, however, that Japan had by no means resigned herself to diplomatic defeat in the peninsula. But

[31] *Id.* to Blaine, enc., February 23, 1891, *ibid.*, Vol. VII, no. 125.
[32] H. B. Hulbert, *The Passing of Korea* (New York, 1906), 127.
[33] Heard to Blaine, June 22, 1891, in Korea: Dispatches, Vol. VIII, no. 175.
[34] Tsiang, "Sino-Japanese Relations, 1870–1894," *loc. cit.*, 104.
[35] See pp. 171–72.

further aggressiveness would have meant war with China, and, in a debate in the Japanese parliament between the pro-war and pro-peace parties in 1885, Ito and Inouye were able to commit their government to a policy of peace. The leader of the war party, General Count Kuroda, alarmed at China's naval expansion after the war with France in Tongking, wished to strike before China would be too strong. Ito, in refutation of this view, and pointing to Japan's annual peace-time deficit, urged a husbanding of resources, further West-ernization, and a strengthening of the navy. He deprecated the seeming increase in Chinese military power and held that China would, after temporary activity, lapse again into sleep. Since her military officers were chosen according to their pro-ficiency with a bow and arrow, and since her civil officials were selected on their ability to write eight-legged essays, he was convinced that any progressive proposal to the Chinese authorities would be buried beneath an avalanche of memo-rials from reactionary elements. Count Inouye also stressed the point that a premature war with China would serve only to benefit Russia. Since the emperor personally backed the peace party, its policy was the one Japan followed after 1885.[36]

The Japanese government, accordingly, viewed the rapid growth of Chinese influence in the peninsula with apparent indifference, holding it to be a matter of comparatively little concern whether or not Korea retained her independence. The *Nichi Nichi Shimbun* was quoted as saying that "If matters in Korea come to a crisis Japanese politicians ought to make up their minds to have nothing to do with that country." [37] Minister Dinsmore in Seoul, reporting that the Japanese rep-resentative there appeared indifferent to Chinese encroach-ments, also indicated the trend of things in Korea as described by the *Nichi Nichi Shimbun:*

[36] Tsiang, "Sino-Japanese Relations, 1870–1894," *loc. cit.,* 105.
[37] Quoted in Dennett, *Americans in Eastern Asia,* 485 n.

. . . she [Korea] has the name of an independent country without the reality. She is going down hill with no probability of being able to recover herself and therefore rather than that she should be exposed to the risk of attack by some strong power it is better for her to become an outer province of China.[38]

For a brief period in 1893 Japan resumed an aggressive policy toward Korea but was forced to abandon it under the realization that China held the whip hand in that area. In 1893 Oishi Masanai replaced Kajiyama as Japan's representative in Korea. Through his arrogance and aggressive attitude concerning the embargo upon the export of beans, which was then the chief difficulty between his country and Korea, Oishi was in sharp contrast to his predecessor.[39] Failing in his attempt to secure access to the king by subterfuge, he delivered an ultimatum demanding compensation within fourteen days for losses due to the embargo.[40] Ito saved the situation by wiring Li Hung-chang and asking him to request Korea to settle the affair.[41] Under China's urging, the Koreans reluctantly satisfied the Japanese claim.

Oishi returned to Japan on June 2, 1893, and was replaced by Otori, whose appointment was said to indicate a conciliatory policy on the part of Japan toward China. With an eye on Russian designs, Japan was presumably broadening her established policy of not making war with China into one of actual cooperation with the Middle Kingdom through the recognition of its position in Korea. This is indicated by Ito's settlement of the bean controversy through the mediation of Li Hung-chang, and by the fact that Otori was credited to Peking as well as to Seoul. These moves, however, were not made without an ulterior motive. As the American representa-

[38] Dinsmore to Bayard, March 27, 1887, in Korea: Dispatches, Vol. IV. no. 20.
[39] Heard to Foster, March 27, 1893, ibid., Vol. IX, no. 376.
[40] Id. to Gresham, May 6, 1893, ibid., Vol. X, no. 396.
[41] Id. to id., May 20, 1893, ibid., no. 399.

tive in Japan viewed it, Japan's policy was to allow Korea to be recognized as belonging to China in order to forestall the designs of any other country and then, when Japan should fight China, Korea could be taken without fear of protest from the European powers.[42] This interpretation appeared to be confirmed by information from Peking which stated that the Japanese representative had proposed to the Chinese government that the two powers cooperate in ousting all Western foreigners from Korea.[43]

At the Tientsin convention of April 18, 1885, China and Japan each agreed not to send troops into Korea except in case of a disturbance "of a grave nature" and then only after previous notification of the other in writing.[44] Obviously, as long as China kept no troops in Korea, Japan could send none without risking the ire of the other powers. But should China be compelled by peninsula disorders to dispatch military forces, Japan could do likewise, and, once in Korea, superior force could achieve what had baffled diplomacy. Such an opportunity presented itself with the rise of the Korean sect of the Tong Hak (*Tung-hsüeh*) or "Eastern Learning" society.[45] Based upon a creed compounded of Confucianism, Buddhism, and Taoism, the organization at first made peaceful attempts to secure redress for the wrong it suffered when its founder was executed as a heretic, and also to get government recognition of its existence. However, the society soon acquired a political complexion, since it gathered in those elements made discontented by years of official oppression. Its religious purpose became secondary to its anti-foreign, anti-Christian, anti-Japanese policies, a transformation which, it was pointed out, indicated the possibility that the Tai-wün-kun was again

---

[42] *Id* to *id.*, July 29, 1893, *ibid.*, no. 428.
[43] *Id.* to Foster, February 10, 1893, *ibid.*, Vol. IX, no. 364.
[44] *Korea: Treaties and Agreements*, 7–8.
[45] For the history of this sect, which dated back to 1859, see W. M. Junkin, "The Tong Hak," in *Korean Repository*, II (1895), 56–60.

making a bid for power through this group.[46] Unconfirmed rumors of uprisings in the south reached the Korean capital, and the foreign legations there received threatening communications presumably from the Tong Hak.[47]

When actual rebellion broke out in the southern provinces of the peninsula, and when the troops sent to quell it were defeated, the Korean king requested Chinese military aid of Li Hung-chang. Though he had refused Yüan Shih-k'ai's plea for troops a month earlier because the king himself had not asked for them, Li was now hesitant to take this step even at the ruler's behest. On June 6, 1894, however, 1500 soldiers were sent from Tientsin, with 725 to follow. According to the American chargé in Peking, Li "formally assured the Japanese Government that these troops shall be withdrawn immediately upon the cessation of hostilities. . . ." [48] Significantly, in the Chinese announcement Korea was referred to as "our tributary state." [49] The Japanese replied on the same day, stating that they were likewise to send a body of troops.[50] Their statement also referred to the words "tributary state" which appeared in the Chinese note, and declared that the Japanese government had never recognized Korea as a tributary state of China.[51] China sent another dispatch on June 9 which pointed out that the Middle Kingdom was merely following the traditional practice of protecting its tributary states and that, as Japan's sole object was the protection of her legation, consulates, and commercial people, there was no need for a large body of Japanese troops, nor for the pres-

---

[46] *Foreign Relations,* 1894, App. I, p. 11; "Russian Documents Relating to the Sino-Japanese War, 1894–1895" (from *Krasny Archiv,* L–LI, 3–63), in *Chinese Social and Political Science Review,* XVII (1933–34), 480–515.

[47] For manifestos and warnings to foreigners, see *Foreign Relations,* 1894, App. I, pp. 8–9, 13–14.

[48] *Ibid.,* 20.

[49] Quoted in Treat, *Diplomatic Relations,* II, 450.

[50] Shuhsi Hsü, *China,* 152.

[51] *Ibid.,* 151–52.

ence in the interior of any of those sent, particularly since Korea had not requested Japanese aid. Japan replied on the twelfth that she had never recognized Korea's tributary position to China, that she had dispatched troops under the treaty of 1882 with Korea, which allowed Japanese guards for Japanese legations, and that she would be the judge as to the disposition of her military forces.[52]

Since the rebellion had been suppressed by the native soldiery before the Chinese arrived, when it was learned that Japan was sending troops without invitation, the Korean king requested the Chinese to leave, and they consented.[53] However, when the 500 Japanese marines who had landed at Chemulpo proceeded to Seoul (the capital) on June 10, the Chinese held their troops at Asan, which was south of the capital and where they were already encamped. On June 13, 800 Japanese soldiers relieved the marines, and some 200 more were distributed between the capital and the coast. On the sixteenth an additional 3000 arrived, and others were reported as being sent to the coastal cities of Fusan and Wünsan.[54]

Mutsu, the Japanese foreign minister, and Otori, the minister to Korea, both assured foreign representatives that the purpose of the Japanese soldiers in Korea was only to protect Japanese persons and property.[55] Yet with the uprising suppressed, Japan refused to remove her troops until the Chinese had withdrawn. On June 16 the Japanese foreign minister proposed to China joint action in suppressing the revolts and in introducing financial, administrative, and military reforms in the Korean government. The Chinese reply pointed out that the rebellion had already been suppressed, that China would not interfere in the internal administration of Korea,

[52] Treat, *Diplomatic Relations*, II, 451.
[53] *Foreign Relations*, 1894, App. I, p. 20.
[54] *Ibid.*
[55] "Russian Documents . . . ," *loc. cit.*, 489–91; Treat, *Diplomatic Relations*, II, 449; *Foreign Relations*, 1894, App. I, p. 21.

and that Japan, having from the very first recognized Korea's independence, certainly had no right to do so.[56]

On June 24, Korea sought to end the deadlock by requesting the Western representatives in Korea to offer the friendly offices of their governments to effect an amiable solution of the situation.[57] Accordingly, the representatives of the United States, Russia, France, and England submitted a joint note to China and Japan suggesting simultaneous withdrawal.[58] To this suggestion the Chinese agreed, but the Japanese reply was evasive.[59]

Japan then took the initiative, and on June 26 Otori had an audience with the Korean king in which he presented a paper by order of his sovereign,

stating that Japan found it necessary, for the mutual welfare of the two countries, to ask that certain radical changes be made in the government and policy of Korea, such changes to be made upon consultation with the Japanese authorities, and until these changes are made in a manner satisfactory to Japan the Japanese troops would not be withdrawn.[60]

Korean delay in setting up a council to hear the Japanese requests brought forth an ultimatum from Otori on the twenty-eighth wherein he demanded to know by the following day whether or not Korea was a tributary of China.[61] This placed Korea in a delicate position, as a definite answer was bound to offend either China or Japan. After several reminders to be prompt had been delivered by the Japanese, the answer, made up of a past statement inspired and approved by China and one inspired and approved by Japan, was delivered. To satisfy Japan the Japanese-Korean treaty of 1876 was quoted to the effect that "Korea, being an in-

[56] Treat, *Diplomatic Relations*, II, 452–53.
[57] Sill to Gresham, June 25, 1894, in Korea: Dispatches, Vol. XI, no. 15.
[58] *Foreign Relations*, 1894, App. I, pp. 23–24.
[59] *Ibid.*, 26–27.
[60] *Ibid.*, 25–26.
[61] Sill to Gresham, July 2, 1894, in Korea: Dispatches, Vol. XI, no. 23.

dependent state enjoys the same sovereign rights as does Japan." [62] Nor could China very well object to the statement, drawn from the Chinese-inspired letter of the Korean king to the President of the United States, which stated, in the English translation, that in both internal administration and foreign intercourse Korea enjoyed complete independence. [63]

On July 14, Japan informed China that the sending of more soldiers to Korea would be considered a hostile act, [64] and on the twentieth she demanded that the Korean government order the Chinese troops already there to leave, intimating Japanese action if a favorable response was not forthcoming. [65] In the early morning of the twenty-third the decisive step was taken when Japanese troops, after some resistance and with some connivance from Koreans within, occupied the royal palace and took possession of the king's person. The Tai-wün-kun then appeared and was made regent. [66] On the following day the now Japanese-dominated Korean government signed an agreement authorizing Japan to expel the Chinese forces. [67] On the twenty-fifth the British steamer *Kowshing,* transporting Chinese troops, was sunk by the Japanese. [68] Three days later the Chinese government acknowledged the outbreak of hostilities; and on August 1 both China and Japan declared war. [69] On the sixteenth Korea announced the abrogation of all treaties and agreements binding her to China. [70]

[62] See p. 131.
[63] Sill to Gresham, July 2, 1894, in Korea: Dispatches, Vol. XI, no. 23. See pp. 145–46.
[64] "A Retrospect, 1894," in *Korean Repository,* II (1895), 32.
[65] *Ibid.*
[66] Sill to Gresham, July 24, 1894, in Korea: Dispatches, Vol. XI, no. 33.
[67] Text in *American Journal of International Law,* I, Supplement (1907), 214.
[68] *Foreign Relations,* 1894, App. I, pp. 41–42, 45–47.
[69] See *ibid.,* 53–54, for statement of Chinese emperor; *Korea: Treaties and Agreements,* 8–10, for Japanese declaration of war.
[70] Sill to Gresham, August 17, 1894, in *Korea: Dispatches,* Vol. XI, no. 43.

During the interval preceding the actual military conflict, China constantly affirmed the position of Korea as that of a nation long dependent on China. Reviewing the events which led to the dispatch of her troops to the peninsula, she cited precedents of previous occasions when similar action had been taken.[71] Japan had been willing earlier to pass over the ceremonial relations between China and Korea, but after 1885 she saw clearly that those relations rested upon a Confucian basis which implied much more than mere ceremony or ritual. For, without altering the principles of the relationship, China had been attaining more and more control in Korea. Hence, before she was completely excluded, Japan decided to destroy the relationship by force. That this was the cause of the war is clearly revealed by the following statement of Count Ito to the Japanese House of Representatives:

There also exists conclusive evidence that on the King of Korea's appealing, or rather being compelled to appeal, to China for the dispatch of troops, China intended by using the suppression of the Tong Hak rebellion as a pretext to destroy the independence of Korea and make her in reality a tributary state. Thereupon our country was obliged to wage war. . . .[72]

After the Japanese forces began pouring into Korea in large numbers, it was soon realized by foreign observers that Japan's objective was not merely to suppress the Tong Haks or to protect Japanese persons and property,[73] but to challenge by force of arms the Chinese claim to Korea as a dependent nation. The charge that Japan started the war as a diversion from domestic embarrassments which the government faced does not, therefore, tell the whole story. As Treat points out:

[71] See *Foreign Relations*, 1894, App. I, pp. 48, 51, 53.
[72] *Japan Daily Mail*, February 25, 1895, quoted in *Foreign Relations*, 1894, App. I, p. 105.
[73] See *ibid.*, 22; "Russian Documents . . . ," *loc. cit.*, 501–502.

In the first place, the Japanese Government instituted a strict censorship of the press in the early days of the dispute; secondly, the issue was not forced upon China, but developed almost two months after the Japanese had first taken offense at the repeated assertion of Chinese suzerainty over Korea; thirdly, public opinion, as reflected in the vernacular press, was strongly of the opinion that Japan should, as Mr. Sill expressed it, "throw off the yoke of Chinese suzerainty" in Korea—it was not necessary for the Government to stir up an imagined *casus belli*, for the irritation produced by Chinese interference in Korea had long been present. . . . The only responsibility which may be attached to the Japanese Government was in the decision, in 1894, to settle once and for all the claim of China to interfere in Korea. . . .[74]

The Western nations apparently were in sympathy with the Japanese stand. For years they had been attempting to define Korea's actual position in the society of nations, and they had long resented both Yüan Shih-k'ai's assumption of a station above that of their own representatives and China's claims to a favorable position not legally hers by Western law. They considered the main cause of the war to be the assertion by China of a superior relation to Korea. When advising the distressed Chinese Foreign Office on the possibilities of peace, Chargé Denby in Peking expressed the Western attitude in these words:

I stated that it would not be proper for me to utter any opinion as to which nation was to blame, but I would express an opinion which generally existed as to one cause of the war. I said that the view was that the attitude of China towards Corea was not consistent; that China had consented that Corea should make treaties with foreign powers; that thereby she admitted the independence of Corea, nevertheless she still claimed a species of suzerainty over her. The Ministers said that the King of Corea had, when he made the treaty with the United States, written a letter to the President, wherein he stated that he was a tributary of China. I

[74] Treat, *Diplomatic Relations*, II, 459–61.

said yes, but that, in the same letter, he stated that he had the right to make treaties as an independent power, and, in the first article of the Japanese treaty with Corea, it is stated "Chosen, being an independent state, enjoys the same sovereign rights as does Japan." [75]

Thus the misunderstanding and conflict over Korea's status which began with the first official Western contact in 1866 continued until the increasing confusion brought about the end of that status. The West held that a nation which possessed the attributes of statehood prescribed by Western international law was sovereign and independent, and that another nation which acknowledged these elements was thereby estopped from claiming the existence of a relation of authority and subserviency between itself and the state whose sovereignty was recognized. China was unable to gain recognition of her claim that, regardless of Korea's status as defined by Western international law, the smaller nation was in truth secured to her, in a relationship entirely apart from Western legal tenets, by a natural, social, Confucian bond.

4. End of the Confucian Relationship

The Sino-Japanese War brought to an end the peculiar relationship between China and Korea, a relationship whose origins went back into the early antiquity of both countries. The loss of this last *shu-pang* ("dependent country") meant also the virtual end of the theory of a Confucian family of nations. Now China stood alone, deprived of her border wardens. With no nation to acknowledge her superior and divine position as the Middle Kingdom, she was henceforth compelled to deal with all on a basis of equality under Western international law.

In summarizing the actions which China had taken concerning Korea's relation to the West and to the Middle King-

[75] Quoted in *ibid.*, 494–95.

dom, one can safely say that behind all of the policies pursued was her constant determination to maintain the traditional *shu-pang* position of Korea. "This peculiar form of subservience based as it is on Confucian theories, which have shaped all Chinese and Korean society and made the people of those countries what they are, must never be lost sight of in studying Korea's relations with and to China." [76] One need not suppose a Chinese desire to modify the accustomed Sino-Korean relationship, or an ambition for overt sovereignty over Korea. Control was established through ideas—Confucian beliefs which automatically led to subservience to China; and with this creed as the very civilization of the two countries, neither desired a change. One cannot suppose that China suddenly in the last of the nineteenth century became an aggrandizing power at Korea's expense. She sought instead merely to maintain the traditional status of Korea; and her actions were replies to outside threats to that status. [77]

Thus when the French in 1866 sought to determine the relationship between China and Korea, the Chinese made no effort to vary from the traditional status. They held, as they always had, that they did not administer Korea's external and internal affairs and hence were not liable for the death of French nationals. A similar position was maintained toward the Americans in 1871. China did advise Korea to give a courteous reception to the Westerners, though she kept asserting that Korea was her dependency. Similarly, a courte-

[76] Rockhill, *China's Intercourse with Korea*, 3.

[77] This is well brought out in the following letter of Sir Robert Hart, written on May 29, 1888, to H. F. Merrill, the head of the Korean customs.

"In all that concerns Korea, the one point to start from is that Korea *is* China's tributary, and that China *will not only* fight anybody rather than give up her suzerainty, *but will* be forced to absorb Korea if troublesome scheming goes on there. It is useless for America to say 'assert your independence!' It is useless for Japan to say 'come to my arms!' . . . The backing that your people [the Americans] are giving the King and the temptations the Japanese are putting in his path are alike pitfalls . . . : if Korea 'flirts' she will lose all her lovers after falling a prey to the monetary power of one of them. . . ." Morse, *International Relations*, III, 15–16 n.

ous reception was advised for the Japanese, whose efforts resulted in Korea's first modern treaty.

China later came to consider this Japanese-Korean treaty as a threat and a prelude, a threat to the status of Korea from Japan and a prelude to similar action by other powers. Unable to protect Korea by force and aiming to balance the political designs of Japan and Russia, Li Hung-chang followed, after 1876, a policy of encouraging Korea to have treaty relations with the Western commercial powers. The admonitions from China ceased to be purely ceremonial, now that a threat existed to the relation, and Korea was urged to make herself physically strong. The power of investiture was used as a basis for removing the Tai-wün-kun, who sought to rule in opposition to China's policies.

Between 1882 and 1885 the Chinese government found it necessary to protect its relationship with Korea by supplying the advisers that Korea needed in such fields as customs and foreign affairs, thus thwarting Western influences which would turn the Korean king toward another country or to a renunciation of his dependent status. This policy was augmented by the dispatch of Chinese troops to quell rebellious factions seeking such ends through the seizure of the king's person.

Despite all these precautions, the Korean king, under Western influences, was weakening in his allegiance to the *shu-pang* status. With this weakening in the ideological control of Confucian principles, China extended her physical domination further and further into such spheres as telegraphs, customs, loans, and foreign relations. A Chinese resident was sent to advise the king on foreign relations, while Chinese capital built the telegraphs and supplied the loans. The result of these endeavors was that by 1894 the Middle Kingdom had attained approximately the degree of control which Western states achieved only through a protectorate established by treaty. When war occurred, her predominance in Korea was recognizable even by Western standards. China, however, thought of her relationship to Korea as remaining, during the entire period, Confucian and alien to any Western status, even though the Chinese policies tended to approximate those of the legalist West.

The entire trend of Chinese policy from 1866 to 1895 was misunderstood by the Western treaty powers, mainly because they made no attempt to fathom the *shu-pang* status and judged the relationship of the two Far Eastern countries by Western international law. Moreover, the West characteristically approached the East as it had approached the rest of the non-European world, assuming the superiority and universality of European legal norms. The initial error in the reasoning of the Western states was their interpretation of China's disavowal of control over the actual administration of Korean affairs as a renunciation of her "suzerainty" and an earnest of Korean independence. The *shu-pang* relation was too casually assumed to be that of a suzerain and vassal, but since China disavowed a vital element of Western suzerainty, the Sino-Korean relationship, of which the West had only vaguely heard, was no longer thought to exist. Korea, then, to those knowing only a theory of legal equality and sovereignty among states, was sovereign and independent.

This thesis was confirmed in the Western mind by China's action in approving a treaty made by Korea with Japan and also by her helping the Western states in later negotiations. Moreover, just as China's disavowal of control over the internal and foreign affairs of Korea estopped any Chinese claim of suzerainty, so the Korean prerogatives of making treaties and carrying on foreign relations seemed definite proof that Korea was a sovereign state. Not only did the treaties acknowledge this equality between the contracting parties, but the king of Korea himself had affirmed it in supplementary letters. The fact that he had also referred to Korea as a *shu-pang* of China was held by Western statesmen to be of no moment, since his government at the same time accepted the responsibility of enforcing the treaties.

Clearly then, as Western observers saw it, any ties existing between China and Korea were of a religious and ceremonial nature and without effect on the terms of a legal document. The West therefore considered Korea legally sovereign and independent, and could point to the admission of China and the declaration of the treaties themselves to substantiate the conclusion. If China claimed a special control over Korea, let her then accept international responsibility for Korea, they argued, since such responsibility was stipulated in the international law by which all were assumed to be bound. As for the ceremonies of tribute and subservience which Korea regularly paid to China, these were thought to represent the full extent of the *shu-pang* status; hence this Far Eastern relationship was held by the West to be of little import.

Consequently, when China was able after 1885 to increase markedly her actual control of Korean affairs, her moves were viewed by the Western states as pure aggression against a sovereign and independent state and as attempts to inaugurate an entirely new Sino-Korean association, though in theory she proceeded on the basis of the *shu-pang* relationship. It has even been held that this attempt to set up a new status for Korea led to the war with Japan, and that the war was not an attempt on Japan's part to destroy an old status.[78] This conclusion was based, however, on the assumption that the evidences of Korea's status which were observed in times when no strain was felt upon it, constituted its limits and entirety—that the payment of ceremonial tribute *was* the status rather than a mere traditional peace-time characteristic of it.

But if there was no more to the *shu-pang* relation than tribute payment, why did Korea follow Chinese instructions

---

[78] See Payson J. Treat, "China and Korea, 1885–1895," in *Political Science Quarterly*, XLIX (1934), 506–43, for this view.

on every issue? And how was China able to achieve in Korea the degree of control she secured after 1885? No treaty gave her the right to remove the Tai-wün-kun and receive the king's thanks for it. No treaty gave her the power to appoint foreign advisers to the Korean departments. No treaty gave her the right to name Yüan Shih-k'ai resident in Korea with control of foreign relations or to elevate him to a rank superior to that of all other foreign representatives located there. Only through a series of some twenty-five treaties was Japan able to achieve a degree of control in Korea comparable with that which China possessed in 1894. If the relationship between China and Korea involved no more than ceremonial tribute, then upon what basis was all this accomplished?

In this connection it is necessary to understand that the *shu-pang* relation was not based on any legal contract exactly defining the rights and obligations of the two parties concerned. It was not possible to say that thus far could China go and no further; that thus far China was obligated and no further. The status was a natural, family relationship, wherein the fact that the elder brother took little interest in the affairs of the younger in times of order and security was no bar to a wider scope of action when the interests of the family were threatened.

To hold further that Korea's treaties with the Western states freed her from any dependent relation to China is a *non sequitur*. Though the treaty of Korea with the United States did acknowledge equality of the two parties, it was no assurance that one of them could not have, and be governed by, a superior in some other system of relations which did not include the United States. That is, to say that Korea's entrance into treaty relations made her independent by international law is to raise the question: By whose international law? In truth, to China and to Korea treaty relations and international law were of no consequence in determining whether Korea acknowledged China's superiority or not, for the *shu-pang* relation had existed long before treaty-making power was viewed as an essential attribute of sovereignty. Obviously, the prevalent confusion over Korea's statehood did not derive from a genuine problem. The Western allegations were completely correct if—and this is a significant point—the first Korean-Japanese or Korean-American treaty is taken as a symbolic act, and if, as a second fundamental assumption, this symbolic act must be regarded as transferring the entire pre-existing system of Far Eastern international relations into the juridical and political framework of the Western state system. That this was not the case in the eyes of either China or Korea is evident from the record. Yet certainly the West had some justification for its conception of the status of Korea. It is entirely logical by Western reasoning that control and responsibility should be within the same sphere. If Korea was subservient to China, then the powers should have looked to China for the enforcement of their Korean treaties. But if China disavowed that responsibility and Korea pledged her own word for the treaty obligations, how, then, could China consistently have claimed the authority to regulate Korea's relations with the Western states? The Western powers were essentially seeking the seat of responsibility in international law. If China had to approve the sending of Korean legations to the West, inferentially she could have disapproved of this and of other treaty commitments. Where, then, would the West have looked for enforcement? Thus Western legalists felt themselves constrained to deny any legal effect of China's claim or of the *shu-pang* relation, believing that no other course was sound.

If the treaty powers had known or cared to find out about the Confucian principles, they might have been able, through Confucian arguments, and without altering the *shu-pang* status, to persuade the Chinese to accept a responsibility for Korea's foreign relations. Within the Chinese family the parent or elder brother, in addition to his right of absolute control over an inferior member of the family in times of stress, was also responsible to the emperor for the misdemeanors of his family. China, the older brother, would therefore by analogy be responsible under Confucian theory for the misdemeanors of Korea. The analogy is not perfect, however, because the Chinese emperor was responsible only to Heaven and in no case to another state. But if the Western powers had used Confucian instead of legal reasoning, and if they had accordingly pointed out to China her obligation as a Confucian nation to her younger brother nation, it is entirely possible that the Chinese would have agreed. Or, had the Western powers accepted the fact that China did exercise the dominant influence over Korea, and had they exerted pressure upon China to secure their demands of Korea, a more successful arrangement might have resulted. Certainly Korea did follow China's advice, and success did attend those efforts which, regardless of any legal status, had recognized the Chinese superiority. Exactly so had the United States been able to secure a treaty with Korea when attempts through other agencies had failed. Exactly so had Japan succeeded in getting a settlement of the "bean controversy" with Korea. Since the Western legal concept of international responsibility was at variance with the Eastern *de facto* system, the West could have arrived at a more satisfactory solution by going outside legal fictions.[79] But such a policy was not pursued. Rather than accept a relationship for which no Western category existed, Western statecraft allowed Korea to maintain a short period of fictional independence after the Sino-Japanese War and before her real status was openly declared by using the purely Western words "protectorate" and "annexation" to describe it.

[79] If, however, there was an emotional dislike for the Chinese claims of superiority over the Koreans and if there was a belief that Korea was, and of right should have been, independent and equal to China in the Western sense, the legal position of the West, exemplified in the arguments of O. N. Denny, offered the best basis for action. See pp. 193 ff.

Part III

KOREA IN THE WESTERN STATE SYSTEM

CHAPTER XI

LEGAL INDEPENDENCE UNDER RIVAL SPONSORSHIP

1. JAPANESE SPONSORSHIP, 1894–1896

THE Sino-Japanese War changed the nature of the problems which Korea faced. Henceforth, she was to witness no clash of systems of international relations. Instead, she was to be involved in the conflicts of diplomatic policies and power politics of states under the Western system, though these disturbances would now take place in a Korea legally independent, yet actually possessing a habit of mind retained from her former Confucian relationship with China. Under the alternate domination of stronger neighbors, she was to be merely a tool for the execution of the international policies of these contending states.

Even before war between China and Japan was declared, the Japanese had made a move which was to be the keystone of their Korean policy during and immediately after the war. This important action was the seizure of the person of the king of Korea [1] and the surrounding of his office with Japanese advisers and with a cabinet of pro-Japanese Koreans, including the Tai-wün-kun, who was virtually the regent.[2] Thus the fiction of Korea's independence could be main-

---

[1] See *Foreign Relations*, 1894, App. I, p. 40. The Japanese guard in the king's palace was replaced on August 25, 1894, by Koreans armed with sticks, who later were given rifles but no ammunition. F. A. McKenzie, *The Tragedy of Korea* (New York, n.d.), 49.

[2] *Foreign Relations*, 1894, App. I, p. 41.

tained, though her government was reorganized actually to serve the interests of the Japanese.

The first action of the new government after the seizure of the palace was the abrogation of the commercial regulations of 1882, which constituted the only legal agreement between China and Korea proclaiming their superior-inferior relation.[3] On August 15, 1894, the president of the Korean Foreign Office, at the insistence of Otori, the Japanese minister, notified the foreign powers of the abrogation of these regulations but offered no explanation beyond the quotation of Otori's note requesting the act.[4] Still closer collaboration of Korea with Japan was guaranteed by their alliance of August 26, 1894, which was to be operative until the conclusion of peace with China. The object of this agreement, according to its first article, was "to maintain the Independence of Korea on a firm footing and to promote the respective interests of both Japan and Korea by expelling Chinese soldiers from Korean territory."[5]

The internal reorganization of the peninsula was not, however, to await the conclusion of peace. Korea's old governmental system, modeled on that of the Ming rulers, had undergone no major change since the foundation of the incumbent dynasty. The king, absolute in theory, was advised by a cabinet, the *Eui-chyüng Pu*, which was made up of a Prime Minister (*Lyung-eui-chyüng*), a Senior Minister of State (*Chwa*), and a Junior Minister (*U*).[6] Between 1882 and 1884 two new departments were created, the Home Office (*Nai-mu Pu*) and the Foreign Office (*Oi A-mun*).[7] To make this machinery of government serve his purpose better, just

[3] See pp. 159 ff.
[4] *Foreign Relations*, 1894, App. I, pp. 55–56.
[5] *Korea: Treaties and Agreements*, 10–11.
[6] Wilkinson, *The Corean Government Constitutional Changes*, 11.
[7] *Ibid.* For the complete organization of the Korean government before 1894, see *ibid.*, 1–41.

before the outbreak of hostilities between Japan and China the Japanese minister in Korea caused a new council to be appointed to consider his requests and to recommend reforms.[8] Known as the "Chamber of Affairs for the State Militant" (*Kun Kuk Keui Mu Ch'yü*), this new advisory body was considered a department within the cabinet, and it proposed, from the end of July, 1894, through the following August, a long series of recommendations. Few of these were put into force, however, since the drive for reform was quietly sabotaged when the council members declined to convene for deliberations.[9] The final session of the group occurred on October 29 [10] shortly after the arrival of Japan's great statesman, Count Inouye.

On the basis of the proposals which the council had made, Inouye drew up twenty recommendations for the reorganization of Korea, and these were presented to the Korean king on November 20.[11] Here, however, the Japanese encountered trouble with the acting regent, the Tai-wün-kun, who refused his assent but who was induced to resign and retire to private life in December.[12] On the seventeenth of the same month, Inouye succeeded in having the non-cooperative Chamber of Affairs for the State Militant dissolved. A new departmentalized cabinet (*Nai Kak*) on the Japanese model was then set up with the following functional divisions: Prime Minister and Vice Prime Minister, Ministers of Home, Law, and War, Departments of Public Works, Agriculture and Commerce, Finance, Foreign Affairs, and Education and Household.[13] Moreover, the *Court Gazette* of December 10 had announced

[8] See p. 209.
[9] See *Foreign Relations*, 1894, App. I, pp. 63–68, for recommendations.
[10] Wilkinson, *The Corean Government Constitutional Changes*, 1–2.
[11] "Great Changes in the Korean Government," in *Korean Repository*, II (1895), 111–18.
[12] *Ibid.*, 112–13; "A Retrospect, 1894," *loc. cit.*, 35.
[13] See "A Retrospect, 1894," *loc. cit.*, 36, for appointees; American minister's comment, *Foreign Relations*, 1894, App. I, pp. 84–85.

the pardon of all who had engaged in the Japanese-inspired *coup* of 1884,[14] and several who had been exiles and branded as traitors before 1894 were included in the new cabinet.[15] The last of Count Inouye's recommendations stated that "For the purpose of securing the independence of Korea the above Article of Reform and National Policy should be presented at the shrine of the Ancestral Temple and be published for the benefit of the people." [16] The king, in a formal ceremony January 7, 1895, swore to observe the twenty recommendations for Korea's reorganization. Naturally, Count Inouye made quite a celebration of the affair despite the fact that the king performed his role in the proceedings with ill grace.[17]

The reforms recommended pertained to the royal succession, the exclusion of the royal household, its affairs, and its members from governmental organization and policy, the necessity of ministerial advice for the king's acts, and revisions of financial, legal, and military matters.[18] Of importance was the initial article which stated that "All thought of dependence on China shall be put away so that the heritage of independence may be secured." [19]

Further indications of Japan's determination to free Korea from the remaining evidences of her *shu-pang* relation to China were given when the *Official Gazette* on January 12, 1895, published the king's approval of a memorial from the prime minister and the eight department heads requesting an elevation of the ruler's title. The Korean king, who had always been known as *Syüng-chyu Syang-tyün* ("His Highness the Lord Paramount"), now became *Tai-kun-chyu*

---

[14] See pp. 170–71.

[15] *Foreign Relations,* 1894, App. I, pp. 84–85.

[16] "Great Changes . . . ," *loc. cit.,* 118.

[17] A. J. Brown, *The Mastery of the Far East* (New York, 1921), 125.

[18] See *Foreign Relations,* 1894, App. I, pp. 94–95; "The King's Oath at the Ancestral Temple," in *Korean Repository,* II (1895), 76–77, for translation of these articles.

[19] "The King's Oath . . . ," *loc. cit.,* 77.

Pyüi-ha ("His Majesty the King"). In keeping with this change, the queens of Korea, who previously had enjoyed a rank no higher than that of the Senior Concubine of the Chinese emperor, were raised from *Wang-pi Tyün-ha* to *Wang-hu Pyüi-ha*.[20] Then in February the ancient arch outside of the west gate of Seoul, traditionally used only by the Korean king on the occasion for greeting the Chinese envoys, was removed.[21] Finally, on April 17, 1895, the treaty of peace between a victorious Japan and a beaten China was signed, in which Japan obtained from China a complete denial of any claim of superiority or interest in Korea. According to Article I of this instrument, known as the Treaty of Shimonoseki, China recognized definitely the "full and complete independence and autonomy of Korea," and further agreed that "the payment of tribute and the performance of ceremonies and formalities by Korea to China, in the derogation of such independence and autonomy, shall wholly cease for the future." [22] Thus Korea had achieved that status for which the Japanese had labored since 1876 when they sought, through Korea's first modern treaty, to divorce that nation from dependence upon the Middle Kingdom.

But the Japanese were determined that the now independent Korea should be developed and controlled in fact by Japan. They therefore took possession of the king's person and excluded, on Inouye's recommendations and by the king's oath, other members of the court, particularly the queen, from interference in the government. The king, however, listened

[20] This change indirectly raised the Korean ruler to a status equal to that of the Chinese ruler. However, the use of the titles in this case is Japanese rather than Chinese. Wilkinson, *The Corean Government Constitutional Changes*, 45.

[21] H. B. Hulbert, *The Passing of Korea* (New York, 1906), 130.

[22] *Korea: Treaties and Agreements*, 11–19; *Treaties and Agreements With and Concerning China, 1894–1919* (J. V. A. MacMurray, ed.) (New York, 1921), I, 18–22; *American Journal of International Law*, I, Supplement 1907, p. 378. China was unsuccessful in an attempt to have included in Article I the recognition of Korea's independence by Japan and an agreement to guarantee mutually the complete neutrality of Korea. See "The Treaty of Peace," in *Korean Repository*, II (1895), 235, for Chinese counter proposals.

less and less to his new advisers, as the queen, a woman of indomitable will, began to oppose the Japanese and again increase her control in governmental affairs.

In the meantime Inouye had returned to Japan, leaving his place in Korea to an individual of much different caliber. General Viscount Muira Goro, the new minister, was a man of military background, scornful of polite diplomacy and a believer in direct action. He found himself, however, checkmated on every hand by the queen. But since the Tai-wün-kun viewed with distaste the power of the queen, who was also his bitter enemy, it was not long before he and Muira were brought together. According to the testimony of the Japanese court which investigated the subsequent happening,[23] the two soon reached an agreement through the Japanese adviser to the Korean War Department, Okamoto Ryunosuke, and the Secretary to the Japanese Legation, Sugimura Fukashi, providing for Japanese aid in murdering the queen. The Tai-wün-kun was then to be placed in control after being bound to pacts insuring his cooperation with the Japanese.[24]

On the eighth of October, 1895, the Tai-wün-kun was escorted to the palace by Japanese-trained Korean detachments and by Japanese who had instructions to kill the queen. While Japanese soldiers from barracks adjoining the palace grounds stood guard, the queen, along with others in the royal entourage, was murdered and her body taken to a near-by grove, saturated with kerosene, and burned. The Japanese minister and his secretary then appeared at the palace, and the king signed several prepared documents appointing certain conspirators to office and agreeing to allow the cabinet to manage the government in the future. On the following day, an edict, not signed by the king, was issued degrading the murdered queen to the lowest rank. Force had again

[23] Transcript of court's findings in "Official Report on Matters Connected with the Events of October 8th 1895, and the Death of the Queen," in *Korean Repository*, III (1896), 122–25.
[24] *Ibid.*

proved, at least temporarily, more effective for the Japanese than diplomacy.[25]

The Japanese triumph was to be short-lived, however. As the part played by the Japanese in the queen's murder became known, a reaction against them and their Korean aides occurred. The people began to take up the cause of their king's dead consort; and the diplomatic representatives in Korea, refusing to recognize her deposition, indicated by their unanimous stand their disapproval of the whole affair.[26] Viscount Muira and the entire staff of the Japanese legation were recalled,[27] and Inouye arrived on October 31 to take charge of Japanese interests. Referring to the shameful incident, Marquis Ito, the Japanese prime minister, emphatically stated:

I believe that it is meant to seek out and punish, if possible, every unworthy son of Japan connected with this crime. Not to do so would condemn Japan in the eyes of the world. If she does not repudiate this usurpation on the part of Tai-Won-Kun, she must lose the respect of every civilised Government on earth.[28]

A preliminary hearing by a Japanese court fully established the fact that Muira made the plans and gave the instructions to kill the queen. The entire group of conspirators was acquitted, however, the court ruling that "notwithstanding these facts, there is no sufficient evidence to prove that any of the accused actually committed the crimes originally meditated by them." [29]

[25] Much material exists on the incident. The more primary sources are: "Official Report on Matters . . . ," *loc. cit.;* Japanese press comment quoted in "The Fate of the Queen," in *Korean Repository,* II (1895), 431–35; "The Official Report," in *Korean Repository,* III (1896), 208–11; Allen to Olney, October 10–22, 1895, in Korea: Dispatches, Vol. XII, nos. 156–63. See also the account of American officer commanding the palace guard, "Correspondence," in *Korean Repository,* III (1896), 216–20; Hulbert, *The Passing of Korea,* 128–47; McKenzie, *Tragedy of Korea,* 51–59; Longford, *Korea,* 339–41.

[26] Allen to Olney, October 17, 1895, in Korea: Dispatches, Vol. XII, no. 160.

[27] *Id.* to *id.,* October 19, 1895, *ibid.,* no. 161.

[28] Quoted in McKenzie, *Tragedy of Korea,* 68.

[29] "Official Report on Matters . . . ," *loc. cit.,* 122–25.

Urged by the other diplomatic representatives in Seoul, the Japanese government agreed to restore the status quo by force if the other powers wished it, but no such request was made. The American minister, who as *doyen* of the diplomatic group had held meetings without the attendance of the Japanese minister, and who in other ways had intervened to aid the beleaguered king against the Japanese, was reprimanded by his government. "Confine yourself strictly [to] protection of American citizens and interests. You have no concern in internal affairs," cabled the American Secretary of State.[30]

On November 27 and 28 the "loyalists," or those seeking to free the king from the Tai-wün-kun and Japanese control, attempted a "rescue" of the monarch. Certain Americans were stationed in the palace to protect him, and, upon the failure of the attempt, eight of the counter-revolutionists were given asylum in the American legation, Minister Sill requesting the use of an American warship to convey them to safety.[31] Sill's request was emphatically refused, and the sheltering of the refugees of the *coup* was condemned.[32] The American minister supported his action by citing the first article of the Korean-American treaty and the obligation therein which bound the United States to exert her good offices in case of oppression or injustice to Korea.[33] He was answered by the assertion that the government of the United States, not its minister in Korea, reserved the right to judge whether good offices should be used.[34]

Yet other governments, notably that of Russia, did not adhere so closely to the legal nature of a minister's function. A Russian policy more aggressive than that of the United States was indicated when Alexis de Speyer arrived to take over the

[30] Telegram, November 20, 1895, in Korea: Instructions, Vol. I.
[31] Sill to Olney, December 2, 1895, in Korea: Dispatches, Vol. XII, no. 175.
[32] Telegram, December 21, 1895, in Korea: Instructions, Vol. I.
[33] See p. 141.
[34] December 31, 1895, in Korea: Instructions, Vol. I, no. 130.

Russian legation in Seoul on January 12, 1896.[35] On the eleventh of the following February, de Speyer allowed his quarters to be used as an asylum for the Korean king and the crown prince, who, despite a heavy guard, had succeeded in escaping from their imprisonment.[36] This liberation of the royal personages destroyed at least temporarily the entire basis of Japanese influence built up since the Sino-Japanese War. Once again in control of his regal powers, the king issued proclamations branding the members of the Japanese-controlled cabinet as traitors, creating a new cabinet, and annulling many of the reform laws which had irritated the Korean people.[37] The Japanese-controlled cabinet fell like a house of cards, several of its members being killed by mobs in the streets before they could make their escape.

As in 1882 and 1884, the Japanese had by rash action again destroyed their influence in Korea. Japan had fought China because of the Chinese refusal to recognize Korea's independence; after China's defeat this independence was fully established through the peace treaty with China and the agreements with Korea. Now that Korea was a sovereign and independent state, Japan resorted to the control of the king's person and the limiting of his power by Japanese and pro-Japanese advisers in order to secure "reforms" in the peninsula. To lose the control of the king—exactly what the Japanese had done—was to lose influence in the government.

[35] Sill to Olney, January 13, 1896, in Korea: Dispatches, Vol. XII, no. 187. De Speyer left to take over the Russian legation in Japan on February 28, 1896. *Id* to *id.*, March 1, 1896, *ibid.*, no. 200.

[36] *Id.* to *id.*, February 11, 1896, *ibid.*, no. 195; *London Times*, February 14, 1896, 5d.

[37] See "Special Supplement to the Korean Repository," in *Korean Repository*, III (1896), 81–94. The Japanese-inspired reform requiring all Koreans to cut off their top-knots and dress their hair in Western fashion was the cause of much agitation. See "The Attack on the Top Knot," *ibid.*, 263–72. See Wilkinson, *The Corean Government Constitutional Changes*, 24–26, for reforms in dress, hats, robes, chairs, insignia, etc.

2. RUSSIAN SPONSORSHIP, 1896–1898

That the king of Korea had been under duress and unable to exercise his powers while in Japanese custody is indicated by the edicts promulgated upon his arrival at the Russian legation. For example, those who had held the highest posts in the kingdom were branded as traitors to be beheaded on sight,[38] and a new cabinet, largely recruited from the "loyalists" who had been refugees in the American and Russian legations, was created. In addition, the obnoxious reforms of costume and hairdress were suspended, all criminals were pardoned, and delinquent taxes were remitted.[39]

The Russians themselves imposed no restraint on the king, nor did they attempt to govern in his name. This was attested by the American minister's report, and the Russian minister earnestly disclaimed any intention of material interference. The British consul was also reported as satisfied with the situation. However, the Russians undoubtedly fell heir to the advisory position which had been previously held by the Japanese and the Chinese. The habit of occupying for centuries the status of an inferior country in the East Asiatic family of nations appeared to persist in the minds of Korea's rulers. The American minister indicated this by the following statements in a telegram to Olney: "I only know that the King and Cabinet defer to Russian opinion in matters of consequence. . . . The King seems to govern with Russia behind the throne." [40]

On the surface it appeared that Russia was merely assuring the liberty of the king and his freely chosen ministers in order to further the inevitable reaction against the Japanese

[38] "Special Supplement . . . ," *loc. cit.*, 84. It was later decreed, however, that the traitors should be held for trial rather than summarily dispatched. See proclamation, *ibid.*, 84–85.

[39] *Ibid.*, 83, 89.

[40] Telegram of Sill to Olney, March 2, 1896, in Korea: Dispatches, Vol. XII, no. 201.

and the reforms they had sponsored,[41] but it later became apparent that she was at the same time taking advantage of her favorable position to advance her own interests and to supplant all other powers as the new "protector" of Korean independence. No effort was made, however, to limit the personal freedom of the king, and in February, 1897, in response to many memorials, he moved without Russian protest to a new palace which had been constructed near the American legation.[42]

In the meantime, through the Korean minister sent in March, 1896, as representative to the Czar's coronation, Russia had negotiated an agreement placing herself in a position not only to control the Korean finances and armed forces, but also, through advice, to direct the policy of the Korean government.[43] That such an agreement existed was indicated when the ambassador to the Czar's coronation returned with the first group of Russians who were to take over the instruction of the Korean army.[44] Though the Korean foreign minister refused to agree to the sending of an additional group of 160 Russian officers and men, still, by September, 1897, there were sixty-six Russian soldiers instructing the Korean army, and the guard at the king's palace was under Russian control.[45] The economic aspects of this penetration were like-

[41] In the fall of 1896 the governmental system was reorganized according to the plan followed before the Japanese reforms, retaining, however, some of the innovations. The sole governing power was returned to the king and the old Council of State (Eui-chyüng Pu) was re-established, the Japanese-inspired cabinet (Nai Kuk) being abolished. For the royal edict effecting these changes, see "The Official Gazette" (compiled from the *Independent*), in *Korean Repository*, III (1896), 500–501. "Constitution of the Council of State" (translation of Ordinance No. 1, September 24, 1896), in *Korean Repository*, III (1896), 404–10. *Foreign Relations*, 1898, pp. 473–75. For a discussion of all the changes in the governmental organization from July, 1896, to January, 1897, see Wilkinson, "The Corean Government," *loc. cit.*, 1–13, 45–56.

[42] Still to Olney, February 22, 1897, in Korea: Dispatches, Vol. XIII, no. 258.

[43] Allen to Sherman, October 2, 1897, *ibid.*, no. 10. The agreement was signed in Moscow on January 9, 1896. Brown, *The Far East*, 142.

[44] Allen to Olney, October 27, 1896, in Korea: Dispatches, Vol. XIII, no. 240.

[45] *Id.* to Sherman, September 17, 1897, *ibid.*, no. 3.

wise not ignored. While the Korean king was yet in the Russian legation, a concession was granted to a Russian company giving it a twenty-year lumber monopoly in the Mu-san district on the Tu-men River and a five-year option to cut timber in the Yalu valley. The Russians also secured a mining concession in Ham Kyang province.[46]

By September, 1897, Russian influence was definitely in the ascendancy in Korea. De Speyer, a man of aggressive temperament, who had replaced the mild-mannered Waeber as Russian minister,[47] had informed the Korean king that henceforth he must take Russian advice on all matters.[48] De Speyer also struck out against the more-than-passing interest and influence of the American missionaries in the nation's affairs by stating that no Korean official who was friendly to the Americans would be retained in office.[49] One sphere which Russia had yet to control was the department of finance, which had been successfully supervised by an Englishman, J. McLeavy Brown, since the spring of 1896. Accordingly, in October, 1897, Minister de Speyer, in a letter to the Korean Foreign Office, and presumably under the agreement signed in Moscow at the time of the Czar's coronation, announced the arrival of Kir Alexeieff to be the "resident" in charge of finance. On November 5 an agreement with the Korean foreign minister [50] conferred this office upon the Russian.[51]

[46] Brown, The Far East, 142. The five-year option limit was extended to twenty years on January 1, 1901.

[47] Allen, A Chronological Index, 36.

[48] Allen to Sherman, September 17, 1897, in Korea: Dispatches, Vol. XIII, no. 3.

[49] Id. to id., October 1, 1897, ibid., no. 9.

[50] Two foreign ministers were removed before one could be found who would sign the agreement with the Russians.

[51] Allen to Sherman, enc., de Speyer's letter; agreement with the foreign minister, in Korea: Dispatches, Vol. XIII, nos. 17, 29. See also "In the Finance Department," in Korean Repository, IV (1897), 434–36. Mr. Brown, however, refused to vacate his position and the matter was not settled until after all Russian advisers were withdrawn in 1898. See pp. 237–40.

It was also through Russian advice that the king of Korea was induced to assume the title of Emperor, and that his country was given a new official name.[52] This move was in line with the original Far Eastern theory that the Chinese emperor was the only ruler not subject and inferior to another, but which later came to view no nation as independent unless it was ruled by an emperor. This additional gesture of independence served, moreover, to weaken the hand of any other state which, by trying to thrust itself into Korean affairs, could be branded by the present protector as an aggressor against that independence. Likewise, the Japanese had been in favor of this move in 1895 when they were in control, the date of assuming the exalted title having then been announced but later postponed.[53] The Russians, who opposed the step under the sponsorship of Japan, now managed it so adroitly that the affair even achieved a degree of spontaneity. Upon an "altar of heaven" the king assumed the title of *Whang Chyui*, and two days later Korea dropped her official name, Chosen, and became the Empire of Dai Han.[54]

With their influence on the wane because of their loss of the new emperor's person, the Japanese could do very little through the Korean government to counteract the rapid rise of Russian prestige in the peninsula. Japan's policy for the time, therefore, appears to have been the advancement of her commercial interests in that area, and, through agreements directly with the Russian government, the limiting as far as possible for Russia's gains there. The first of these compacts, known as the Waeber-Komura agreement, was signed May

[52] The official name of Korea since 1392 had been Chao-hsien or Chosen.
[53] "The Emperor of Korea," in *Korean Repository*, II (1895), 435–38; T. H. Yun, "The Whang-Chei of Dai Han, or the Emperor of Korea," in *Korean Repository*, IV (1897), 385.
[54] For documents and description of the ceremony, see Yun, "The Whang-Chei . . . ," *loc. cit.*, 385–90; Allen to Sherman, October 14, 20, 1897, in *Korea: Dispatches*, Vol. XIII, nos. 18, 24; *Foreign Relations*, 1898, pp. 484–87; *London Times*, October 16, 1897, 5e.

14, 1896, four months after the king escaped from his pro-Japanese advisers.[55] Both parties pledged themselves to leave the matter of the king's stay in the Russian legation to his own discretion, agreeing, however, to advise his departure when there were no further doubts as to his safety. The Japanese, to insure that safety, promised to take measures to control those of their subjects inclined to favor direct and violent action. They were constrained, moreover, to recognize the new cabinet, which had replaced the one of their choice, as "liberal and moderate men" appointed by the king "of his own free will." The number of troops and the number and location of telegraph guards which Japan could maintain in Korea were also definitely limited.

In the following month Japan sought by the Lobanoff-Yamagata agreement,[56] to block the Russian pathway to increased power through loans, and to checkmate Russian control of the Korean armed forces and police. By this compact both Russia and Japan agreed to lend money to Korea only by "mutual accord" and to leave to Korea "so far as the financial and economical situation of that country" would permit them to do so, "the creation and maintenance of an armed force and of a native police in sufficient proportions to maintain internal order without foreign aid." Russia later evaded this attempt to restrict her freedom of action by asserting that her agreement with Korea to furnish military and financial guidance had been signed previously and could not be affected by the more recent Russo-Japanese understandings.[57]

[55] Text in *Korea: Treaties and Agreements*, 21–22; *British and Foreign State Papers*, LXXXVIII, 472–73.

[56] Text in *Korea: Treaties and Agreements*, 23–24; *British and Foreign State Papers*, LXXXVIII, 471–72.

[57] See comments of the *Japan Mail*, November 27, 1897, and the *Japan Times*, November 19, 1897, on Russia's actions, quoted in "The Press on the Situation," in *Korean Repository*, IV (1897), 468–71. See the conversation of Count Hayashi with Count Muravieff, *The Secret Memoirs of Count Tadasu Hayashi* (A. M. Pooley, ed.) (New York, 1915), 91–93.

In 1897 an ill-advised act by the Russian representative in Korea initiated diplomatic competition which led up to the Russo-Japanese War. The incident in which de Speyer overstepped himself, known as the Deer Island episode, concerned a small island in the harbor of the southern port of Fusan. In August, 1897, Mr. Waeber, then the Russian representative, had selected twenty acres on the island as a location for a Russian coaling station despite the fact that J. McLeavy Brown, at that time Chief Commissioner of Customs, had two years earlier marked off much of this plot and reported it to the Foreign Office as the site for the general foreign settlement of Fusan. De Speyer was now determined to have Waeber's action legalized, notwithstanding the protests of the representatives of the other powers and the fact that Japanese citizens had purchased privately some of the land claimed. Extravagant demands of land for Russia in the foreign settlements of other ports were also made. Mr. de Speyer's belligerent attitude engendered in the Korean officials a reluctance to accord Russia even the requested coaling base on Deer Island. When de Speyer sought the approval of the Council of State, the Korean foreign minister, though introducing the measure, immediately absented himself from the deliberations. Wholesale cabinet changes were then made under Russian pressure, and an acting foreign minister who would favor the demand was appointed.[58] Without Council approval, and finding the Foreign Office deserted, the acting minister personally wrote to the Russian minister and to the dean of the diplomatic corps sanctioning Russia's claim.[59]

Public disapproval mounted at this action. Three times the entire Council of State offered its resignation to the king, and the foreign minister submitted a personal memorial asking his own dismissal and punishment. When a compromise, ar-

[58] Allen to Sherman, March 19, 1898, in Korea: Dispatches, Vol. XIV, no. 89.
[59] For text of notes, see "The Deer Island Episode," in *Korean Repository*, V (1898), 111–12.

ranged between the Korean Foreign Office and the Russian legation secretary, was ignored by de Speyer, the matter appeared deadlocked.[60]

De Speyer, however, decided to force the issue and to gamble all of Russia's influence in Korea to achieve his point. He therefore delivered to the Korean government on March 7, 1898, the following note, which approached an ultimatum in its tone and content.

Recently I have been informed that there exists a deplorable condition of affairs in Seoul; many idlers among your people, claiming to be gifted politicians, create disturbance by opposing Russian interests. This state of affairs naturally causes great surprise to my Imperial Sovereign, the Emperor of Russia. At the request of your Imperial Sovereign and your government, the Russian government had sent military instructors to drill the soldiers and to guard the palace, and an advisor for your finance department. This action on the part of my government plainly indicates Russia's intention of helping your country as a neighbor and her desire to strengthen your independence. But your government did not seem to appreciate the importance of Russia's action at the time and now your government freely prevents Russia from accomplishing the advantages and beneficial results for your country which she intended. The present attitude of your government is so plain that Russia cannot endure this condition much longer. Therefore my emperor has graciously ordered me to report fully to your emperor and inquire of your government definitely whether Korea still desires to be benefitted by Russia's help or not, and if the military instructors and finance advisor are not considered necessary by your emperor and your government, my government will make some other arrangement according to the circumstances, but your government must maintain your independence in the future according to its ability.[61]

News of the ultimatum served to solidify the rising feeling against Russia, and demands to accept the Russian offer of

[60] For a recital of these events, see *ibid.*, 109–13; *Foreign Relations*, 1898, pp. 475–77.

[61] Quoted in "Right About Face," in *Korean Repository*, V (1898), 113.

withdrawal from Korea came from all sides. In addition to the numerous memorials from private individuals, the pressure of an organization known as the Independence Club was of great influence. This society had been founded by a Korean who had studied in America and who had Anglicized his name from Shü Chai Pil to Dr. Phillip Jaisohn. Through the pages of its journal, the *Independent*, which was written half in English and half in native script (*on-mun*), this group had long opposed the growing control of Russia. They now proceeded to hold mass meetings. Questioning the hand that the recently established Russo-Korean bank had in governmental affairs, they broadened their opposition to include the entire sphere of Russian influence.[62] This popular backing was augmented by that of former Korean ministers, the present cabinet, and the Japanese minister, Mr. Kato. The king decided to view as a valid offer the threats of de Speyer to withdraw all Russian assistance, and, to the extreme discomfiture of the Russian representative, he accepted it. His acceptance expressed the appreciation of the Korean government for Russia's past aid and explained: "Your officials have accomplished their work and it is convenient for us to have them relieved from our service. I feel grateful to you for suggesting the idea of relieving these officials." [63]

De Speyer had thus been made a victim of his own designs. He had gambled the whole advantageous position of Russia and had lost. Having made the offer, he could do little now but withdraw, and blaming his defeat on Dr. Jaisohn and the Japanese,[64] he was relieved of his post. The Russo-Korean bank was closed, the Russian military advisers went to Port

[62] See *ibid.*, 114, for the memorial of the Independence Club; also "The Independence Club," in *Korean Repository*, IV (1897), 281–87; T. H. Yun, "Popular Movements in Korea," in *Korean Repository*, V (1898), 465–69.

[63] "Right About Face," *loc. cit.*, 115; for the advice of the Japanese minister, see "The Secret Memoirs," *loc. cit.*, 96; see also *London Times*, March 19, 1898, 7a, and March 22, 5b, for the Russian viewpoints.

[64] Allen to Sherman, March 19, 1898, in Korea: Dispatches, Vol. XIV, no. 89; "The Secret Memoirs," *loc. cit.*, 97.

Arthur, and the Russian financial experts were assigned to the legation at Tokyo.[65]

3. *De Facto* INDEPENDENCE

Japan, quick to take advantage of the weak diplomatic position of Russia, secured the Nishi-Rosen agreement in the same month of the Russian debacle, whereby she bound Russia, and herself as well, "to take no measure in respect to the appointment of military instructors or financial advisors, without arriving beforehand at a mutual agreement on the subject." She also secured a pledge from Russia recognizing the "wide development taken by the commercial and industrial enterprise of Japan in Korea" and agreeing in no way to hinder "the development of commercial and industrial relations between Japan and Korea." Both parties, furthermore, recognized definitely "the Sovereignty and entire independence of Korea" and pledged themselves "mutually to abstain from all direct interference in the internal affairs of that country." [66]

For the period of about a year after this, Korea was free from the overlordship of any country, and during this interim she approached nearer to a state of *de facto* independence and sovereignty than at any time since her legal independence was first asserted. Being only recently released, however, from the status of a nation traditionally under the hand of a stronger power, she made little showing of an ability to control her own affairs properly. Since the king had divested himself of his Japanese and progressive advisers in 1896, the Korean government had become more and more conservative, tending toward the revival of administration on the Confucian

[65] Allen to Sherman, April 12, 1898, in Korea: Dispatches, Vol. XIV, no. 96.
[66] Text of Nishi-Rosen agreement, *Korea: Treaties and Agreements,* 24–25, and *British and Foreign State Papers,* XCII, 1068–69.

pattern rather than on that of the West.[67] The king had re-established his power to rule absolutely and was soon surrounded by ministers and palace favorites, described by the American minister as a "corrupt cabal." [68] Persons out of power continued to agitate for a change, and in July, 1898, a conspiracy to force the reactionary ruler's abdication and place a Japanese-schooled prince on the throne was discovered.[69] In September an attempt was made to poison the king and the crown prince. Though both of these acts were unsuccessful, they indicated the degree of disorganization and intrigue existing in the country.[70]

The Independence Club was very active during this period. Advocating reform and stability in the Korean government as well as maintenance of the nation's independence, the group kept up a constant stream of memorials to the king. Its endeavors were rewarded in some measure by the king's selection in October, 1898, of what was termed a "model cabinet" of patriotic, honest, and forward-looking Koreans of the best type.[71] But the ousted cabinet members were able to convince the ruler that both the Independence Club and the cabinet it sponsored were committed to a policy of deposing him and setting up a republic. The result was the dismissal of the cabinet, the disbanding of the Club, and the arrest of its leaders on November 5.[72] Ensuing protests and demonstrations by the followers of the deposed group were combated by summoning into the city the members of the Peddlers' Guild.[73] Subsequent riots were at last ended by the

---

[67] See "Reaction," in *Korean Repository,* III (1896), 334–36; "Reformation, Revision, Regulation," in *Korean Repository,* IV (1897), 192–95.

[68] Allen to Sherman, July 18, 1898, in Korea: Dispatches, Vol. XIV, no. 125.

[69] *Ibid.*

[70] See "Abdication, Acclamation, Assassination," in *Korean Repository,* V (1898), 342–49, for discussion of these two incidents; and Allen to Day, September 17, 1898, in Korea: Dispatches, Vol. XV, no. 145.

[71] Allen to Day, October 13, 1898, in Korea: Dispatches, Vol. XV, no. 152.

[72] *Id.* to Hay, November 14, 1898, *ibid.,* no. 161.

[73] *Id.* to *id.,* November 28, 1898, *ibid.,* no. 162.

re-establishment and recognition of the Independence Club and the granting of freedom of speech and assembly. Yet when later meetings and speeches exceeded moderate bounds, the leaders of this progressive group were again taken into custody, and reactionary elements once more were given free rein.[74] The situation was such that in December, 1898, Kato, the Japanese representative in Korea, in indicating future Japanese policy, stated: "Korea is steadily retrograding. Her so-called independence is an idle legend. She is absolutely without strength to be independent." [75]

In appraising the international status of Korea from the Sino-Japanese War to the turn of the century, one may say that she had now entered fully into the Western state system and renounced completely her allegiance to an international order founded on Confucian principles. Nevertheless, her actual position among the sovereign and independent states of the world was still dictated to a considerable degree by her former habits of subservience to and reliance on a stronger nation. Along with the retarding effect of this tradition, there was the almost hopeless physical condition of the nation, a nation corrupt, undeveloped, archaic, surrounded by powers overwhelmingly larger, and buffeted about by the stresses of modern power-politics.

Legally, Korea was an independent and sovereign state. Beyond the general recognition of independence given by the Western states in their pre-1894 treaties with her, the recognition of her complete independence was accorded by China in the Treaty of Shimonoseki, by Japan in the agreements with Korea, and by Russia in the agreements with Japan. Thus each of those nations most tempted to challenge her independence had specifically attested her legal existence.

Yet the actual status of Korea in this period exhibited little of the elements of *de facto* independence. It is to be doubted that the assertions of Japan and Russia of a desire to main-

[74] See Yun, "Popular Movements in Korea," *loc. cit.*, 465–69.
[75] Quoted in an editorial in the *Japan Mail*, December 6, 1898.

tain that independence were based on a genuine intention to see Korea completely secure in her territorial integrity and sovereignty. Japan had first used the assertion of Korean independence to break China's hold on the peninsula, but the independence myth also served the Japanese as a basis for the post-war control of Korea wherein reforms introduced to secure that independence allowed them to direct Korean policy and thereby to secure valuable concessions for themselves as well. When the Japanese lost control of the royal person, Russia, the succeeding protector, likewise advanced the independence theory as against the Japanese.

It need not be decided here as to which, if either, of these two powers was merely trying to thwart the designs of the other against Korea's sovereignty.[76] It is of importance, however, to note the circumstances under which both Japan and Russia were able, in turn, to exert such a controlling influence over Korean affairs. There undoubtedly existed a habit of mind in the Koreans, bred during centuries under the aegis of China, which made them susceptible to advice from stronger nations. Japan, however, impatient with slow diplomatic methods, attempted to bolster her influence by keeping the Korean king a virtual prisoner and giving orders instead of advice. The Russians, on the other hand, allowed the monarch full liberty, and as long as they made no attempt to force their opinions on him, their advice was generally followed to the prosperity of their interests. Eventually the efforts of a small group of Koreans, genuinely desiring the sovereignty and independence of their country from all foreign control, were instrumental in giving Korea a brief opportunity to govern herself. But by lapsing into a period of reaction and misgovernment, even by Asiatic standards, the nation invited still further outside interference.

---

[76] On this point see Tyler Dennett, *Roosevelt and the Russo-Japanese War* (New York, 1925), 97–101, and Ariga Nagao, quoted in René Terriou, *Le statut international de la Corée anterieurement au 29 Août 1910* (Paris, 1911), 107.

CHAPTER XII

LOSS OF INDEPENDENCE

1. Russo-Japanese Rivalry, 1900–1904

A T THE turn of the century, rivals in the Korean area were facing issues which were to be decided five years later by war. Under the Nishi-Rosen agreement, both Russia and Japan were limited in the matter of direct interference in the affairs of Korea and in the privilege of supplying advisers to her military staff. Japan, however, had secured in this agreement a recognition of her special commercial interests in the peninsula, and after 1899 she began to construct a basis for political action through these economic concessions.

In July, 1888, the Japanese completed their telegraph line from Fusan to Seoul, and in September, 1898, they obtained concessions permitting them to build a railway between these two points and another between the capital and the seaport of Chemulpo.[1] The American minister reported in October of 1898 that many Japanese were in the interior of Korea in violation of the treaty arrangements which limited foreigners to the open ports,[2] while in the areas around the open ports it was discovered that important and strategic property had been purchased by Japanese individuals.[3] Sure signs of Japan's accelerated commercial penetration were her establishment in Chemulpo and Seoul of offices of the Bank of Japan,[4]

[1] Brown, *The Far East*, 151–52.
[2] Allen to Day, October 20, 1898, in Korea: Dispatches, Vol. XV, no. 153.
[3] See Masampo incident, p. 246.
[4] Allen, *A Chronological Index,* 42, 44.

and her securing of valuable whaling rights in February of 1900, a mining concession in August, and a general fisheries convention in October.[5] Mr. G. Hayashi, who had replaced the less aggressive Kato as Japanese minister to Korea, described the position of his government as follows:

> Our policy in Korea is very simple; it consists of our abstinence from all innovation in the internal affairs of this country and to make possible the development of our economic interests. This policy has received the approval of the great majority of our countrymen and we do not have any reason to change it.[6]

Yet the Japanese pushed their averred economic interests with a political passion. They attempted to wrest a vital link in the Seoul Electric Railway from the control of an American company, centering their complaint on the spot where the tracks of the American line crossed those of their own Seoul-Chemulpo road. Their purpose was to force the Seoul railroad to remove its tracks from the populous area through which it ran, in order that they might get a right of way for the Japanese line from Fusan to Seoul.[7] Moreover, a report came from the American minister that they were interfering with a plan to set up a Korean-American bank,[8] and also that they were evading the Nishi-Rosen restriction on military advisers by sending their officers to Korea and having them naturalized.[9]

Despite her set-back of 1898,[10] Russia was busily engaged in an effort to combat the growing Japanese influence. In pursuing her ends, however, she made greater use of politics than did the Japanese. With the return of A. Pavlov as Russian representative to Korea at the beginning of 1900, the Russian government sought to block or to reciprocate the

[5] *Ibid.*, 42; Brown, *The Far East*, 152.
[6] Quoted by Terriou, *Le statut international*, 82.
[7] See *Foreign Relations*, 1900, pp. 771 ff.
[8] Allen to Hay, September 25, 1900, in Korea: Dispatches, Vol. XVI, no. 282.
[9] *Id.* to *id.*, August 31, 1900, *ibid.*, no. 275.
[10] See pp. 237–39.

actions of Japan by keeping in power those Koreans who were hostile to the Japanese.[11] Pavlov was able to establish a connection with Yi Yong Ik, a corrupt official and one of the king's closest advisers, who in April of 1900 had granted to the Russian Count Henry Keyserling a whaling concession, setting aside land in several ports for the processing of the catch.[12] When the southern port of Masampo was opened to accommodate Keyserling's concession, Pavlov promptly staked off a strategically placed area at that point. The Russians found, however, when they attempted to occupy the claim, that the land had all been previously purchased from its Korean owners by Japanese citizens. Pressure was then brought to bear on the Korean government to invalidate these sales; bribery was resorted to, and the Russian fleet appeared at Chemulpo. But the firm stand of Japan caused Russia to be satisfied with a less strategic area at Masampo, and her attempts to secure other well-placed areas on the southern coast brought to light the fact that the Japanese had, through their citizens, already pre-empted much of the land desired.[13] The Russians were quite naturally affronted by these *sub rosa* activities of Japan in securing important areas in the Korean port settlements,[14] while the Japanese press, on the other hand, was already talking of war with Russia and citing the fact that the time for such action was now ripe.[15]

[11] Hulbert, *The Passing of Korea*, 169.

[12] See *Foreign Relations*, 1899, pp. 484–88, for text of the agreement.

[13] For Masampo incident, see Brown, *The Far East*, 143–44; Allen to Hay, March 19, 1900, in Korea: Dispatches, Vol. XVI, no. 235; *British Documents on the Origin of the War, 1898–1914* (G. P. Gooch and Harold Temperley, eds.) (London, 1929), II, 32–33.

[14] Allen to Hay, November 18, 1899, in Korea: Dispatches, Vol. XV, no. 214.

[15] *Japan Daily Mail*, December 7, 1899, March 30, 31, 1900; *Kobe Chronicle*, March 23, 29, 1900, in Korea: Dispatches, Vol. XV, no. 215; Allen to Hay, December 12, 1899, April 5, 1900, *ibid.*, Vol. XVI, no. 239.

2. The Anglo-Japanese Alliance and the War with Russia

An Anglo-Japanese alliance, concluded on January 30, 1902,[16] was a definite result of the tension in Korea. Count Hayashi, in his early conversations with Lord Lansdowne, British foreign minister, had stated that Japan's first and last wish was the protection of her Korean interests and the prevention of interference in the affairs of the peninsula by any other country.[17] The purpose of the alliance was further indicated in the first article of the formal treaty, wherein the parties recognized that Japan "is interested in a peculiar degree politically as well as commercially and industrially in Korea. . . ." Despite an appearance of calm and indifference over this agreement, the Russians were reported to have been greatly discomforted by it, viewing it as a "diplomatic check, if not defeat." [18] France and Russia responded to the newly made pact by a declaration which indicated that their Dual Alliance, in existence since 1895, was now to be considered as extending to the Far East as well as to areas formerly designated.[19]

The Korean emperor, at first viewing the Anglo-Japanese and the Russian-French understandings with misgiving, instituted a reform movement to allay the threat which these agreements portended for his country. However, he later came to view them as, in effect, neutralizing Korea and therefore making her position secure. Since Russian and Japanese influences appeared equally divided, his reform attempts were dropped, and the corrupt and extravagant government of the peninsula continued, with the oppressed people on the point

[16] *British and Foreign State Papers*, XCV, 83–84.

[17] *The Secret Memoirs*, 134.

[18] Sir C. Scott to Marquess of Lansdowne, February 20, 1902, in *British Documents*, 130–31.

[19] For this declaration of March 16, 1902, see *Korea: Treaties and Agreements*, 34–35. On the Anglo-Japanese alliance, see Chang Chung-fu, *The Anglo-Japanese Alliance* (Baltimore, 1931) ; *The Secret Memoirs; British Documents, II*, pp. 89–137.

of revolt.[20] The alliances of Japan with England and of Russia with France merely brought about a breathing spell in the clash of interests in Korea. In the face of imminent conflict, this lull was used by both Russia and Japan to arrange for the benevolent neutrality of another country or for active aid if the opposing side should be made up of more than one power. The struggle for dominance in Korea then continued.

Early in April, 1901, Russia was able to secure from the Korean emperor a promise not to grant any more of his country's mining concessions to foreigners, and further to lease his personal mines only to Russians when he wished foreigners to operate them. It was also agreed at this time that Russia was to furnish any foreign capital borrowed for the construction of the Seoul-Wu-ji railroad.[21] Further indication of this aggressive policy was given on April 13, 1901, when Russia notified Korea of her intention to exercise the option of cutting timber in the Yalu valley as provided in her agreement of April, 1896, with Korea.[22] Since this agreement stipulated that the Russian interpretation should prevail in case of dispute over the concession, subsequent Korean and Japanese protests were of little avail. Moreover, Russia interpreted the Yalu concession to embrace all streams draining into the Yalu River, thus giving her the control of a vast area in northern Korea. She therefore constructed forts to protect this territory, sent "frontier guards" to patrol it, and selected the favorable port of Yongampo, near the mouth of the Yalu River, as a shipping outlet for the timber it contained, although Yongampo was far removed from the actual forest area involved.

By 1903 friction in the Yalu region had strained Russo-Japanese relations to the breaking point. After October the

[20] Allen to Hay, May 31, 1902, in Korea: Dispatches, Vol. XVIII, no. 470.
[21] Brown, The Far East, 144.
[22] See p. 234.

Japanese merchants and bankers in Seoul began calling in their money and refusing to make loans. At the end of the year the foreign legations were securing guards for their establishments, and the Japanese were reported by the American minister to be landing supplies, guns, and ammunition in Korea.[23]

Events on the peninsula were not, however, the sole cause of the Russo-Japanese War. Russian advances into Manchuria after the Boxer Rebellion had also alarmed Japan. Despite her agreements with China for the withdrawal of troops, Russia appeared as determined to control Manchuria as Japan was to control Korea.[24] Japan therefore sought to settle the tension both in Manchuria and Korea by opening direct negotiations with her rival. Accordingly, the Japanese foreign minister, Baron Komura, suggested to the Czar's government a joint "examination of the condition of affairs in the Extreme East where their Russian and Japanese interests meet, with a view to a definition of their respective special interests in those regions." [25] To Korino, the Japanese minister at St. Petersburg, he described as follows his concern over a matter more serious to Japan than the Russian advance into Manchuria:

Russia stationed on the flank of Corea would be a constant menace to the separate existence of that Empire, and in any event it would make Russia the dominant power in Corea. Corea is an important outpost in Japan's line of defense, and Japan consequently considers the independence of Corea absolutely essential to her own repose and safety. Japan possesses paramount political

---

[23] See Allen to Hay, April 24, 1903, in Korea: Dispatches, Vol. XIX, no. 604; id. to id., May 26, 1903, ibid., Vol. XX, no. 612; Brown, The Far East, 144–46.

[24] See British Documents, II, 197–207, for negotiations concerning the evacuation of Manchuria. See ibid., II, 211, for the British military intelligence estimate of Russia's position in Manchuria.

[25] Archives Diplomatiques (Paris, 1861–1914), XCI–XCII, 845.

as well as commercial and industrial interests and influence in Corea which, having regard to her own security, she cannot consent to surrender to, or share with, any other Power.[26]

The negotiations, continued over a six months' period, were unsuccessful. Russia was willing to acknowledge Japanese predominance in Korea, provided Japan would guarantee Korea's independence; and Japan was prepared to make a similar conditional acknowledgment in regard to Russia's position in Manchuria. But the Russians held that Manchuria was out of the Japanese sphere of influence and should not be dealt with in the treaty, and their obvious delaying tactics and playing for time led to rupture of the conference. In ending the negotiations, the Japanese foreign minister, through his representative in St. Petersburg, said in part:

The Government of His Majesty the Emperor of Japan regard the independence and territorial integrity of the Empire of Corea as essential to their own repose and safety, and they are consequently unable to view with indifference any action tending to render the position of Corea insecure.

The successive rejections by the Imperial Russian Government . . . of Japan's proposals . . . regarded as indispensable to assure the independence and territorial integrity of the Corean Empire and to safeguard Japan's preponderating interests in the Peninsula . . . have made it necessary for the Imperial Government seriously to consider what measures of self-defense they are called upon to take.[27]

Japan severed diplomatic relations with Russia on February 6, 1904, and Japanese ships attacked Port Arthur in the night of February 8. On the following day two Russian ships were attacked in the Korean harbor of Chemulpo. As in 1894, Japan did not declare war until after her first blow had been delivered, the formal announcement being made on Febru-

26 *Ibid.*, 844.
27 *Ibid.*, 894–95.

ary 10. Moreover, she ignored the Korean declaration of neutrality issued prior to the opening of hostilities.[28]

Those who ruled Korea were not greatly disturbed over the effect upon their country of a Russo-Japanese war. As early as 1900 Minister Allen had assured the Korean king that America and the other treaty powers would make it difficult for any one nation to take away the independence of his nation. Concerning this assurance, the American minister reported to Secretary Hay in Washington:

I reminded him of the promise made in these treaties that the treaty powers would assist Korea in time of distress, by their good offices, and recalled to his mind the fact that in 1894, at the time of the Japan-Chinese War, when he had asked the good offices of the United States he had not asked in vain, for Secretary Gresham had promptly sent a very strong telegram to the Japanese Government in reply to this appeal, which act, I could not but believe, had had much to do with the ultimate course of Japan in respecting and fully establishing Korean independence.[29]

To the Koreans such a statement was likely to convey the wrong impression. With a habit of mind which led them to look to some superior state for protection, and with little understanding of Western legal concepts such as "good offices," these assurances were considered an indication that the Americans would act as their benevolent "elder brother." [30] When hostilities were clearly imminent, Korea therefore issued a

[28] See *ibid.*, 843–98, for the entire Komura-Korino correspondence. English and European attitudes on the negotiations in *British Documents*, II, pp. 197–252. For Russian documents see, "On the Eve of the Russo-Japanese War" (from *Krasny Archiv*, II, 7–54, *Historical Journal of the Central Archives of RSFSR*, Moscow), in *China Social and Political Science Review*, XVIII (1934–35), 572–94; XIX (1935–36), 125–. 9. See *Foreign Relations*, 1904, p. 414, for the Japanese declaration of war.

[29] Allen to Hay, August 31, 1900, in Korea: Dispatches, Vol. XVI, no. 275.

[30] In 1897 the Korean king, in the first audience given to Allen as American minister, referring to the position of the United States as the first Western nation to enter treaty relations, stated: "We feel that America is to us as our Elder Brother." *Id.* to Sherman, September 13, 1897, in Korea: Dispatches, Vol. XIII, no. 1.

proclamation of neutrality [31] and took no steps to put her own house in order as a means of discouraging outside interference. Pertinent here is the instance of a conversation between F. A. McKenzie and the emperor's minister Yi Yong Ik, held several days prior to the outbreak of hostilities, in which Mc-Kenzie urged that Korea undertake reforms to save herself from impending extinction. The minister quickly retorted that Korea was in no danger, since her independence was guaranteed by America and Europe. "It does not matter what the other nations are doing," he continued. "We have this day sent out a statement that we are neutral and asking for our neutrality to be respected."

"Why should they protect you if you do not protect yourself?" asked McKenzie.

"We have the promise of America," answered Yi. "She will be our friend whatever happens." [32]

3. Establishment of the Protectorate

Through the decisive military victories of the Japanese over Russia in their war of 1904–1905, the only remaining opponent of Japan in Korea was vanquished. Japan then took immediate steps to place Korea in such a position that, though still legally independent, she would no longer be a field for international intrigue. Her status as a protectorate was the result.

The concept of a protectorate in international law is by no means clearly defined. "Actually the term is less a description of a status than a category for classifying a number of anomalous international relationships. . . ." [33] Yet it has

[31] *United States Senate Documents,* 64 Cong., 1 Sess. (1916) XLII, No. 342, pp. 8–9, for notification of neutrality.

[32] F. A. McKenzie, *Korea's Fight for Freedom* (New York, 1928), 77–78.

[33] A. H. Feller, "Protectorate," in *Encyclopedia of Social Science* (New York, 1934), XII, 567.

always involved the idea of subordination of one state to another, generally through a contractual agreement.[34] While the connotation has even been broadened to cover colonial relationships not governed by international law,[35] the essential characteristic of a true protectorate is its attribute of a relationship under international law.[36] The protector, in return for his protection, exercises varying degrees of control over the external or internal affairs of the protected state. In the nineteenth century, the term was employed in non-European areas mainly to indicate a semi-sovereign position, a step toward annexation.[37]

Even before she signed the treaty of peace with Russia in September, 1905, Japan was able to secure a degree of control in Korean affairs which placed Korea completely within the Japanese orbit except for her foreign relations. Two days before the declaration of war [38] the Japanese took possession of the Korean capital and surrounded the palace of the emperor with troops.[39] A protocol was signed as early as February 23, 1904, which laid the foundation for the Japanese pro-

[34] Frantz Despagnet, *Essai sur les protectorats* (Paris, 1896), 51. T. Baty, "Protectorates and Mandates," in *British Yearbook of International Law*, II (1921–22), 109, n. 2, holds that a protectorate may be established tacitly, as in the relationship of Russia to Bulgaria between 1878–85.

[35] See André Devaulx, *Les protectorats de la France en Afrique* (Domois-Dijon, 1903) ; M. F. Lindley, *The Acquisition and Government of Backward Territory in International Law* (London, 1926), 182–88.

[36] Feller, "Protectorate," *loc. cit.*, 570. See, with reference to the Tunis and Morocco nationality decrees, *Publications of the Permanent Court of International Justice, Collection of Advisory Opinions* (Leyden, 1923), Series B, no. 4, p. 27, wherein the court states: "The extent of the powers of a protecting State in the territory of a protected State depends, first, upon the Treaties between the protecting State and the protected State establishing the Protectorate, and, secondly, upon the conditions under which the Protectorate has been recognized by third Powers as against whom there is an intention to rely on the provisions of these Treaties."

[37] Lindley, *Backward Territory*, 182; E. D. Dickinson, *Equality of States in International Law* (Cambridge, 1920), 241.

[38] See *Foreign Relations*, 1904, p. 414, for an official translation of the Japanese declaration of war.

[39] McKenzie, *Tragedy of Korea*, 108.

tectorate and excluded the threat of competition by other states.[40] Under its terms the government of Korea agreed to place "full confidence" in the Japanese government and to "adopt the advice of the latter with regard to improvements in administration." In return, Japan definitely guaranteed "the independence and territorial integrity" of Korea. Further concessions to the Japanese, however, gave them the right to intervene as they saw fit to protect that territorial integrity, and also assured them that Korea would not conclude without Japanese assent any agreement with a third power which would be "contrary to the principles of the present protocol."

Thus, to counterbalance her responsibility for Korean independence, Japan gained authority to block the efforts of any power to secure the position that Russia had held in the peninsula. Korea could make no treaties with other countries threatening Japanese interests, and she bound herself to "adopt the advice" of Japan in regard to governmental improvements. The notice of this agreement sent to the other states indicated that it was "to facilitate military operations . . . and also . . . to prevent future complications. . . ."[41] The American minister to Tokyo stated that all his information led him to believe that Japan had "every intention of respecting the integrity of the Korean Empire."[42]

Once again under the advice of the Japanese, the Korean emperor in May, 1904, issued a series of decrees, one of which annulled all agreements and concessions previously secured by Russia.[43] Another, renouncing the absolute power of the Korean emperor, declared that all contracts with foreigners must henceforth have the approval of the Korean minister of

[40] For the text of this agreement, see *Foreign Relations*, 1904, p. 437; for Chinese text see Allen to Hay, February 27, 1904, in Korea: Dispatches, Vol. XX, no. 681.

[41] *Foreign Relations*, 1904, p. 437.

[42] Griscom to Hay, March 17, 1904, *ibid.*, 438.

[43] Allen to *id.*, May 19, 1904, in Korea: Dispatches, Vol. XXI, no. 741.

finance. This embraced practically every type of negotiation that the government might undertake.[44]

These May edicts were followed in August by an additional agreement entrusting to Japan the appointment of the advisers to the Korean finance and foreign affairs departments [45] and requiring the counsel of these advisers before action could be taken.[46] In the same month Japan appointed Metega financial adviser and D. W. Stevens, an American, adviser to the Department of Foreign Affairs.[47] In the meantime Japanese Minister Hayashi had secured the privilege of audience at any time with the Korean emperor, and Mr. Kato, another Japanese, was installed as adviser to the Royal Household Department, which handled all affairs of the royal family.[48]

The Koreans did not take kindly to these innovations. As adventurers poured into the country, the early disciplined action of the Japanese had given way to brutal arrogance. For instance, an unsuccessful attempt was made to secure for Japanese colonists all the waste lands in Korea whose title rested in the emperor, and thousands of Koreans were forced to work as coolies for the Japanese army. Personal property was seized, and complaints were of no avail. Severe punishment was meted out, however, by the Japanese military courts for violations by Koreans of Japanese orders.[49]

The Korean emperor, alarmed at the increasing Japanese control, viewed it as a threat to his country's independence. He still labored, however, under the impression that Korea would be protected, particularly by the United States. In

[44] *Id.* to *id.*, May 24, 1904, *ibid.*, no. 744.

[45] Text in *Foreign Relations,* 1904, p. 439.

[46] "All matters concerning finance" and "all important matters concerning foreign relations" were the phrases used.

[47] See Allen to Hay, October 20, 1904, in Korea: Dispatches, Vol. XXI, no. 813, for Metega's contract giving power of veto over all matters.

[48] *Id.* to *id.*, September 6, 1904, *ibid.*, no. 790.

[49] *Id.* to *id.*, October 11, 1904, *ibid.*, Vol. XXI, no. 804; McKenzie, *Tragedy of Korea,* 108–29, goes into detail on this subject.

September, 1904, secretly and at the emperor's request, the former Korean minister to the United States wrote a letter to Charles W. Needham, Counselor at the Korean legation in Washington, requesting the United States to aid his homeland. The dispatch mentioned the earlier conversations which the minister had had with Secretary Hay and, referring to what he described as Hay's assurances of aid to Korea, continued:

Now the war between Russia and Japan has not yet been settled, still the Japanese stretch their hands by force upon Korea and it will result in the domestic affairs and the foreign relations of Korea passing entirely into the hands of Japan, and the independence of Korea will be lost.

Is it not regrettable? . . .

At this critical time of danger we need your kind assistance; therefore I beg to ask that you will take the opportunity to describe the condition of Korea to the President and to the Secretary of State, and help to maintain the independence and integrity of the imperial household of Korea.[50]

The steady advance of Japan continued. At the beginning of 1905 she took over the policing of the Korean capital and placed a Japanese police inspector in every province.[51] In January, Minister Hayashi presented to the emperor a series of demands designed to achieve internal reform in Korea. One significant requirement was the reduction of the Korean army to 800 "Imperial Guards." Others were the abolition of the Korean department of posts and telegraphs, the appointment of Japanese-speaking Koreans to provincial offices, and the recall of the Korean legations abroad. To climax his program Hayashi demanded indemnity for every Japanese killed by Koreans in the previous ten years.[52] These demands aroused a storm of protest among Koreans.

[50] Allen to Hay, September 30, 1904, *ibid.*, no. 799.
[51] *Id.* to *id.*, December 16, 1904, *ibid.*, no. 839.
[52] *Id.* to *id.*, January 12, 1905, *ibid.*, Vol. XXII, no. 859.

Yet governmental policy was so greatly swayed by the Japanese that when a memorial condemning the demands was submitted to the Korean emperor by a group of his eminent countrymen, the memorialists were arrested.[53] In April the Japanese were able to secure the control of the postal, telegraph, and telephone services, thereby also acquiring the authority to speak for Korea at all future international conventions in regard to these matters.[54]

International approval was to be bestowed upon the policies of Japan in Korea through the new Anglo-Japanese agreement of August 12, 1905, the Taft-Katsura conversations in the preceding July, and finally the Treaty of Portsmouth, signed September 5 as a conclusion of the Russo-Japanese War. Whereas the earlier alliance of 1902 between England and Japan had provided for the joint recognition of the independence of Korea,[55] that of 1905 made no mention of Korea's status beyond the assertion that,

Japan possessing paramount political, military, and economic interests in Corea, Great Britain recognizes the right of Japan to take such measures of guidance, control, and protection in Corea as she may deem proper and necessary to safeguard and advance those interests. . . .[56]

The British knew, however, of Japan's intention of establishing a protectorate over Korea, and their approval is attested by the following extract from Lord Lansdowne's dispatch to the British ambassadors in Russia and France on September 6:

The new Treaty no doubt differs at this point conspicuously from that of 1902. It has, however, become evident that Corea, owing to its close proximity to the Japanese Empire, its inability to

[53] *Id.* to *id.*, March 14, 1905, *ibid.*, no. 882.
[54] Text of agreement in *Foreign Relations*, 1905, pp. 625–26.
[55] See p. 247.
[56] *British and Foreign State Papers*, XCVIII, 136–38.

stand alone, and the danger arising from its weakness, must fall under the control and tutelage of Japan.[57]

In July, 1905, President Theodore Roosevelt likewise gave his approval to the policies of Japan. Through the conversations between his Secretary of War, W. H. Taft, and Count Katsura, Japanese premier and foreign minister, Katsura denied any designs of his country upon the Philippine Islands, and in return Mr. Taft thus expressed his personal opinion:

. . . the establishment by Japanese troops of a suzerainty over Korea to the extent of requiring that Korea enter into no foreign treaties without the consent of Japan was the logical result of the present war and would directly contribute to permanent peace in the East.[58]

This opinion became that of the President and of the United States government when Mr. Roosevelt cabled Taft on July 29, 1905: "Your conversation with Count Katsura absolutely correct in every respect. Wish you would state to Katsura that I confirm every word you have said." [59]

To the approval of the United States and Great Britain, that of Russia was added through the treaty ending her war with Japan.[60] In Article II of this instrument, known as the Treaty of Portsmouth,[61] Russia not only acknowledged Japan's paramount interests in Korea, but agreed specifically never to contest them or the measures taken thereunder. The article stated:

The Imperial Russian Government, recognizing that Japan has paramount political, military and economic interests in Korea,

[57] *British Documents,* IV, 174–75.

[58] Quoted in Dennett, *Roosevelt and the Russo-Japanese War,* 113–14.

[59] Quoted in H. F. Pringle, *Theodore Roosevelt* (London, 1932), 384.

[60] The American minister in Korea had been privately approached by the Korean emperor through his chamberlain and asked if the United States would favor a Korean attempt to be represented in the peace negotiations between Japan and Russia. The response was evidently not encouraging, as no action was taken. See Morgan to Secretary of State, July 20, 1905, in Korea: Dispatches, Vol. XXII, no. 7.

[61] Text in *Foreign Relations,* 1905, pp. 824–28.

agrees not to interfere or place obstacles in the way of any measure of direction and protection, and supervision which the Imperial Government of Japan may deem necessary to adopt in Korea.

With recognition by these powers of her position as the exclusive protector of Korea, Japan proceeded to lay plans which would guarantee that her policies in that country would receive representation abroad only through Japanese channels.[62] Before the final signing of the treaty ending the war with Russia, rumors were current that all foreign legations were to be withdrawn from the peninsula kingdom. The American minister was forced to deny an unauthorized report that, at a meeting of all the foreign representatives in Korea, they had agreed to request their governments to withdraw them. He did say, however, that the Japanese minister had intimated his government's expectation that the legations would in time be closed. The emperor and his Korean advisers, on the other hand, were represented as earnestly hoping that Korea's legal status of independence might be saved and that the prophesied departure of foreign governmental agents would not be made.[63]

Beginning in October, 1905, pressure by the Japanese minister was applied on the Korean emperor and his advisers to force their consent to complete Japanese supervision of Korean affairs, together with control over the nation's foreign relations. The ruler of the victimized country was described as resisting all such demands and looking to the United States for aid under the treaty of 1882.[64] Since the Korean legation in Washington was represented as sympathetic with the Japanese, and since it would inform them immediately should an official appeal be made, a personal messenger was sent. Homer B. Hulbert, a teacher and an American of long residence in

[62] The counselors in the Korean legations at Paris, Washington, and Berlin, the only ones employing foreigners, had already been discharged on July 15. See Morgan to Secretary of State, July 18, 1905, in Korea: Dispatches, Vol. XXII, no. 6.

[63] *Id.* to Root, August 30, 1905, *ibid.*, no. 15.

[64] *Id.* to *id.*, October 19, 1905, *ibid.*, no. 23.

260 KOREA AND THE OLD ORDERS

Korea, left for the United States to lay before the President evidence justifying the exercise of American good offices in behalf of the helpless nation under the treaty of 1882.[65]

The Japanese, however, were to move more swiftly. Marquis Ito reached the peninsula early in November and in an audience with the Korean emperor on the eleventh delivered to him an autographed letter from the Emperor of Japan which stated:

I, the Emperor of Japan, hereby congratulate your Majesty on the restoration of peace in the Far East, and in order that the friendly relation of our two nations shall become a degree closer, I hereby send my special embassador.

I also wish to inform your Majesty that I shall hereafter guard the integrity of Korea and vouchsafe the personal safety of the Imperial Household.[66]

On the fifteenth he had another audience and presented these proposals: First, the Korean department of foreign affairs was to be abolished, future diplomatic functions to be handled by a special council at Tokyo; second, the Japanese minister at Seoul was thereafter to be termed the "General Superintendent or Director"; third, the Japanese consular representatives at the capital and in the different ports were to be termed "Superintendents." [67]

The reply of the Korean emperor to these proposals was as follows:

I had heard of late newspaper rumors of a treaty concerning a protectorate; but never doubting His Majesty, the Japanese Emperor's sincerity in His Majesty's late declaration of war against Russia that "Japan will preserve the independence and integrity of Korea," and also in the treaty made and signed at Seoul last year between your empire and my land, in which was the statement that

[65] *Id.* to *id.*, October 19, 1905, *ibid.*, no. 19.
[66] Allen Papers. See a varying paraphrase of this letter in G. T. Ladd, *In Korea with Marquis Ito* (New York, 1908), 254–55.
[67] Allen Papers.

Korea's independence will be upheld; I had not given credit to such reports and congratulated myself upon having the privilege of welcoming you as His Majesty's representative, never doubting but that your mission was for a friendly purpose. But now you propose these three articles that were beyond my slightest apprehension.[68]

In spite of the urging of Marquis Ito, the conversation ended without the emperor's assenting to the Japanese proposals. Since the emperor excused his recalcitrance by expressing a desire first to discuss the matter with his ministers and to ascertain the feeling of the people, Ito could offer no valid objection, but he warned the hesitant ruler against any attempt to stir up the Korean people.[69]

On the two days following their emperor's refusal to sanction Ito's plan, the members of the Korean cabinet were subjected to intense pressure in order to secure their approval of the proposed reforms. When this group also refused, Ito secured a joint audience with them and the emperor but had no better success. His further attempts to get personal audiences were also unsuccessful. Concentrating again on the emperor's advisers, he was able at one o'clock on the morning of November 18 to secure the signatures of five of the eight. There are, however, definite indications that intimidation was used in winning even this bare majority, particularly in the instance of Han Kyu Sul, the prime minister, who refused to sign and was out of the room when majority consent was given. The Korean emperor did not sign the agreement then or later.[70]

Korea thus entered upon a new phase of her existence. Heretofore all the nations who had at various times achieved

<hr />

[68] *Ibid.* Cf. McKenzie, *Tragedy of Korea,* 132; Ladd, *In Korea,* 256 ff.

[69] See McKenzie, *Tragedy of Korea,* 132–33; Ladd, *In Korea,* 254–61, for accounts of this conversation.

[70] Allen Papers; McKenzie, *Tragedy of Korea,* 134–37. Even Ladd, *In Korea,* 261–67, is unable to dispel completely the atmosphere of duress surrounding these proceedings.

predominance in Korea had maintained the fiction that their functions were purely advisory. Now Japan had overstepped this position and assumed direct control. The declaration of the Japanese government, accompanying the announcement of the treaty, justified the move by "the unwise and improvident action of Korea, more especially in the domain of her international concerns," and stated that

To permit the present unsatisfactory condition of things to continue unrestrained and unregulated would be to invite fresh difficulties, and Japan believes that she owes it to herself and to her desire for the general pacification of the extreme East to take the steps necessary to put an end once and for all to this dangerous situation. Accordingly, with that object in view and in order at the same time to safeguard their own position and to promote the wellbeing of the Government and people of Korea, the Imperial Government have resolved to assume a more intimate and direct influence and responsibility than heretofore in the external relations of the Peninsula.[71]

The terms of the new system of Japanese control over Korean affairs were substantially those which Ito had presented on November 15.[72] The three important articles were as follows:

I. The Government of Japan, through the department of foreign affairs in Tokyo, will hereafter have control and direction of the external relations and affairs of Korea and the diplomatic and consular representatives of Japan will have the charge of the subjects and interests of Korea in foreign countries.

II. The Government of Japan undertake to see to the execution of the treaties actually existing between Korea and other powers, and the Government of Korea engage not to conclude hereafter

[71] *Foreign Relations*, 1905, p. 613.

[72] See p. 260. A provision in the preamble stated that the terms were to serve "until the moment arrives when it is recognized that Korea has attained national strength," and an extra article provided for the maintenance of the welfare and dignity of the Imperial House. A text of the agreement is in *Foreign Relations*, 1905, pp. 612–13.

any act or engagement having an international character, except through the medium of Japan.

III. The Government of Japan shall be represented at the court of His Majesty the Emperor of Korea by a resident general, who shall reside at Seoul primarily for the purpose of taking charge of and directing the matters relating to diplomatic affairs. He shall have the right of private and personal audience of His Majesty the Emperor of Korea. The Japanese Government shall have the right to station residents at the several open ports and such other places in Korea as they may deem necessary.

Such residents shall, under the direction of the resident general, exercise the powers and functions hitherto appertaining to Japanese consuls in Korea, and shall perform such duties as may be necessary in order to carry into full effect the provisions of this agreement.

Thus Japan had at last attained exclusive control of Korea's destinies as against any other power.

4. Efforts to Save Korea's Independence

The policy of the American government toward Korea had already been established by Roosevelt's approval of the Taft-Katsura conversations of July, 1905, and by his note to Hay on the twenty-eighth of the preceding January in which he stated: "We cannot possibly interfere for the Koreans against Japan. They could not strike a blow in their own defense." [73] It is therefore not surprising that Hulbert, who had been in

[73] Quoted in Dennett, *Roosevelt and the Russo-Japanese War*, 110. H. N. Allen mentions an interview that he had with President Roosevelt in September, 1903. Allen states that he tried then to show the President that the administration was wrong in lending sympathy to the Japanese as it was leading them on to war with Russia. "But the President showed most unmistakably that that was just what he wanted to see." Allen Papers. Accordingly, when the Japanese minister in Washington notified the American Secretary of State of the conclusion of the agreement on November 23, Secretary Root, much to the satisfaction of the Japanese and without Korean confirmation, on the following day instructed the American minister in Korea to close his legation and withdraw from Korea. Telegram, November 24, 1905, in Korea: Instructions, Vol. II; paraphrase in *Foreign Relations*, 1905, p. 631.

Washington since November 18 endeavoring to intercede for Korea, was unable to secure an interview with the President. Though his letter from the Korean emperor [74] was placed before Mr. Roosevelt by Secretary Root, a reply was made only after the United States government had taken official cognizance of the Japanese-Korean agreement and closed the legation in Korea. Mr. Roosevelt's reply, addressed to Mr. Root, is as follows:

I have read carefully through the letter of the Korean Emperor handed to you by Mr. Hulbert. . . . I understand from you that the Korean representatives here, so far as you know, are unacquainted with the existence of such a letter and that Mr. Hulbert understands that it is the wish of the Emperor that the existence of the letter should be kept secret and nothing said to anyone about it, and particularly not to the Japanese. Of course, these facts render it impossible for us to treat the letter as an official communication, for there is no way in which we could officially act without violating what Mr. Hulbert says is the Emperor's wish. Moreover, since the letter was written we have been officially notified that the Korean Government has made the very arrangement with Japan which in the letter the Emperor says he does not desire to make. All things considered I do not see that any practical action on the letter is open to us.[75]

The matter, however, was not so easily disposed of. On December 11, 1905, Mr. Hulbert received a cablegram from the emperor of Korea declaring "the agreement of November 17 to be null and void because it was obtained by force." The message further stated that "a protest should be lodged at once" and insisted that Hulbert "arrange in the best possible manner the termination of this agreement within a reasonable time." [76] On the same day the Korean minister to France, then in the United States as "special envoy without creden-

[74] Text of emperor's letter in McKenzie, Korea's Fight, 102–103.
[75] Quoted in Dennett, Roosevelt and the Russo-Japanese War, 304–305.
[76] Korea: Notes from, United States Department of State.

tials," called on Mr. Root, related a similar story, and branded the treaty an invalid instrument. To the Korean, however, the refusal of the United States to become involved was made even more definite than previously to Hulbert, for in the meantime Secretary Root had received official notice of the agreement from the Korean legation in Washington and was also informed that this agency had transferred its functions and effects to the Japanese embassy there. Said Secretary Root:

> In view of this official communication, it is difficult to see how the Government of the United States can proceed in any manner upon the entirely different view of the facts which you tell us personally you have been led to take by the information which you have received. It is to be observed, moreover, that the official communications from the Japanese Government agree with the official communications from the Korean Government, and are quite inconsistent with your information.[77]

The American Department of State also advanced a legal argument that the earlier agreements of February 23, 1904, and August 22, 1904, whose validity was not contested,[78] "appear to be of such a character as practically to give Japan control over the foreign relations of Korea. . . . Those previous relations of control," the argument concluded, "amount to a complete bar to any interference by the United States under the treaty of 1883." [79]

It is not generally known that besides Mr. Hulbert and the Korean minister to France, a third person was also seeking the aid of the United States in the effort to save the Korean Empire from complete Japanese control. This person was H. N. Allen, who had been in Korea since 1884 and a

[77] Letter of December 19, 1905, in Korea: Notes to, United States Department of State; also printed in *Foreign Relations*, 1905, pp. 629–30.

[78] See pp. 253 ff., and *Foreign Relations*, 1904, pp. 437, 439.

[79] Memorandum of Department of State, December 18, 1905, in Korea: Notes from; Letter, December 19, 1905, in Korea: Notes to; also *Foreign Relations*, 1905, pp. 629–30.

member of the American legation there since 1889.[80] A long-time personal friend of the Korean emperor, Allen, upon his return to the United States, also attempted to help the unfortunate monarch. Through the firm of Collbran and Bostwick, an American company in Korea, the emperor transferred $10,000 of his personal funds to finance Allen's fight. A message in code was also sent, as well as blank sheets of paper each stamped with the emperor's seal. Because of the inability of the ruler to communicate with his legations except through the Japanese, the code message was to be translated and written on the blank papers for delivery to the Korean legations in London, Paris, Berlin, and Washington. Presumably, these missives were to instruct the legations to refuse recognition of the recent treaty and the Japanese-inspired instructions. But, since the matter had to be handled without the knowledge of the Japanese, of whom the emperor, recalling the murder of his wife, might well be afraid, and who would be sure to force a retraction of his act should it be made public, no communication to secure a translation of the message could be had with the Korean legation. Allen made extended efforts to secure the services of Joseph H. Choate as attorney for his case. Finally, because of the emperor's inability to assert his claim openly, and President Roosevelt's policy of giving Japan a free hand in Korea, Allen concluded that insufficient evidence existed to warrant further pursuance of his cause. The unspent funds were then returned to the emperor, and all hope of American aid was abandoned.[81]

During this period, from 1900 through the Russo-Japanese War, the declared Japanese policy of maintaining the independence of Korea gradually became secondary to the more expedient policy of "paramount interests." Japan's proced-

[80] Allen was the American minister from July, 1897, to March, 1905.

[81] This material is all found in the Allen Papers, the blank sheets with the emperor's seal, the untranslated message, as well as the extensive correspondence of Allen in his attempt to secure adequate legal counsel.

ure of building up strong commercial interests in Korea, as against the Russian technique of political control, gave her a most favorable basis for the later claim of special interests in the peninsula, political as well as commercial. This claim was first recognized by her alliance with Great Britain in 1902.[82] In making it, Japan was challenging Russia, and Russia's refusal to give her a clear field in Korea led to the war. Yet up to the actual outbreak of hostilities Japan still officially predicated her policy upon a desire to maintain Korean independence.

With Russia removed from the scene, Korea, whose previous sovereignty and independence were legally complete, entered upon a new international status—that of a protectorate. The step into this status was not a long one, since her previous condition of independence was merely diplomatic, not actual.[83] Moreover, she had been governed under foreign advice before, and by the agreements of February and August, 1904,[84] somewhat habitually bound herself by international agreement to accept the exclusive advice of outsiders, this time that of the Japanese. Although susceptibilities might be soothed, and perhaps certain diplomatic difficulties avoided by still referring to Korea as independent, in reality she was a Japanese protectorate.[85]

Any doubt as to this status was certainly dispelled by the agreement of November, 1905, in which Korea lost all control over her foreign relations. "A stipulation placing all its foreign affairs in the hands of its protector is regarded by most authorities as depriving the protected State of its inter-

---

[82] Russia had, however, previously recognized Japan as having special commercial interests in Korea by the Nishi-Rosen agreement.

[83] T. J. Lawrence, *War and Neutrality in the Far East* (London, 1904), 208–18.

[84] See pp. 253 ff.

[85] Lawrence, *The Far East*, 219; see also Francis Rey, "La situation internationale de la Corée," in *Revue Générale de Droit International Public*, XIII (1906), 40–58.

national character." [86] But though it be agreed that Korea did give up her international status in the Western family of states, she still existed in fact as an international personality, for Korean affairs after 1905 cannot be considered as purely a matter of constitutional law. As long as the Japanese continued to act in the name of the separate entity of Korea and her emperor, a small vestige of her international status remained, though this condition has been termed "a protectorate of the strictest kind known to international law." [87]

The belief of the emperor of Korea that the United States would save his country from falling under the control of the Japanese is one of the striking aspects of this period. And this confidence was not without foundation, for Article I of the terms of the treaty between the United States and Korea stated: "If other Powers deal unjustly or oppressively with either Government, the other will exert their good offices, on being informed of the case, to bring about an amicable arrangement, thus showing their friendly feelings." [88]

It is important here to note that the term "good offices" has a definite meaning in Western international law. Under it a third state may offer itself as a means of bringing about negotiation in an international dispute and yet avoid the charge of unfriendly intervention. Should the contending states accept this offer, the way is then open for mediation through the third state.[89] The United States was therefore not bound to take cognizance of any condition in Korea until notified by the Korean government. The attempt of Minister Morgan to point out, in the face of Japan's action, the Amer-

---

[86] Baty, "Protectorates and Mandates," loc. cit., 110; see also Emmerich de Vattel, The Law of Nations (New York, 1796), Bk. I, Chap. I, sec. 11.

[87] "The International Status of Korea," in American Journal of International Law, I (1907), 448.

[88] United States Statutes at Large, XXIII, 720.

[89] Wheaton, International Law, sec. 73; J. B. Moore, Digest of International Law (Washington, 1906), VII, secs. 1064–65; A. E. Hindmarsh, Force in Peace (Cambridge, 1935), 18–19; G. G. Wilson, Handbook of International Law (St. Paul, 1927), sec. 89.

ican obligations under Article I of the American-Korean treaty, brought the logical reminder from Secretary Root that "Fulfillment of article one is for Korea to question. . . ."[90] Likewise, the efforts of individuals to enlist the aid of the United States in branding the treaty of 1905 invalid were confronted by official notice from both the Japanese and Korean governments that the treaty was in force.

Finally, the United States claimed that the earlier Japanese-Korean agreements of 1904 had created in themselves a Japanese protectorate which, as Korea had made no appeal then, now served as a bar to action under the treaty of 1882.[91] It should be mentioned, however, that this position, though legally valid, was based upon the fact that the United States did not want to prevent the control of Korea by Japan. The independence of Korea was held of lesser import than the general peace of Asia, and a Japanized Korea preferable to a Russianized one.[92]

To Korea, however, the clause in the treaty with the United States did not appear a merely legal phrase subject to an interpretation which would rob it of its spirit. The United States was viewed as a nation having no territorial or political ambitions in Korea and one which could be relied on to check those states who did have. This impression was due, first, to the earlier actions of the United States, such as that in 1894, when Korea had asked the good offices of the American government because of the Sino-Japanese War.[93] In the second place, the personal attitudes and sympathies of the American diplomatic representatives had given Korea the impression that the United States would protect her. The Americans had been the most ardent supporters of Korean

[90] Telegram, Root to Morgan, November 3, 1905, in Korea: Instructions, Vol. II.
[91] See p. 265; see also Vattel, *The Law of Nations*, Bk. I, Chap. XVI, sec. 199.
[92] Dennett, "American Good Offices in Asia," *loc. cit.*, 22–24.
[93] See p. 209.

independence, whether against Chinese pretensions of suzerainty or Japanese attempts at dominance.

For example, H. N. Allen, American minister to Korea from 1897 to 1905, was a close personal friend of the Korean monarch and had given him assurances that the United States would make it "difficult for any one nation to ruthlessly take away this [Korean] independence." [94] When the Japanese began consolidating their position in the peninsula after February, 1904, Allen indicated to his superiors that the king "falls back in his extremity upon his old friendship with America. It is my endeavor to soothe him all I can," he continued.[95] Though Allen asserted he had not encouraged the ruler to dispatch anyone to the United States to secure aid under the treaty, to Secretary Hay he wrote:

At the same time I may as well inform you that the Emperor confidently expects that America will do something for him at the close of this war, or when opportunity offers, to retain for him as much of his independence as is possible. He is inclined to give a very free and favorable translation to Article I of our treaty. . . . I trust to be able to prevent a direct invocation of this treaty, however, though I am obliged to assure His Majesty that the condition of Korea is borne in mind by the United States Government who will use their good offices when occasion occurs.[96]

It is not therefore strange that when the Japanese began pressing the Korean emperor to agree to the treaty depriving him of control over his foreign relations, the new American minister reported that it was the United States to whom the ruler looked to save for him the last vestige of his international status.[97]

A third factor in creating the belief that America would save Korea from calamity was the Korean habit of mind

[94] Allen to Hay, August 31, 1900, in Korea: Dispatches, Vol. XVI, no. 275.
[95] *Id.* to *id.*, April 14, 1904, *ibid.*, Vol. XXI, no. 720.
[96] *Ibid.*
[97] Morgan to Root, October 19, 1905, *ibid.*, Vol. XXII, no. 23.

which viewed the United States not as bound legally to extend "good offices" in certain rigidly defined circumstances, but, instead, as cast in the Far Eastern role of the "elder brother" of Korea.[98] That is, to those who knew little of the legal implications of "good offices," the phrase was interpreted as meaning benevolent assistance in time of stress. That an "elder brother" would refuse that assistance because of legal technicalities was incomprehensible to the Korean rulers.

[98] See statement of the Korean emperor to Allen, 251 n.

CHAPTER XIII

LOSS OF INTERNATIONAL PERSONALITY, 1905–1910

1. THE RESIDENCY-GENERAL OF JAPAN

FROM 1905 to 1910 Korea appeared to remain an empire with its ruling dynasty on the throne. Actually she experienced more complete foreign domination than under either the Mongols or the residency of Yüan Shih-k'ai. The Japanese, by giving the country the Western status of a protectorate, had effectively removed it from international concern, and the futile attempts of the Korean monarch to secure international condemnation of the legality of the protectorate were to lead to his abdication. Later, his land was to be annexed to the Japanese Empire, and Korea was to disappear completely as an international personality *de jure* and *de facto*.

Within a month from the time that the other powers had been notified of the November 17 agreement transferring Korean foreign relations to Japan, the Japanese government had issued the decrees which would set up, within the broad terms of the treaty, the Residency-General. The *Tokan-fu,* literally "Supervisory Office," was set up by decree on December 20, 1905, under the control of the *tokan* or "resident general." The resident general was to be "under the direct control" of the Japanese emperor, but was not to have direct access to him. Instead the new official was to deal through the Japanese foreign minister in matters concerning foreign affairs and through the premier in all other matters.[1]

---

[1] Imperial Ordinance, no. 267, in *Foreign Relations,* 1906, II, 1025.

The treaty of November 17 outlined the resident general's function as primarily one of control and direction in diplomatic matters, but the Imperial Ordinance limited his duties to the control of consular matters and the supervision of business in Korea pertaining to foreigners, leaving the purely diplomatic sphere to be handled through the Foreign Office in Tokyo. The resident general, however, was given supervision of all government functions previously placed under Japanese advice, such as those of the Department of Finance. All Japanese employed by the Korean government were subject to his orders, and he could call on the Japanese military forces in Korea to preserve order.[2]

The administration of those matters under Japanese direction was to be carried out through Korean officials. This meant that the resident general would transmit his orders to the Korean government for execution, though in urgent cases he could deal directly with the local authorities. In matters under his jurisdiction he could issue ordinances, backed by small fines and imprisonment, and he had the authority to suspend the operation of any Korean law deemed contrary to treaty, Japanese law, or the public interest. Under the resident general the local "residents" were to be appointed, their number, location, and jurisdiction being at his discretion. In addition to the army and the Japanese-advised native police, a special Japanese police force was attached to each Residency and to the Residency-General.[3]

The status of aliens in Korea, other than Japanese, remained as before the treaty of 1905, foreign consuls having both civil and criminal jurisdiction over their nationals. To clarify its position in this respect, on November 22, 1905, the Japanese government addressed a note to the treaty pow-

[2] *Ibid.*

[3] *Annual Report on Reforms and Progress in Korea* (Seoul, 1907–11), 1908, pp. 31–33. In November, 1906, the Residency police numbered 558, the native force 734 Japanese and 2067 Koreans. The size of the Japanese gendarmery is not known.

ers promising that "in assuming charge of the foreign relations of Korea and undertaking the duty of watching over the execution of the existing treaties of that country, they [the Japanese government] will see that those treaties are maintained and respected, and they also engage not to prejudice in any way the legitimate commercial and industrial interests of these Powers in Korea." [4]

As set forth in the preceding paragraphs, it is clear that under the 1905 agreement the Japanese made no attempt to reorganize Korean administration, but sought, by placing supervisors in every department, to control the native system and its administrators. Looking to this end, they closed their consulates in Korea and put the Residency-General into operation there on February 1, 1906.[5] Their strict supervision of the Korean government, however, and their control of its diplomatic service did not exempt the Japanese from all repercussions resulting from their Korean policies. The emperor of Korea, who had refused to sign the treaty validating these reforms, and who had previously denounced its legality, still opposed Japan; and while the Japanese could prevent non-cooperative Koreans from holding office, they had as yet no control over the advisers whom the emperor chose to keep at the palace. A coterie opposing the Japanese was thus able to find sanctuary in the imperial household. In addition the emperor himself had been secretly in touch with Koreans in Russia and China, through whom he continued to seek international intervention in his own behalf.

In July, 1906, Marquis Ito sought to regulate this still uncontrolled sphere in the interest of Japan. On the second day of the month, taking the Japanese adviser on police affairs and a body of police to the palace, the resident had an extended consultation with the Korean emperor. The *Japan Times* the next day described the conversation as follows:

4 *Ibid.,* App. F, p. 109.
5 *Foreign Relations,* 1906, II, 1023.

Among other things the marquis pointed out the absolute necessity of clearing the court of all sorts of evil characters . . . who
daily and nightly infest the palace and whose increasing machina-
tions seriously imperil the friendship between Japan and Korea,
and dangerously compromise the dignity and safety of the Korean
Imperial House. In order to save the Emperor the annoyance and
dangers caused by these persons, the resident-general suggested
the advisability of replacing the incompetent palace guards by a
more efficient force of constables under the Japanese police advisor,
to which the Emperor readily consented.[6]

The emperor was also directed to take steps to prevent the
dispatch of his aid and sympathy to anti-Japanese Korean
groups in China and Russia. As a result of these measures for
"pacification of the court," and with the palace now being
guarded by a body of Japanese constables, to which 360 others
were soon to be added, the emperor was little more than a
prisoner.[7]

The Japanese determination to exploit fully all powers
granted by treaty was shown in their attitude toward the
status of foreign representatives in Korea. In March, 1906,
the American government requested the government of Japan
to approve a proposal entitling the American representative
in Korea "Agent and Consul-General," a customary designation for such an official in dependent countries. Since the title
"Agent and Consul-General" denoted diplomatic functions
as well as consular duties,[8] Marquis Saionji, the Japanese foreign minister, refused his consent and pointed out that Japan
would control all Korean diplomatic matters from Tokyo,
thus making necessary only consular representation of the
United States in Korea.[9]

A similar situation, less amicably dealt with, was that in-

[6] *Ibid.*, 1042–43.
[7] See *ibid.*, 1042–44, for Japanese newspaper comments on this more re-
strictive policy.
[8] Ernest Satow, *A Guide to Diplomatic Practice* (London, 1922), I, 246.
[9] See *Foreign Relations*, 1906, II, 1033–35, for this correspondence.

volving Mr. Plançon, the Russian consul-general. Here a controversy arose because the credentials of the Russian representative were addressed to the emperor of Korea. The Japanese, by virtue of their complete control over all of Korea's foreign relations, objected to this, claiming the power to grant an exequatur for the performance of the duties of consul in Korea. After negotiations between the Japanese and Russian representatives in St. Petersburg and Tokyo, Russia was forced to draft new credentials addressed to the Japanese government rather than to that of Korea.[10]

2. The Hague Peace Conference and the Abdication

By 1907 the Japanese appeared to have matters in Korea arranged so that the policies they were employing there could receive only that favorable representation abroad which would be given by their own agents. This seemed assured since Korea's foreign affairs were being handled through Tokyo, and since her emperor had been relieved of his many non-official advisers and was being kept in his palace guarded by Japanese police. Nevertheless, when Mr. Hulbert (the American teacher who had pleaded the emperor's cause in the United States in 1905) departed suddenly from Seoul, some conjecture arose, though even his closest friends were unaware of what was brewing.[11]

Toward the end of June, 1907, Koreans and Japanese alike were astonished when, under Hulbert's advice, a deputation appeared at the Hague Peace Conference bearing credentials authorized by the emperor of Korea. By some means the emperor had been able to sign a document on April 20 appointing to the conference three Koreans as "Delegates Extraordinary and Plenipotentiary." The appointees were Prince Yi Wi-chyong, a member of the imperial family, and two other

10 *Ibid.*, 1044–46.
11 Ladd, *In Korea*, 83 ff.

Koreans of high rank. Their mission was financed with money advanced by the emperor himself. The imperial credentials described the business of the delegates as follows:

As the independence of Korea has been known to all the Powers with which she has ever been in friendly relation, we have, for this reason, the right to send delegates to all international conferences which can be convoked for any purpose. But by the terms of the treaty of November 18th, 1905, which was extorted from us by force, the Japanese by menace and by a violation of all international equity deprived us of the right of direct communication with the friendly Powers.

Not recognizing this act on the part of the Japanese, we hereby appoint . . . Delegates . . . for the purpose of making clear to the representatives of the Powers the violation of our rights by the Japanese and the dangers which presently threaten our country; and also to reestablish between my country and the foreign Powers the direct diplomatic relations to which we are entitled by the fact of our independence.[12]

On June 29 the deputation had presented themselves to M. Nelidoff, president of the Hague conference, to protest against the fact that Korea was not invited to the convention and also against the violation of Korean sovereignty by Japan. M. Nelidoff, however, refused to receive the group, on the grounds that he was unable to give audience to a foreign deputation which had not been recommended and invited by the Dutch government.[13] Subsequent efforts to establish themselves officially through the Dutch foreign minister, M. Van Tets, were of no avail. Upon being informed that Marquis Ito had interrogated the Korean emperor and secured a denial of all knowledge of the deputation and its actions,[14] the group declared through the *Courrier de la Conférence* that their credentials "are perfectly authorized and bear the signature

[12] Photograph of imperial credentials in Prince Ye We Chong's "A Plea for Korea," in *Independent*, LXIII (1907), 425.

[13] *London Times*, July 1, 1907, 5a.

[14] *Ibid.*, July 6, 1907, 7b.

and seal of the Emperor Yi Hyeng" but that "the Emperor, being a prisoner of the Japanese, is not at liberty officially to declare the truth as this might entail grave personal consequences." [15] But the deputation was unsuccessful, for, not having been officially invited, they were denied a hearing. The *London Times* was of the opinion that with the momentous work before the conference, it had no time for lost causes and submerged nationalities, which might disrupt that harmony so necessary for the accomplishment of its tasks.[16]

The Korean emperor revealed by his attempt to get a hearing at the Hague that he still trusted the powers—particularly the United States—to come to his aid if he could but let them know officially that he considered the treaty of November, 1905, void. After the Hague fiasco, however, he could have little faith left that aid against Japan might come from either Europe or America. As an additional worry, he now had the indignant Japanese to face for what they considered a violation of the treaty.

The news of the Korean deputation at the Hague conference caused much concern in Japan, and many discussions were held by the Japanese regarding what action they should take. Count Okuma was said to have stated that if the Korean emperor had authorized a scheme so lacking in common sense, he might properly be placed under restraint as not being in his right mind. Count Inouye was of the opinion that the stubborn ruler should be brought to Japan where, seeing that country's advancement, he would voluntarily cease his unfriendly attitude.[17] The *Japan Mail* stated that the unanimous opinion of the press and of the political parties was that such measures should be adopted "as would effectively prevent the recurrence of similar incidents." [18]

[15] Quoted in *ibid.*, July 8, 1907, 5a.
[16] *Ibid.*, July 8, 1907, 5a.
[17] Ladd, *In Korea,* 417–18.
[18] Quoted in *ibid.*, 419.

The Japanese government publicly announced on July 16 that it was determined to "go along with the opinion of the people" and adopt toward Korea "a strong line of action." [19] Viscount Hayashi, the Minister of Foreign Affairs, proceeded in person to Korea to consult with Marquis Ito. On July 17, the day before Hayashi's arrival, the Korean cabinet, presumably under Ito's orders,[20] called upon their emperor and proposed as an alternative to his abdication that he sign with his own seal the agreement of November 17, 1905, which gave Japan control of Korea's external relations but which had been signed by only five of the eight of the Korean cabinet; [21] that he accept the appointment of a regent; and that he proceed to Tokyo and apologize personally to the emperor of Japan.[22]

The enraged emperor at first refused. Pressure was continued, and finally, with all hope of foreign aid gone and with his own cabinet members urging his abdication, he weakened at three o'clock in the morning of the nineteenth, after being subjected to constant urging since 4:45 P.M. the previous day, and agreed to retire in favor of the crown prince.[23] Perhaps the best proof that the monarch accepted only under duress was the following statement which he signed for the Minister of Justice: "In abdicating my throne I acted in obedience to the dictate of my conviction; my action was not the result of any outside advice or pressure." [24]

[19] *Ibid.*
[20] It is the height of naïveté to suggest that the subsequent cabinet action was purely voluntary and would have been attempted without Ito's orders or, at least, his approval.
[21] See p. 261.
[22] T. F. Millard, *America and the Far Eastern Question* (New York, 1909), 131.
[23] For the decree of abdication, see McKenzie, *Tragedy of Korea*, 159–60.
[24] Quoted in Ladd, *In Korea*, 424.

3. COMPLETE JAPANESE ADMINISTRATION

In abdicating, the emperor did not view his influence in the affairs of Korea as being at an end. The crown prince, who assumed the throne, was of feeble intellect, and the emperor therefore felt that he himself would be able to continue to rule through his son. His hopes were short-lived, however, for the Japanese, having placed the imperial authority in such inept hands, were now able to secure without effort the imperial assent to a thorough reorganization of Korean-Japanese relations. A new agreement was signed on July 24, 1907, which removed from the Korean authorities any vestige of power to make decisions or to exercise governmental functions. The brief but comprehensive terms were as follows:

I. The Government of Korea shall act under the guidance of the Resident General in respect to reforms in administration.

II. The Government of Korea engage not to enact any laws, ordinances or regulations, or to take any important measures of administration without the previous assent of the Resident General.

III. The judicial affairs in Korea shall be set apart from the affairs of ordinary administration.

IV. The appointment and dismissal of all high officials in Korea shall be made upon the concurrence of the Resident General.

V. The Government of Korea shall appoint as Korean officials the Japanese subjects recommended by the Resident General.

VI. The Government of Korea shall not engage any foreigner without the concurrence of the Resident General.

VII. Art. 1 of the Protocol between Japan and Korea signed on the 22nd of August, 1905, shall hereafter cease to be binding.[25]

Whereas the earlier agreements put Japanese advisers in every sphere of Korean administration, that of July 24 placed in Japanese hands the actual functions of government. Under

[25] *Annual Report*, 1907, App. G. This agreement was that in which Korea agreed to accept a Japanese financial adviser, now no longer necessary with the increased Japanese control.

it no law, ordinance, or important administrative act could be made or executed without the approval of the resident general. He controlled the appointment and dismissal of all officials and could place in the governmental organization such of his own nationals as he might choose.

Various innovations fortified Japan's position on the peninsula. New regulations for the imperial household were promulgated on November 29, 1907. By their terms two thirds of its offices were abolished, a separate accounting bureau was set up for it, and access to the emperor was possible only through the Minister of the Household. A Japanese became the Director of the Police for the entire country, and in each province the police forces were under Japanese leadership. The special Japanese police attached to the Residency-General were incorporated into a new Korean constabulary, of which they constituted the nucleus.[26] Described as mercenaries, the Korean soldiers were held not to constitute "a perfect instrument of national defense."[27] Accordingly, the Korean army was ordered disbanded on August 1, 1907.

Toward the end of 1907, Marquis Ito, then in Japan, specifically denied that annexation of Korea was contemplated. He deprecated the use of military force exclusively in administering the country and in quieting the uprisings that had been frequent there since the abdication of the emperor.[28] Yet the Japanese had to increase the police forces and the gendarmery on the peninsula through the years 1908 and 1909 as the Korean "righteous army" kept up constant warfare against the foreign administration.[29] In July, 1909, when Marquis Ito was appointed president of the Japanese Privy Council, Viscount Sone, his deputy, succeeded him in Korea and continued his policies.[30]

[26] Ibid., 32–33.
[27] Ibid., 35.
[28] Japan Times, September 20, 1907, in Foreign Relations, 1907, pp. 774–75.
[29] Annual Report, 1908, p. 2; ibid., 1909, p. 2.
[30] Ibid., 1909, p. 1.

During these years Korea's few contacts with other countries were all handled by the Japanese. These included a new agreement with China concerning certain Chinese settlements, and the acknowledgment by Japan of the validity of some of the earlier Chinese loans to Korea. Further agreements with China were one disposing of the controversy over the Chientao region on the Tu-men River, which area, though inhabited by large numbers of Koreans, the Chinese claimed, and another settling the question about timber-rafting on the Yalu River. The Russians were also reimbursed for the large coal depot they had secured before 1904 at the southern port of Masampo.[31]

4. ANNEXATION

Marquis Ito, whose policy in Korea he himself had described as one of exercising "power and kindness side by side," and which was definitely opposed to the annexation of the country he administered,[32] was not viewed favorably by either the military party in Japan or the Japanese army in Korea. Even though he received outward cooperation from the military forces in Korea, the army remained a power he was not able completely to control.[33] Furthermore, the continued existence of groups of insurgent Koreans made necessary its expansion and constant use in the peninsula.[34]

Certain events led the Japanese to inaugurate in Korea a policy of repression, obviously best accomplished through their annexation of the entire country. These were a series of assassinations of natives and of foreigners who were working with the Japanese, which culminated in the assassination of Prince Ito himself. While on a trip in North China and Manchuria, Ito was killed by Koreans in the city of Harbin in

---

[31] For further discussion of these settlements, see *ibid.*, pp. 7–13.
[32] *Japan Times*, September 20, 1907, in *Foreign Relations*, 1907, p. 775.
[33] Millard, *The Far Eastern Question*, 130.
[34] *Annual Report*, 1908, pp. 77 ff.; *ibid.*, 1909, pp. 45 ff.

October, 1907.[35] In addition, Mr. W. D. Stevens, an American who had been employed by the Japanese in 1904 as adviser to the Korean foreign affairs department, was assassinated in 1908 in San Francisco,[36] and an unsuccessful attempt was made against the life of the Japanese-controlled Korean prime minister Yi Wan-yong.

These events enabled the military party in Japan to secure the acceptance of its program. The plans of this group came to fruition in July, 1910, when Viscount Sone was replaced by Count Terauchi, an avowed exponent of a more drastic policy in Korea. Formerly a member of the Japanese general staff and minister of war during the Russo-Japanese conflict, Terauchi was an exponent of the extreme military view that the Koreans must either be absorbed or decimated.[37] This view was justified as follows by the Japanese-controlled *Seoul Press:*

The present requires the wielding of an iron hand rather than a gloved one in order to secure lasting peace and order in this country. . . .

Japan is in this country with the object of promoting the happiness of the masses. She has not come to Korea to please a few hundred silly youngsters or to feed a few hundred titled loafers. . . . She must be prepared to sacrifice anybody who offers obstacles to her work. Japan has hitherto dealt with Korean malcontents in a lenient way. She has learned from experience gained during the past five years that there are some persons who cannot be converted by conciliatory methods. There is but one way to deal with these people, and that is by stern and relentless methods.[38]

The *Japan Mail* also approved the new program, stating that "The policy of conciliation is all very well in the hands of such a statesman as the late Prince Ito, but failing a successor to

[35] *Ibid.*, 1909, pp. 46–47.
[36] *Ibid.*, 1908, pp. 83–84.
[37] McKenzie, *Korea's Fight*, 174.
[38] Quoted in *ibid.*, 175.

Prince Ito, more ordinary methods will be found safer as well as more efficacious." [39]

Even before Ito's assassination had given Japan a pretext for repressive measures in Korea, a policy looking toward annexation had been decided upon.[40] This culminated in the signing of a memorandum on July 12, 1909, by the resident general and the Korean prime minister, whereby Korea transferred to Japan her entire judicial administration, including the prisons.[41] In consequence, the courts were thenceforth administered and supported by the Japanese government, although Koreans, with certain exceptions, were still subject to Korean law. The general effect of the agreement was to extend the Japanese judicial and penal system to the peninsula.[42]

According to the Japanese, the assassinations, actual and attempted, had "induced certain classes of Koreans to tender to their Sovereign and the Resident-General a petition for Annexation." [43] Authorized to arrange for the solution of the question of annexation, and still retaining his portfolio as minister of war in the Japanese government, Count Terauchi was appointed resident general May 30, 1910, and arrived in Seoul on July 23.[44] On the following day, the nature of impending events was disclosed by a short memorandum, cosigned by the new resident general and the Korean minister of the interior, placing at Japan's disposal the entire police function of the Korean government except custody of the imperial palace, and handling that by consultation between the Japanese and the household minister.[45] The resident general had previously controlled only the police at the treaty ports

[39] Quoted in *ibid.*, 175–76.
[40] *Annual Report*, 1910, p. 10.
[41] Text in *ibid.*, App. A.
[42] See *ibid.*, 1909, pp. 32–40.
[43] *Ibid.*, 1910, p. 11.
[44] *Ibid.*
[45] Text in *Foreign Relations*, 1910, p. 678.

and those attached to the courts, while the Korean government had charge of the native police force and the Japanese war department directed the gendarmery. Now, with the gendarmery as a nucleus, all of these agencies were combined in a single department under the resident general.[46] The American ambassador in Tokyo described this reorganization as "another step in the almost completed transfer to Japan of all real governmental powers in Korea." He indicated the situation more definitely by saying that

Japan at present has direct control of foreign, military, railway, post and telegraph, judicial, prison and police affairs, while the Korean Government must obtain the preliminary approval of the resident general in all matters relating to the enactment of laws and in all important matters of administration. . . .[47]

The month of August, 1910, saw the Korean emperor renounce his sovereignty and Korea become completely extinct as an international personality. On August 22, after approval by the emperor of Japan and his privy council on one hand, and by the emperor of Korea on the other, the treaty of annexation was signed at Seoul by Viscount Terauchi and Yi Wan-yong, the Korean prime minister.[48] The terms involved a complete and permanent cession of sovereignty by Korea and an acceptance and complete annexation by Japan. The imperial family of Korea and their heirs were to be given suitable titles and to receive annual grants sufficient for the maintenance of their position. As for the nonroyal Koreans, the Japanese agreed to confer peerages and monetary grants on those deserving recognition for meritorious services and, further, to protect the persons and property of all who were law-abiding. Koreans loyal to the new regime would also be employed in the public service as far as circumstance permitted.

[46] *Ibid.*, 677.
[47] *Ibid.*, 678.
[48] Text in *Annual Report*, 1910, App. A; *Foreign Relations*, 1910, pp. 682–83.

The treaty, together with rescripts of the Japanese and Korean emperors, a declaration to the powers, and a proclamation by the resident general, was promulgated on August 29, 1910. The Japanese emperor justified his policy of annexation on the grounds that he attached the "highest importance to the maintenance of permanent peace in the Orient and the consolidation of lasting security to our Empire. . . ." [49] In phrases reminiscent of the memorials formerly sent by Korean kings to the emperors of China, the Korean emperor, on the other hand, proclaimed his unworthiness and his inability to effect reforms, and was hence "constrained to believe it wise to entrust Our great task to abler hands. . . ." [50] The office of resident general was replaced by that of governor general, and Japan took up her first important responsibility as an imperial power.

To the foreign powers having treaties with Korea, Japan sent a declaration of complete annexation.[51] Since the annexation automatically extinguished their agreements with Korea, Japan's existing treaties, so far as practicable, were to be extended to the new increment of territory in matters relating to foreigners and foreign trade. Foreign residents were to have, as far as conditions permitted, the same rights and immunities as in Japan, the protection of those rights being in all cases subject to Japanese jurisdiction. Thus the extraterritorial privileges hitherto enjoyed by the treaty powers came to an end, though cases actually pending were allowed to remain in the consular courts until final decision. As a concession, Japan agreed to maintain for a ten-year period the current import and export duties even as against herself, and the treaty powers were likewise to retain coastwise fishing privileges for a similar period.

In the resident general's proclamation of annexation, the

---

[49] Rescript, *Annual Report*, 1910, App. B.
[50] *Ibid.*, App. C.
[51] Text in *ibid.*, App. D.

ideas peculiar to the Far East were not all forgotten. Japan and Korea were referred to as being bound by a "brotherly feeling," and the Japanese administrators were urged in dealing with Koreans to "always bear in mind that they are our brothers. . . ." [52] But that Japan was to be the "elder brother," and even the "master" as well, is indicated by the conclusion of the Japanese official's proclamation:

No leniency will be shown to those who, entertaining malicious motives, try to obstruct the carrying out of any administrative measures. But all those who behave themselves loyally and abide by law peacefully shall receive unto their posterities the benefits of a judicious and benevolent rule. You, people of *Chosen*,[53] should therefore take due cognizance of the new regime and be careful not to go astray.[54]

The news of Korea's annexation could not but be viewed by other states as a foregone conclusion. It had been shown at the Hague Peace Conference that no power was interested enough to contest Japan's claims on her. Internationally, therefore, Korea had been extant in name only, though as long as Japan even pretended to act for the emperor and government of Korea, a small vestige of her international personality remained. In fact, so complete was the Japanese control by 1910 that the formal annexation could have been viewed by other states more as a matter of constitutional law than of international law. The move was quite generally looked upon as the favorable solution of a problem long disturbing the Far East.[55]

[52] *Ibid.*, Apps. E and F.
[53] The name of Korea, officially *Dai Han*, was changed to *Chosen*, a term having no character denoting a separate state or nation. *Foreign Relations,* 1910, p. 684.
[54] *Annual Report,* 1910, App. E.
[55] See "The Annexation of Korea to Japan," in *American Journal of International Law,* IV (1910), 923–25.

CHAPTER XIV

CONCLUSION

K OREA occupies a position unique in modern history because of her many rapid changes of status. In a little more than two decades she passed from membership in a closed East Asiatic state system which gave her a peculiar status unknown to Western international law, to become legally a sovereign and independent political entity in the Western system, then, under that system, to the status of a protectorate, and finally, to complete extinction through annexation. In such a short period it was impossible for the Koreans to attain a full understanding of the nature and duties of a sovereign state, encumbered as they were by centuries of teachings and practice which cast them in a role of subservience to China, and by a civilization and a conception of society, government, and the world completely alien to that held by the West.

To those accepting Confucian ideology, the world stood as a single unit. Under the aegis of Heaven, according to this belief, there existed a pre-established world pattern wherein all things had a definite and proper relation to all other things. In their proper place all things were good, and evil was a disharmony resulting from a disturbance of the natural order. Since the social order and the natural order were both within the natural plan, disharmony in nature was an indication of disorder in the social structure.

The social order was built upon the five personal relationships of parent and child, husband and wife, ruler and subject, elder and younger brother, and friend and friend. *Li,* or the rules of proper conduct, set the standard for each of these relationships. By the observance of *li* each would perform his proper function according to the world pattern, whereupon harmony would exist. Equality was productive only of rivalry and contention. Hence, a hierarchy of superiors and inferiors was established through the social order. The purpose of all restraint, all government, was that of encouraging the observance of those rules which would achieve harmony and order in the world. The method of achieving order was not by fiat of law, but by reason, example, and conversion.

China was the Middle Kingdom, to whose ruler Heaven had given its mandate, to whom Heaven looked for the proper ordering of things. The parts of the world not pervaded by Chinese culture could only be in disorder, and were at best barbarian nations according to the Chinese conception. The Son of Heaven, viewing the whole world as his family, was in duty bound to extend order even to the barbarians through example and teaching. In the course of time these barbarian regions would become amenable to reason and example. When they understood the correct relations between the various orders of humanity, they would practice the rules of proper conduct, be taken into the natural order, and become filial sons in an international family.

This family was regulated by the same rules as the natural family, the relationship being, for the most part, that of parent and son, though China's relationship to Korea after the seventeenth century was termed that of elder to younger brother. International order was therefore merely the extension of the social order into the world sphere. A nation's duties and privileges were governed by the same rules that preserved harmony in the family and in society. Obviously, then, the East Asiatic Confucian society, national and international, was familistic and natural, not legal. It lacked such Western concepts as those of law, the state, sovereignty, and the legal equality of states.

Korea did not begin to achieve a full status within this Confucian familistic system until about the seventh century A.D. Before that time the Korean peninsula was viewed as definitely barbarian and, as a matter of course, received the treatment accorded all such areas near China. The Chinese policy of preserving peace on the borders of the Middle Kingdom was to secure the cooperation, by force if necessary, of friendly chieftains of the barbarian tribes. Barbarian princes were either conquered or subsidized in order to keep them from raiding Chinese territory; they might be given titles as border protectors and invested with authority from the Son of Heaven. Although the barbarians remained ignorant of their position in the world order and of their proper relationship to the Middle Kingdom, they did develop an appreciation of China's military might and mature civilization.

As the Confucian culture became dominant in China and spread into the Korean peninsula, it conquered where armies had failed. In consequence of this phenomenon, the rulers of the petty Korean nations came to view investiture by the emperor of China, the Son of Heaven, as necessary to their right to rule, or as a delegation by the world ruler of the authority he possessed from Heaven. Viewing themselves as lesser members of the imperial family, these Korean rulers showed their respect by sending tribute to the Son of Heaven and accepting from him their investiture, along with gifts and admonitions concerning the preservation of the natural order.

When barbarians from the areas north and west of China succeeded in overthrowing the reigning Chinese dynasty, Korea, in accordance with the legitimism fundamental to Confucian teaching, gave up her allegiance to the orthodox Chinese rulers only under duress and returned to them at the first opportunity. The Mongols, for instance, being rejected as barbarians by the Koreans, found it most difficult to control the peninsula. Without the sanction of the Confucian familial relationship, they had to use force and direct rule to hold Korea's allegiance.

After the last half of the fourteenth century the relations between Korea and China achieved a regularization which was disrupted only in the nineteenth century by contacts with the Western states. During this long period Korea was considered a lesser nation. The various lesser nations in the East Asiatic Confucian system [1] existed on a *fan-ch'en* basis, that is, as "border wardens" to the Middle Kingdom and its Son of Heaven, and they were termed *shu-pang* or dependent nations. Korea, as the closest of the *shu-pang*, stood in the relation to China as a younger to an elder brother, the latter also possessing, as head of the Confucian family of nations, the powers of the father. Consequently, the relations between these two nations were regulated, not by law, treaty, or agreement of any kind, but by *li*, the rules of proper conduct, which governed the five great relations that made up all social existence.

In this association China was to give the benevolent protection and advice that a parent or elder brother might properly give. Korea, in turn, owed that respect and submission which a younger brother or son should show to his elder brother or parents. There were, therefore, no definite legal limits concerning what China could or could not do. Legalistic formulation would merely have distorted the true relationship and prevented its adjustment to the varied situations of actual life. The relationship was natural, familial, not legal.

In times of peace, when no strain existed on the relationship, it was signalized by certain regular forms of intercourse such as the sending of tribute, the return of gifts, the dispatch

[1] At the beginning of the nineteenth century the lesser nations in the system were Korea, Liu-ch'iu, Annam, Laos, Siam, Burma, and Sula. Areas such as Tibet, Mongolia, and Turkestan were not separate nations but were governed more as provinces. Japan had at various times acknowledged and renounced an inferior status in the East Asiatic system.

of imperial missions to confer investiture or offer congratulations, and other acts of ceremony. When harmony existed
these were the only outward tokens of the inward status of
being a *shu-pang*, a nation related to China as a son or respectful younger brother to his father or elder brother. Just
as ceremony alone marked the natural father's control over
his son in ordinary circumstances, so China received only
these outward tokens from Korea. Yet as the Chinese father
in times of crisis had absolute control, even unto death, so the
Chinese state in the nineteenth century exercised a like privilege in increasing her control over Korea. No legal contract
was necessary for China to take such action; no legal contract fixed the limits to which she might go. Who could say,
"This much aid shall the parent or elder brother give, and
no more"?

When the Western states began their eastward march in
the latter part of the nineteenth century, they brought with
them a concept of "international law" which they considered
to be universal in scope. In their attempts to deal with Korea,
however, they found that a relationship existed between that
country and China which they could not understand. Search-
ing back into the categories which their international system
listed, they hit upon that of suzerain and vassal as most nearly
fitting this East Asiatic relationship, and they then proceeded
to apply the legal attributes of vassalage to the non-legal
status of a *shu-pang*. Since they understood that a suzerain
always handles his vassal's foreign relations, when China
refused responsibility for Korea's acts the Western states accepted the refusal as a renunciation of suzerainty. Therefore, particularly after China encouraged Korea to sign treaties with the West to balance power against power, Korea was
viewed as sovereign and independent, and all Chinese claims
concerning her were rejected as pure ceremony and of no
legal effect.

China endeavored to have included in the early Western

treaties a recognition of the Confucian relationship. When this failed, she adopted the expedient of complementing each treaty with a letter attesting the inferior position of Korea with respect to that of the Middle Kingdom. But the admissions that the Korean king was *tzü chu* (master of himself) were translated into "independent" and "sovereign," and the Western states were thus further convinced of the lack of justification for China's claims. According to the non-legalist Confucian reasoning, however, Korea, the younger brother, was capable of being "master of himself" without renouncing his obligations to the elder brother, China.

With no competitors, China had been willing for centuries to exercise only the outward ceremonies of the central nation over its *shu-pang*. But with powerful Western states and a Westernized Eastern state vying with one another in Korea, and affirming that by *their* international law Korea was sovereign and independent, China decided to take steps to protect this dependent member of her family. In keeping with the *shu-pang* status, and not needing to secure any further agreements with Korea, she proceeded to place her own advisers in the spheres of customs and foreign affairs of the Korean government. The reigning Korean monarch was upheld as against revolutionary factions and intervention was used to correct those conditions which might serve as a basis for intrusion by other states.

After 1885 the Confucian relationship weakened as the king of Korea came under the influence of foreigners who urged that he assume the sovereign and independent status legally his. China, therefore, sent Yüan Shih-k'ai as Chinese resident to Korea to direct affairs, particularly in the diplomatic and consular fields. Her early policy of encouraging the foreign states to make treaties of friendship with Korea she also gradually changed to an attempted exclusion of all foreign influence. By 1894, still on the *shu-pang* basis and without the necessity of a legal agreement for each advance made,

China had achieved a *de facto* control over Korea which no Western supporter of Korean independence could deny. It was to overthrow this Chinese position that Japan resorted to war in 1894.

Under the assumption that the *shu-pang* relationship was that of vassal and suzerain, the Westerners, unable to comprehend a subservient relation not based on force, by adroit legal reasoning were able to prove conclusively that Korea was not a vassal, that China was not suzerain, and that Korea was a sovereign and independent state. The logic of this may have been unassailable under Western international law, but to both China and Korea the relationship between them was still that of *shu-pang* despite the Western interpretations of "suzerain" and "vassal." Under the assumption that China had nothing but a religious and ceremonial connection with Korea, Westerners viewed her growing *de facto* control of Korea as pure and unjustified power politics directed against an independent state. Supported by this assumption, Japan was able to end by force the age-old relationship between the two continental states.

When the Sino-Japanese War ended Korea's attempt to be a member of the Western state system and to retain as well the peculiar Confucian relationship to China, Korea became, legally, completely sovereign and independent. Actually, with a habit of subservience to a stronger power extending over centuries, she vacillated between the alternate overlordship of her two strongest neighbors, Russia and Japan. Her independence was merely a diplomatic fiction, since each of these two powers, only to check the designs of the other, loudly asserted its existence. This competition for dominance, plus the Manchurian issues, ended in war between Russia and Japan. The independence of Korea then was paid less lip service, and "paramount interests" became the basis of Japanese policy.

Korea soon went under the protectorship of Japan, first

with Japanese advisers in each Korean department of government, and later with actual administration through Japanese officers. The Koreans, who had been amenable to a Confucian relationship with China, naturally chafed under the Westernized control of the Japanese, which was administered with little attempt at conciliation. But the minds of the Korean king and his closest advisers harbored a ray of hope, particularly after the Russo-Japanese War, in a touching belief that under the Treaty of 1882 the United States could be relied upon to save Korea from extinction as an international personality. For, after centuries under a non-legal Confucian elder brother–younger brother relationship, those who ruled Korea had no conception of the limited obligation implied by a treaty guarantee of "good offices." When the king felt the independence of his country threatened by the Japanese, he therefore confidently sought American aid. Rebuffed, he appealed to the international peace conference at The Hague, only to be again refused. This act cost him his throne. Sporadic opposition to the foreign control continued, however, and Japan was forced to use sterner measures. Her first attempt at indirect rule of another nation subsequently ended with the annexation of the nation, and with the adoption of a policy of repression and absorption in dealing with it.[2]

The Japanese policy of absorption was not particularly successful. The Korean peninsula was never thoroughly subdued, and expatriated Koreans in the United States and

---

[2] F. A. McKenzie quotes a conversation, held about 1906–1907, with "one of the most influential Japanese in Korea," who described Japan's policy as follows: "You must understand that I am not expressing official views, but if you ask me as an individual what is to be the outcome of our policy, I can only see one end. This will take several generations but it must come. The Korean people will be absorbed in the Japanese. . . . There are only two ways of colonial administration. One is to rule over the people as aliens. This you English have done in India, and, therefore, your Indian Empire cannot endure. India must pass out of your rule. The second way is to absorb the people. This is what we will do. We will teach them our language, establish our institutions, and make them one with us." McKenzie, *Tragedy of Korea*, 145–46.

throughout the world have long been laying plans for the future independence of their homeland.[3] The policy of future freedom for Korea, announced at the Cairo conference November 22–26, 1943, has now changed the independence movement from its status of little more than a localized conspiracy to a matter of world policy.[4]

Korea, as the first major step in Japanese expansion, was the stepping stone to the "incident" in China which, in turn, was later broadened into a plan for a "new order" for the entire Pacific. At least on the Asiatic mainland it now appears that Japan was not seeking actual dominium of territory but was rather attempting to re-establish the outward forms of a closed regional international system—a "Middle Kingdom" and surrounding satellites—such as China once headed. Ignoring the legal concept of the sovereignty and juridical equality of states, she set up a group of entities subservient to her will and bound to her by ties which defy accurate legal definition. This system has been called one in which, "instead of the clear-cut lines of jurisdiction and independence so dear to the heart of the usual positivist, is found a condition of legal osmosis with Japanese and Chinese oozing into one another in most shocking fashion." [5] When the past history of the Far East is brought to mind, this "osmosis" is not so shocking, for in this particular aspect, the "new order" was indeed reminiscent of that Confucian system which so confounded the Western visitors of a century ago.

The Japanese-proposed new East Asiatic order lacked, however, the ethical basis which the former Chinese system possessed. Since it was only the Japanese who believed that

[3] See C. W. Kendall, *The Truth About Korea* (San Francisco, 1919), and *Korea Must Be Free* (Washington, 1930). For current activities see "Free Korean Movement," in *China At War*, VIII (1942), 22–24, *Korean Liberty Conference* (Washington, 1942), and *New York Times*, March 1, 1942, I, 10:1, IV, 6:2.

[4] *New York Times*, December 2, 1943, I, 1:8, 3:2, 3, 4.

[5] Payson Wilde, "What Is the Trouble with International Law?" in *American Political Science Review*, XXXII (1938), 493.

their emperor was the descendant of the Sun-Goddess and rightful ruler of the world, their control, as a consequence, could be extended and maintained only through force. Furthermore, to use the Confucian patterns and precepts for ruling and at the same time deny them as a guide for rulers, to reject the theory that a ruler governs under Heaven's mandate only so long as he is virtuous, made any revived Far Eastern order of the Japanese a mere façade for the exploitation of the neighboring peoples.

Nevertheless, Confucian concepts are still effective in the Far East, and if international society is to be reorganized on regional lines, that of East Asia, with its traditions of unity, of superior and inferior, of familistic government, will probably revert to an order more closely bound to its common civilization. After a century of experiment with the alien legal concepts of interstate relations introduced by Europe and America, the Far East may find in an indigenous system that community of ideas necessary for the peaceful relationship of all its peoples.

APPENDIXES

APPENDIX A

Treaties and Agreements with and Concerning Korea

February 26, 1876	Japan and Korea	Treaty of Kang-wha
August 24, 1876	Japan and Korea	Agreement for Trade
October 14, 1876	Japan and Korea	Agreement for Trade at Fusan
January 30, 1877	Japan and Korea	Agreement for Settlement at Fusan
July 3, 1877	Japan and Korea	Agreement for Shipwrecks
December 20, 1877	Japan and Korea	Agreement for Coal Depots
May 20, 1878	Japan and Korea	Agreement for Shipwrecked Koreans
August 30, 1879	Japan and Korea	Agreement for Opening of Wün-san
August 4, 1881	Japan and Korea	Agreement for Land Rent at Wün-san
May 22, 1882	United States and Korea	Treaty
June 6, 1882	Great Britain and Korea	Treaty (unratified)
June 30, 1882	Germany and Korea	Treaty (unratified)
August 30, 1882	Japan and Korea	Agreement re Emeute of 1882
September, 1882	China and Korea	Regulations for Overland Trade
October 31, 1882	Japan and Korea	Agreement for Travel and Trade
March, 1883	China and Korea	Regulations for Liaotung Trade
July 25, 1883	Japan and Korea	Agreement for Trade
July 25, 1883	Japan and Korea	Agreement for Port Limits
July 27, 1883	Japan and Korea	Agreement for Treatment of Japanese Fishermen
September, 1883	Japan and Korea	Agreement for Settlement at Jenchuan
November 26, 1883	Great Britain and Korea	Treaty of Seoul
November 26, 1883	Germany and Korea	Treaty of Seoul
April 1, 1884	China and Korea	Agreement for Chemulpo Settlement

June 25, 1884	Russia and Korea	Treaty of Seoul
June 26, 1884	Italy and Korea	Treaty of Seoul
October 3, 1884	General Agreement for Chemulpo Settlement	
November 11, 1884	Japan and Korea	Agreement for Remission of Indemnity
January 9, 1884	Japan and Korea	Agreement *re* Emeute of 1884
April 18, 1885	China and Korea	Convention of Tientsin
June 4, 1886	France and Korea	Treaty of Seoul
August 20, 1888	Russia and Korea	Treaty for Tumen River Trade
November 12, 1889	Japan and Korea	Agreement for Fisheries
July 23, 1892	Austria-Hungary and Korea	Treaty of Tokyo
August 16, 1894	Abrogation of Chinese-Korean Treaties	
August 26, 1894	Japan and Korea	Treaty of Alliance
April 17, 1895	Japan and China	Treaty of Peace
May 14, 1896	Japan and Russia	Agreement Relative to Korea
June 9, 1896	Japan and Russia	Agreement Relative to Korea
April 25, 1898	Japan and Russia	Agreement Relative to Korea
September 11, 1899	China and Korea	Treaty
October 3, 1900	Japan and Korea	Agreement for Fisheries
March 23, 1901	Belgium and Korea	Treaty of Seoul
April 17, 1901	France and Korea	Postal Agreement
January 30, 1902	Great Britain and Japan	Treaty of Alliance
March 19, 1902	France and Russia	Announcement Relative to Korea and Anglo-Japanese Alliance
July 15, 1902	Denmark and Korea	Treaty of Seoul
February 23, 1904	Japan and Korea	Protocol of Alliance
August 22, 1904	Japan and Korea	Agreement for Financial and Diplomatic Advisers
April 1, 1905	Japan and Korea	Agreement for Transfer of Communication Services to Japan
August 12, 1905	Great Britain and Japan	Treaty of Alliance
August 13, 1905	Japan and Korea	Agreement for Coastwise and Inland Water Navigation
September 5, 1905	Japan and Russia	Treaty of Peace
November 17, 1905	Japan and Korea	Convention for Transfer of Korean Foreign Relations to Japan
October 19, 1906	Japan and Korea	Agreement for Exploitation of Yalu and Tumen Forest Regions

July 24, 1907	Japan and Korea	Convention Relative to Japanese Administration in Korea
July 12, 1909	Japan and Korea	Memorandum Giving to Japan the Administration of Justice in Korea
June 24, 1910	Japan and Korea	Memorandum Giving to Japan the Administration of Police in Korea
August 22, 1910	Japan and Korea	Treaty of Annexation

APPENDIX B

CHRONOLOGY OF KOREAN RULERS, KINGDOMS, AND DYNASTIES

The Viscount of Chi and his descendants (legendary) .... 1122 (?)–193 B.C.
Wei Man, his son, and grandson ...... 193–108 B.C.
Direct administration in the north of the peninsula by Han China ...... 108 B.C.–A.D. 300 (?)
Sam Kuk (Three Kingdoms)
    Kaokuli .... 37 B.C.–A.D. 668
    Pai-chi .... 18 B.C.–A.D. 660
    Hsin-lo (Silla) .... 57 B.C.–A.D. 935
Wang (Kao-li) .... A.D. 918–1389
Li (Chao-hsien) .... A.D. 1392–1910

APPENDIX C

CHRONOLOGY OF CHINESE DYNASTIES

Hsia (legendary) ....to 1765 (?) B.C.
Shang ....1765 (?)–1123 (?) B.C.
Chou ....1122 (?)–256 B.C.
   Ch'un Ch'iu (Spring and Autumn
     Epoch) ....770–473 B.C.
   Chan Kuo (Warring State Epoch) ..473–221 B.C.
Ch'in ....221–206 B.C.
Former Han (including Wang Mang) ..202 B.C.–A.D. 25
Later Han ......................A.D. 25–220
The Three Kingdoms .............A.D. 221–277
The Six Dynasties and the Northern
   and Southern Dynasties .........A.D. 265–588
Sui ...........................A.D. 589–619
T'ang ..........................A.D. 620–906
Wu-Tai (Five Dynasties) .........A.D. 907–960
Sung ..........................A.D. 960–1280
Yüan (the Mongols) .............A.D. 1280–1367
Ming ..........................A.D. 1368–1643
Ch'ing (the Manchus) ...........A.D. 1644–1912

SELECT BIBLIOGRAPHY

I. BIBLIOGRAPHIES

Cordier, Henri, *Bibliotheca Sinica*. 4 vols., Paris, 1904–1907.

————, *Bibliotheca Sinica: Supplément*. Paris, 1924.

Courant, Maurice, "Introduction to the 'Bibliographie Coreene'" (Mrs. W. Massy Royds, trans.), in *Transactions of the Korea Branch of the Royal Asiatic Society*, XXV (1936), 1–99.

Friederici, Charles, *Bibliotheca Orientalis*. 2 vols., London, 1876–1883.

Müller, August (later Ernst Kuhn and Lucian Scherman), *Orientalische Bibliographie* [1887–1911]. 25 vols., Berlin, 1888–1922.

Nachod, Oskar, *Bibliographie von Japan, 1906–1935*. 5 vols., Leipsig, 1928–1937.

Trollope, M. N., "Corean Books and Their Authors," in *Transactions of the Korea Branch of the Royal Asiatic Society*, XXI (1932), 1–104.

Underwood, H. H., "Occidental Literature on Korea," in *Transactions of the Korea Branch of the Royal Asiatic Society*, XX (1931), 1–15.

————, "A Partial Bibliography of Occidental Literature on Korea from Early Times to 1930," in *Transactions of the Korea Branch of the Royal Asiatic Society*, XX (1931), 17–198.

————, "Supplement to a Partial Bibliography of Occidental Literature on Korea from Early Times to 1930," in *Transactions of the Korea Branch of the Royal Asiatic Society*, XXIV (1935), 23–48.

II. PRIMARY SOURCES

A. Manuscripts

Allen, H. N., Papers. New York Public Library.

Foulk, George C., Papers. New York Public Library.

China: Dispatches. 130 vols. United States Department of State.
China: Instructions. 7 vols. United States Department of State.
Korea: Dispatches. 22 vols. United States Department of State.
Korea: Instructions. 2 vols. United States Department of State.
Korea: Notes from. United States Department of State.
Korea: Notes to. United States Department of State.

B. Occidental Documents

Archives Diplomatiques. 112 vols., Paris, 1861–1914.
British and Foreign State Papers. 136 vols., London, 1841–1938.
British Documents on the Origin of the War, 1898–1914 (G. P. Gooch and Harold Temperley, eds.). 13 vols., London, 1929.
Carnegie Endowment for International Peace. *Korea: Treaties and Agreements.* Washington, 1921.
"Captain Basil Hall's Account of His Voyage to the West Coast of Corea in 1816," in *Transactions of the Korea Branch of the Royal Asiatic Society,* IX (1920), 1–37.
Congressional Record. Washington, 1873—.
Dennett, Tyler, "Documents, American Choices in the Far East in 1882," in *American Historical Review,* XXX (1924–25), 84–108.
"First Steps of Russian Imperialism in the Far East, 1888–1903" (from *Krasny Archiv,* LII, 54–124), in *Chinese Social and Political Science Review,* XVIII (1934–35), 236–81.
Hamel, Hendrick, "An Account of the Shipwreck of a Dutch Vessel on the Coast of the Isle of Quelpaert, Together with a Description of the Kingdom of Corea," in *Transactions of the Korea Branch of the Royal Asiatic Society,* IX (1918), 91–148.
M'Leod, John, *Narrative of a Voyage in His Majesty's Late Ship Alceste to the Yellow Sea Along the Coast of Corea.* London, 1817.
"On the Eve of the Russo-Japanese War" (from *Krasny Archiv,* II, 7–54, *Historical Journal of the Central Archives of RSFSR,* Moscow), in *China Social and Political Science Review,* XVIII (1934–35), 472–94; XIX (1935–36), 125–39.
Papers Relating to the Foreign Relations of the United States, 1861–1928. Washington, 1862–1943.

Publications of the Permanent Court of International Justice. Collection of Advisory Opinions. Series B. No. 4. Leyden, 1923.

"Russian Documents Relating to the Sino-Japanese War, 1894–1895" (from *Krasny Archiv*, L–LI, 3–63), in *Chinese Social and Political Science Review*, XVII (1933–34), 480–515, 632–70.

Treaties and Agreements With and Concerning China, 1894–1919 (J. V. A. MacMurray, ed.). 2 vols., New York, 1921.

United States House Executive Documents, 28 Cong., 2 Sess., No. 138. "Extensions of American Commerce—Proposed Mission to Japan and Corea." Washington, 1845.

———, 48 Cong., 2 Sess., No. 163. "Military Instructors for Corea: Message from the President of the United States." Washington, 1885.

United States Senate Documents. 64 Cong., I Sess., No. 342. "Occupation of Korea by Japan." Washington, 1916.

United States Statutes at Large. 56 vols., Washington, 1850–1943.

C. Translations from the Orient

Annual Report on Reforms and Progress in Korea. Seoul, 1907–11.

The Book of Lord Shang (J. J. L. Duyvendak, trans.). London, 1928.

Brewitt-Taylor, C. H., *San Kuo, or Romance of the Three Kingdoms.* 2 vols., Shanghai, 1925.

Chang T'ing-yu and others, *Ming Shih* (History of the Ming Dynasty). Wuchang, 1877.

The Chinese Classics (James Legge, trans.). 8 vols., London, 1861–72.

"Constitution of the Council of State" (translation of Ordinance No. 1, September 24, 1896), in *Korean Repository*, III (1896), 404–10.

"Corea: Extracts from M. F. Scherzer's French Translation of the Chao-hsien-chih" (Charles Gould, trans.), in *Journal of the North China Branch of the Royal Asiatic Society*, XVIII (1884), 25–36.

Gale, J. S., "Korean History (Selections from Native Writers)," in *Korean Repository*, III (1896), 183–88.

308 SELECT BIBLIOGRAPHY

Gale, J. S., "Korean History (Translations from the Tong-gook T'ong-gam)," in *Korean Repository*, II (1895), 321–27.

"Korean Relations with Japan, The Cheung-jung Kyo-rin-ji," in *Korea Review*, III (1903), 294–300, 347–49, 394–98, 438–43, 492–97; IV (1904), 9–13.

Li Hung-chang, *Memoirs of Li Hung Chang* (William Francis Mannix, ed.). Boston, 1913.

"The Official Gazette" (compiled from the *Independent*), in *Korean Repository*, III (1896), 500–501.

"Official Report on Matters Connected with the Events of October 8th 1895, and the Death of the Queen," in *Korean Repository*, III (1896), 120–42.

Pan Ku, *Han-shu Pu-shu* (History of the Former Han Dynasty) (Wang Hsien-ch'ien, ed.). Changsha, 1900.

———, *The History of the Former Han Dynasty* (H. H. Dubs, trans.). Baltimore, 1938–.

Parker, E. H., "On Race Struggles in Corea" [Translated from Chao-hsien chapters in *Early Han-shu* (200 B.C.–A.D. 1) and *After Han-shu* (A.D. 1–A.D. 200)], in *Transactions of the Asiatic Society of Japan*, XVIII (1890), 157–228.

The Sacred Books of the East (F. Max Müller, ed.). 50 vols., Oxford, 1879–1910.

The Sacred Edict (F. W. Baller, trans.). Shanghai, 1917.

Se-Ma Ts'ien, *Les mémoires historiques* (Edouard Chavannes, trans.). 5 vols., Paris, 1895.

The Shu King (W. G. Old, trans.). London, 1904.

Tcheou-Li ou Rites des Tcheou (Edouard Biot, trans.). 2 vols., Paris, 1851.

The Works of Hsüntze (H. H. Dubs, trans.). London, 1928.

III. SECONDARY SOURCES

A. Books

Allen, H. N., *Things Korean*. New York, 1908.

———, *A Chronological Index: Some of the Chief Events in the Foreign Intercourse of Korea from the Beginning of the Christian Era to the Twentieth Century*. Supplement for 1901–1902. Seoul, 1901.

———, *Korea, Fact and Fancy: Being a Republication of Two Books Entitled "Korean Tales" and "A Chronological Index."* Seoul, 1904.

Backhouse, E.; and Bland, J. O. P., *Annals and Memoirs of the Court of Peking.* London, 1914.

Bau, M. J., *The Foreign Relations of China.* New York, 1921.

Bishop, I. L., *Korea and Her Neighbors.* 2 vols., London, 1898.

Bland, J. O. P., *China, Japan and Korea.* London, 1921.

Bodde, Derk, *China's First Unifier.* Leyden, 1938.

Brown, A. J., *The Mastery of the Far East.* New York, 1921.

Carles, W. K., *Life in Corea.* New York, 1888.

Chang Chung-fu, *The Anglo-Japanese Alliance.* Baltimore, 1931.

Cordier, Henri, *Histoire générale de la Chine.* 4 vols., Paris, 1920.

Costin, W. C., *Great Britain and China, 1833–1860.* Oxford, 1937.

Couling, Samuel, *The Encyclopedia Sinica.* Shanghai, 1917.

Creel, H. G., *Sinism, A Study of the Evolution of the Chinese World-View.* Chicago, 1929.

———, *Studies in Early Chinese Culture.* Baltimore, 1937.

Curzon, G. N., *Problems of the Far East.* London, 1894.

Dallet, Charles, *Histoire de l'église de Corée.* 2 vols., Paris, 1874.

Dennett, Tyler, *Americans in Eastern Asia.* New York, 1922.

———, *Roosevelt and the Russo-Japanese War.* New York, 1925.

Denny, O. N., *China and Korea.* Shanghai, 1888.

Despagnet, Frantz, *Essai sur les protectorats.* Paris, 1896.

Devaulx, André, *Les protectorats de la France en Afrique.* Domois-Dijon, 1903.

Dickinson, E. D., *Equality of States in International Law.* Cambridge, 1920.

Djang Chu, Chinese Suzerainty. Unpublished Ph.D. dissertation, Johns Hopkins University, 1935.

Douglas, Robert K., *Li Hungchang.* New York, 1895.

Dubs, H. H., *Hsüntze, The Moulder of Ancient Confucianism.* London, 1927.

Du Halde, J. B., *The General History of China* (R. Brookes, trans.). 4 vols., London, 1736.

Escarra, Jean, *Le droit chinois.* Paris, 1936.

Federal Council of the Churches of Christ in America, *The Korean Situation.* New York, 1919.

Fenwick, Charles G., *International Law*. New York, 1934.
Fitzgerald, C. P., *Son of Heaven, A Biography of Li Shih-Min, Founder of the T'ang Dynasty*. London, 1933.
Forke, Alfred, *Die Gedankenwelt des Chinesischen Kulturkreises*. Munich, 1927.
————, *The World Conception of the Chinese*. London, 1925.
Foster, J. W., *American Diplomacy in the Orient*. Boston, 1903.
Fung Yu-lan, *A History of Chinese Philosophy* (Derk Bodde, trans.). Peiping, 1937.
Gale, J. S., *The Unabridged Korean-English Dictionary*. Seoul, 1931.
Gibert, Lucien, *Dictionnaire historique et géographique de la Mandchourie*. Hong Kong, 1934.
Giles, H. A., *A Chinese-English Dictionary*. Shanghai, 1912.
Goodrich, L. C.; and Fenn, H. C., *A Syllabus of the History of Chinese Civilization and Culture*. New York, 1934.
Granet, Marcel, *Chinese Civilization* (K. E. Innes and M. R. Brailsford, trans.). New York, 1930.
Griffis, W. E., *Corea, The Hermit Nation*. London, 1905.
Herrman, Albert, *Historical and Commercial Atlas of China*. Cambridge, 1935.
Hershey, A. S., *The Essentials of International Public Law and Organization*. New York, 1930.
Hindmarsh, A. E., *Force in Peace*. Cambridge, 1935.
Hiroshi Ikeuchi, "A Study on Lo-lang and Tai-fang, Ancient Chinese Prefectures in Korean Peninsula," in *Memoirs of the Research Department of the Toyo Bunko*, VI (1932), 79–95.
————, "A Study on the Fuyü," in *Memoirs of the Research Department of the Toyo Bunko*, VI (1932), 23–60.
Hsieh, Pao Chao, *The Government of China (1644–1911)*. Baltimore, 1925.
Hsü, L. S., *The Political Philosophy of Confucianism*. London, 1932.
Hsü, Shuhsi, *China and Her Political Entity*. New York, 1926.
Hughes, E. R., *The Invasion of China by the Western World*. London, 1937.
Hulbert, H. B., *The History of Korea*. 2 vols., Seoul, 1905.
————, *The Passing of Korea*. New York, 1906.

Ireland, Alleyne, *The New Korea*. New York, 1926.

Japan by the Japanese (Alfred Stead, ed.). London, 1904.

Joseph, Philip, *Foreign Diplomacy in China, 1894–1900*. London, 1928.

Kawakami, K. K., *American-Japanese Relations*. New York, 1912.

Kendall, C. W., *The Truth About Korea*. San Francisco, 1919.

Kolnai, Aurel, *The War Against the West*. New York, 1938.

Korea Must Be Free. Washington, 1930.

Korff, Baron S. A., *Russia's Foreign Relations During the Last Half Century*. New York, 1922.

Kuno, Yoshi S., *Japanese Expansion on the Asiatic Continent*. 2 vols., Berkeley, 1937–40.

Ladd, G. T., *In Korea with Marquis Ito*. New York, 1908.

Lattimore, Owen, *Manchuria, Cradle of Conflict*. New York, 1932.

Lawrence, T. J., *War and Neutrality in the Far East*. London, 1904.

Lawton, Lancelot, *Empires of the Far East*. 2 vols., London, 1912.

Li Chi, *Manchuria in History: A Summary*. Peiping, 1932.

Liang Ch'i-ch'ao, *History of Chinese Political Thought*. New York, 1930.

Lindley, M. F., *The Acquisition and Government of Backward Territory in International Law*. London, 1926.

Linebarger, P. M. A., *Government in Republican China*. New York, 1938.

Lobanov-Rostovsky, Prince A., *Russia and Asia*. New York, 1933.

Longford, J. H., *The Story of Korea*. London, 1911.

MacNair, H. F., *Modern Chinese History: Selected Readings*. Shanghai, 1927.

———, *The Real Conflict Between China and Japan*. Chicago, 1938.

Martin, W. A. P., *A Cycle of Cathay*. New York, 1897.

Mayers, William F., *The Chinese Government*. Shanghai, 1886.

McKenzie, F. A., *Korea's Fight for Freedom*. New York, 1928.

———, *The Tragedy of Korea*. New York, n.d.

Michael, Franz, *Origin of Manchu Rule in China*. Baltimore, 1942.

Millard, T. F., *America and the Far Eastern Question*. New York, 1909.

Moore, J. B., *Digest of International Law*. 8 vols., Washington, 1906.

Morse, H. B., *The International Relations of the Chinese Empire.* 3 vols., London, 1918.

Morse, H. B.; and MacNair, H. F., *Far Eastern International Relations.* Boston, 1931.

Murdoch, James, *A History of Japan.* 3 vols., London, 1925–26.

Oppenheim, L., *International Law.* 2 vols., London, 1937.

Oxenham, E. L., *Historical Atlas of the Chinese Empire.* London, 1898.

Paullin, C. O., *Diplomatic Negotiations of American Naval Officers, 1778–1883.* Baltimore, 1912.

Pauthier, G., *Histoire des relations politiques de la Chine avec les puissances occidentales.* Paris, 1859.

Price, E. B., *Russo-Japanese Treaties of 1907–1916.* Baltimore, 1933.

Pringle, H. F., *Theodore Roosevelt.* London, 1932.

Reischauer, R. K., *Early Japanese History.* 2 vols., Princeton, 1937.

Rockhill, W. W., *China's Intercourse with Korea from the XVth Century to 1895.* London, 1905.

Russell, F. M., *Theories of International Relations.* New York, 1936.

Sands, W. F., *Undiplomatic Memories.* New York, 1930.

Sansom, G. B., *Japan, A Short Cultural History.* New York, 1936.

Satow, Ernest, *A Guide to Diplomatic Practice.* 2 vols., London, 1922.

Schuman, F. L., *Europe on the Eve.* New York, 1939.

The Secret Memoirs of Count Tadasu Hayashi (A. M. Pooley, ed.). New York, 1915.

Shryock, J. K., *The Origin and Development of the State Cult of Confucius.* New York, 1932.

Steiger, G. N., *A History of the Far East.* Boston, 1936.

Terriou, René, *Le statut international de la Corée anterieurement au 29 Août 1910.* Paris, 1911.

Thomas, E. D., *Chinese Political Thought.* New York, 1927.

Treat, Payson J., *Diplomatic Relations Between the United States and Japan, 1853–1895.* 2 vols., Stanford, 1932.

——, *The Far East.* New York, 1935.

Vattel, Emmerich de, *The Law of Nations.* New York, 1796.

Verbrugge, R., *Yuan Chi-K'ai: sa vie—son temps.* Paris, 1934. (IV of series entitled *Les grandes figures de l'orient.*)

Wheaton, Henry, *Elements of International Law.* Boston, 1866.

White, Trumball, *The War in the East, Japan, China and Corea.* Philadelphia, 1895.

Wieger, P. Leon, *Textes historiques, histoire politique de la Chine.* 2 vols., Paris, 1929.

Wilhelm, Richard, *Geschichte der chinesischen Kultur.* Munich, 1928.

Wilkinson, W. H., *The Corean Government Constitutional Changes, July 1894 to October 1895, With an Appendix on Subsequent Enactments to 30th June 1896.* Shanghai, 1897.

Williams, S. Wells, *The Middle Kingdom.* 2 vols., New York, 1883.

Willoughby, W. W.; and Fenwick, C. G., *Types of Restricted Sovereignty and of Colonial Autonomy.* Washington, 1919.

Wilson, G. G., *Handbook of International Law.* St. Paul, 1927.

Wu, K. C., *Ancient Chinese Political Theories.* Shanghai, 1928.

B. Periodical Literature

"Abdication, Acclamation, Assassination," in *Korean Repository,* V (1898), 342–49.

"The Annexation of Korea to Japan," in *American Journal of International Law,* IV (1910), 923–25.

Appenzeller, H. G., "Ki Tza, The Founder of Korean Civilization," in *Korean Repository,* II (1895), 81–87.

———, "The Opening of Korea: Admiral Shufeldt's Account of It," in *Korean Repository,* I (1892), 56–62.

Aston, W. G., "Early Japanese History," in *Transactions of the Asiatic Society of Japan,* XVI (1889), 39–75.

———, "Hideyoshi's Invasion of Korea," in *Transactions of the Asiatic Society of Japan,* VI (1878), 227–45; IX (1881), 87–93, 213–22; XI (1883), 117–25.

"The Attack on the Top Knot," in *Korean Repository,* III (1896), 263–72.

"Baron von Möllendorff," in *Korean Review,* I (1901), 245–52.

Baty, T., "Protectorates and Mandates," in *British Yearbook of International Law*, II (1921–22), 109–21.

Britton, R. S., "Chinese Interstate Intercourse Before 700 B.C.," in *American Journal of International Law*, XXIX (1935), 616–35.

Cable, E. M., "United States–Korean Relations, 1866–1871," in *Transactions of the Korea Branch of the Royal Asiatic Society*, XXVIII (1938), 1–230.

Chung, Kei Won; and Hourani, G. F., "Arab Geographers on Korea," in *Journal of the American Oriental Society*, LVIII (1938), 658–61.

"Correspondence," in *Korean Repository*, III (1896), 216–20.

Cory, Ralph M., "Some Notes on Father Gregorio de Cespedes, Korea's First European Visitor," in *Transactions of the Korea Branch of the Royal Asiatic Society*, XXVII (1937), 1–55.

Courant, Maurice, "La Corée jusqu'au IX⁰ siècle ses rapports avec le Japon et son influence sur les origines de la civilisation japonaise," in *T'oung Pao*, IX (1898), 1–27.

"The Deer Island Episode," in *Korean Repository*, V (1898), 109–13.

Dennett, Tyler, "American Good Offices in Asia," in *American Journal of International Law*, XVI (1922), 1–24.

———, "Early American Policy in Korea, 1883–1887," in *Political Science Quarterly*, XXXVIII (1923), 82–103.

"The Emperor of Korea," in *Korean Repository*, II (1895), 435–38.

Fairbank, J. K., "Tributary Trade and China's Relations with the West," in *Far Eastern Quarterly*, I (1942), 129–49.

Fairbank, J. K.; and Têng, S. Y., "On the Types and Uses of Ch'ing Documents," in *Harvard Journal of Asiatic Studies*, V (1940), 1–71.

———, "On the Ch'ing Tributary System," in *Harvard Journal of Asiatic Studies*, VI (1941), 135–246.

"The Fate of the Queen," in *Korean Repository*, II (1895), 431–35.

Feller, A. H., "Protectorate," in *Encyclopedia of Social Science*, XII, 567–71. 15 vols., New York, 1934.

Gale, J. S., "The Fate of the General Sherman: From an Eye Witness," in *Korean Repository*, II (1895), 252–54.

———, "Han-yang (Seoul)," in *Transactions of the Korea Branch of the Royal Asiatic Society*, II (1902), 1–43.

———, "The Influence of China Upon Korea," in *Transactions of the Korea Branch of the Royal Asiatic Society*, I (1900), 1–24.

"Great Changes in the Korean Government," in *Korean Repository*, II (1895), 111–18.

"His Majesty, the King of Korea," in *Korean Repository*, III (1896), 423–30.

Hu Shih, "Wang Mang, The Socialist Emperor of Nineteen Centuries Ago," in *Journal of the North China Branch of the Royal Asiatic Society*, LIX (1928), 218–30.

Hulbert, H. B., "The Ancient Kingdom of Karak," in *Korea Review*, II (1902), 541–46.

———, "The Itu," in *Korean Repository*, V (1898), 47–54.

———, "The Korean Alphabet," in *Korean Repository*, I (1892), 1–9.

———, "Korean History," in *Korea Review*, I (1901), 29–48, 77–96, 125–44, 177–92, 221–40, 273–88, 317–36, 369–84, 417–32, 465–80, 513–28, 561–76; II (1902), 33–48, 81–96, 129–44, 177–92, 225–40, 273–88, 321–36, 369–84, 417–32, 465–80, 513–28, 561–76; III (1903), 33–48, 81–96, 129–44, 177–92, 225–40, 273–88, 321–36, 369–84, 417–37, 465–80, 513–28, 561–76; IV (1904), 33–48, 81–96, 129–44, 177–92, 225–40, 273–88, 321–36, 369–84, 417–32, 465–80, 513–28, 561–76.

———, "Korean Survivals," in *Transactions of the Korea Branch of the Royal Asiatic Society*, I (1900), 25–50.

———, "The Mongols in Korea," in *Korean Repository*, V (1898), 133–43.

———, "National Examination in Korea," in *Transactions of the Korea Branch of the Royal Asiatic Society*, XIV (1923), 9–32.

"In the Finance Department," in *Korean Repository*, IV (1897), 434–36.

316   SELECT BIBLIOGRAPHY

"The Independence Club," in *Korean Repository*, IV (1897), 281–87.

"The International Status of Korea," in *American Journal of International Law*, I (1907), 444–49.

J. R., "The Rise and Progress of the Manjows," in *Chinese Recorder*, VII (1876), 155–68, 235–48, 315–29; VIII (1877), 1–24, 196–208, 361–80.

Jamieson, G., "The Tributary Nations of China," in *China Review*, XII (1883), 94–109.

Jones, G. H., "Historical Notes on the Reigning Dynasty," in *Korean Repository*, III (1896), 343–49, 392–95; IV (1897), 18–22, 121–28, 220–27.

———, "The Japanese Invasion," in *Korean Repository*, I (1892), 10–16, 46–50, 116–21, 147–52, 182–88, 217–22, 308–11.

———, "Sketches of a Hero," in *Korean Repository*, V (1898), 319–27.

———, "The Taiwon Kun," in *Korean Repository*, V (1898), 241–50.

Junkin, W. M., "The Tong Hak," in *Korean Repository*, II (1895), 56–60.

"The King's Oath at the Ancestral Temple," in *Korean Repository*, II (1895), 76–77.

Krauel, A., "Applicabilité du droit des gens européen à la Chine," in *Revue de Droit International et de Législation Comparée*, IX (1877), 387–404.

Landis, E. B., "Notable Dates of Kang-Wha," in *Korean Repository*, IV (1897), 245–48.

Lin, T. C., "Li Hung-chang: His Korea Policies, 1870–1885," in *Chinese Social and Political Science Review*, XIX (1935–36), 202–33.

London Times (1882–1910).

MacNair, H. F., "Some Observations on China's International Relations," in *Journal of the North China Branch of the Royal Asiatic Society*, LVI (1925), 1–29.

Martin, W. A. P., "Traces of International Law in Ancient China," in *Chinese Recorder*, XIV (1883), 380–93.

Mörsel, F. H., "Events Leading to the Emeute of 1884," in *Korean Repository*, IV (1897), 95–98, 135–40, 212–19.

Nagaoka, M. N., "La guerre russo-japonaise et le droit international," in *Revue de Droit International et de Législation Comparée*, VI, II série (1904), 461–515.

Nelson, M. Frederick, "Feudalistic Propaganda in Modern Japan," in *Amerasia*, II (1938), 444–51.

Noble, H. J., "The United States and Sino-Korean Relations, 1885–1887," in *Pacific Historical Review*, II (1933), 292–304.

"The Official Report," in *Korean Repository*, III (1896), 208–11.

Oh, M. W., "The Two Visits of the Rev. R. J. Thomas to Korea," in *Transactions of the Korea Branch of the Royal Asiatic Society*, XXII (1933), 95–123.

Ohlinger, F., "The Three Female Sovereigns of Korea," in *Korean Repository*, I (1892), 223–27.

"Our Little Battle in Corean Waters," in *Overland Monthly*, VIII, 2d series (1886), 125–28.

Paik, George, "The Korean Record on Captain Basil Hall's Voyage of Discovery to the West Coast of Korea," in *Transactions of the Korea Branch of the Royal Asiatic Society*, XXIV (1935), 15–19.

Parker, E. H., "China's Relations with Foreign Tribes," in *China Review*, XIV (1885), 12–14.

———, "The Manchus," in *Transactions of the Asiatic Society of Japan*, XV (1887), 83–92.

———, "The Manchu Relations with Corea," in *Transactions of the Asiatic Society of Japan*, XV (1887), 93–95.

———, "A Chinese View of Corea," in *Chinese Recorder*, XVIII (1887), 70–73.

Paullin, C. O., "The Opening of Korea by Commander Shufeldt," in *Political Science Quarterly*, XV (1910), 470–99.

Pollard, R. T., "American Relations with Korea, 1882–1895," in *Chinese Social and Political Science Review*, XVI (1932–33), 425–71.

"The Press on the Situation," in *Korean Repository*, IV (1897), 468–71.

"Reaction," in *Korean Repository*, III (1896), 334–36.

"Reformation, Revision, Regulation," in *Korean Repository*, IV (1897), 192–95.

"A Retrospect, 1894," in *Korean Repository*, II (1895), 29–36.

Rey, Francis, "La situation internationale de la Corée," in *Revue Générale de Droit International Public*, XIII (1906), 40–58.

"Right About Face," in *Korean Repository*, V (1898), 113–17.

Sansom, G. B., "An Outline of Recent Japanese Archaeological Research in Korea in Its Bearing Upon Early Japanese History," in *Transactions of the Asiatic Society of Japan*, VI, 2d series (1929), 5–19.

Schwarzenberger, Georg, "The Rule of Law and the Disintegration of the International Society," in *American Journal of International Law*, XXXIII (1939), 56–77.

Scott, James, "Stray Notes on Corean History and Literature," in *Journal of the North China Branch of the Royal Asiatic Society*, XXVIII (1898), 214–32.

"Special Supplement to the Korean Repository," in *Korean Repository*, III (1896), 81–94.

Takayanagi, Kenzo, "A Japanese View of the Struggle in the Far East," in *International Affairs*, XVIII (1939), 29–55.

Treat, Payson J., "China and Korea, 1885–1895," in *Political Science Quarterly*, XLIX (1934), 506–43.

"The Treaty of Peace," in *Korean Repository*, II (1895), 235.

Trollope, M. N., "Kang-Wha," in *Transactions of the Korea Branch of the Royal Asiatic Society*, II (1901), 1–36.

Tsiang, T. F., "The Origin of the Tsungli Yamen," in *Chinese Social and Political Science Review*, XV (1931–32), 92–97.

————, "Sino-Japanese Diplomatic Relations, 1870–1894," in *Chinese Social and Political Science Review*, XVII (1933–34), 1–106.

Wilder, Payson, "What Is the Trouble with International Law?" in *American Political Science Review*, XXXII (1938), 478–94.

Wilkinson, W. H., "The Corean Government," in *Korean Repository*, IV (1897), 1–13, 45–56.

Yamagata, I., "Japanese-Korean Relations After the Japanese Invasion of Korea in the XV Century," in *Transactions of the Korea Branch of the Royal Asiatic Society*, IV (1913), 1–11.

Ye We Chong, Prince, "A Plea for Korea," in *Independent*, LXIII (1907), 423–26.

Yun, T. H., "Popular Movements in Korea," in *Korean Repository*, V (1898), 465–69.

———, "The Whang-Chei of Dai Han, or the Emperor of Korea," in *Korean Repository*, IV (1897), 385–90.

INDEX

ST. MARY'S COLLEGE OF MARYLAND LIBRARY
ST. MARY'S CITY, MARYLAND